Using Educational Technology with At-Risk Students

Greenwood Professional Guides in School Librarianship

Using Educational Technology with At-Risk Students
A Guide for Library Media Specialists and Teachers

Roxanne Baxter Mendrinos

Greenwood Professional Guides in School Librarianship
Harriet Selverstone, Series Adviser

GREENWOOD PRESS
Westport, Connecticut • London

Library of Congress Cataloging-in-Publication Data

Mendrinos, Roxanne.
    Using educational technology with at-risk students : a guide for
library media specialists and teachers / Roxanne Baxter Mendrinos.
        p.   cm. — (Greenwood professional guides in school
librarianship, ISSN 1074–150X)
    Includes bibliographical references and index.
    ISBN 0–313–29369-4 (alk. paper)
    1. School libraries—United States—Data processing.   2. Computer-
assisted instruction—United States.   3. Dropouts—United States.
4. Instructional materials centers—United States—Data processing.
I. Title.   II. Series.
Z675.S3M3339   1997
027.8´0285—dc21   96–51139

British Library Cataloguing in Publication Data is available.

Library of Congress Catalog Card Number: 96–51139
ISBN: 0–313–29369-4
ISSN: 1074–150X

First published in 1997

Greenwood Press, 88 Post Road West, Westport, CT 06881
An imprint of Greenwood Publishing Group, Inc.

Printed in the United States of America

The paper used in this book complies with the
Permanent Paper Standard issued by the National
Information Standards Organization (Z39.48–1984).

10 9 8 7 6 5 4 3 2 1

Copyright Acknowledgments

Grateful acknowledgment is given to AIM LAB from the College of Agricultural,
Consumer and Environmental Sciences at the University of Illinois at
Urbana-Champaign for permission to reprint Figures 5.1–5.7

Selected graphic images (Figures 5.8–5.11) reprinted courtesy of Environmental Systems
Research Institute, Inc. Copyright © 1994 Environmental Systems Research Institute, Inc.
All rights reserved.

Contents

Illustrations

FIGURES

Change in Education and Technology in the Information Age

1

THE INFORMATION TECHNOLOGY REVOLUTION

World society is in the midst of the information technology revolution that is changing the basic roots of nationalistic society and cultural development and its educational foundations. Following the agricultural dominance in the 1700s came the Industrial Revolution, which affected life in the nineteenth and twentieth centuries. Now, in the latter part of the twentieth century, we are in the midst of an information technology revolution. Dybkjaer-Christensen in "Info-Society 2000," his report to the Danish Parliament, stated, "A revolution is in progress, a world-wide short circuit of time, space, people and processes." The contours of the Information Society are shaped by the ability to communicate instantaneously worldwide, thereby demonstrating the irrelevance of geographic distances. According to Toffler (1990), the power of the 1990s flows to those with the skill to transform data into information and insight.

The info-society welcomes an anarchistic exchange of ideas, debate, and communication. The electronic form of communication eliminates social conventions, niceties, and unnecessary verbiage. Time and space are coveted. Both good and evil appear unobstructed at this point, governed only by the ethics of those who participate. This worldwide global communication network, the Internet (or network of networks), links governments, schools, libraries, businesses, the underworld, and the individual. It is a way of communicating among a variety of computer networks that use a set of technical rules known as the Transmission Control Protocol/Internet Protocol (TCP/IP protocols). No one is deprived of access, all one needs is a computer, a modem, and an Internet account.

The 1980s emphasized the importance of the computer as a tool to be integrated into the curriculum. The 1990s brings the full potential of the Information Age to the doorstep of the classroom and the library media center through the expanded world of telecommunications. Electronic mail is delivered immediately or at the very least within twenty-four hours. It is cheaper than phone or fax. Huge files of text, audio, video, satellite images, and graphics can be transferred in a matter of seconds or minutes depending on the size of the file and the speed of the available data lines. With the aid of the latest graphical-user interface browsers such as the Netscape Navigator, searching on the Internet is easy and user-friendly.

Electronic library catalogs showcase books, videos, and collections of major and minor universities and colleges. No longer should students, faculty members, or library media specialists be confined by the inadequacies of their library collection. Electronic museums bring the wealth of the Smithsonian and the Louvre to the desktop of the computer user, with works of art and biographies of the artists.

Electronic publishing of magazines, journals, and newspapers is a growing reality. As of April 1995, over 120 newspapers are offered in electronic format including the *New York Times*. *Time* and the *New Republic* are among several dozen magazines that are making subscriptions available on the Internet's World Wide Web and through online utilities such as CompuServe and America Online (Ziegler 1995, 1). Not only are we able to read this month's issue but we have the ability to search for specific key words in back issues of the magazine.

The technology in a globally networked environment is profoundly changing the way we live and work. There are 35 million users on the Internet, and this is expected to increase to close to 100 million users worldwide. Commercial connections are growing faster than educational ones (*Computer World* 1995, 65). Most wide area Internet connection providers are privately owned and will carry any traffic users will pay for. In fact since 1988, the Internet has doubled in size. "Internet usage has doubled every year since 1970 and it is estimated that there will be 200 million Internet users by the year 2000, an estimated 53% of Americans will be Web users" (Key Internet Demographics, 1997). Commerce is expected to increase from $150 billion to $200 billion by the year 2000 according to the International Data Corporation (Key Internet Demographics, 1997).

More and more businesses are advertising their products on the global network—artists are exhibiting their creations, researchers worldwide are collaborating on experiments, and physicians are providing diagnoses from centers of medicine to physicians in remote areas as well as suggesting possible cures to problem illnesses. Universities and colleges are expanding their boundaries by offering courses over the Internet to students throughout the world. "According to the American Library Association, 44% of public libraries offer Internet access in 1996 up from 21% in 1994.

They estimate Internet access in public libraries will increase to 67% in 1997" (Key Internet Demographics, 1997).

Those who have the knowledge and the keys to the utilization of information technology will be in an outstanding position to influence and be part of this growing economic development. The Information Age economy is characterized by information as a commodity, in a global structure; democratic access creating an equal playing field for those who have the tools to play; instantaneous action; and the need for education around the world to update skills and train employees. Information translates into knowledge and power.

As of 1995, the info-society appears to be a more open and decentralized society with uncontrolled access to information, communication, and debate. This may change if countries such as Singapore put in place censorship instruments to limit this completely free access and if the U.S. Congress and legislatures of other countries enact laws to protect young people from pornography and illegal solicitation. The need for technology to be an inherent part of the education and thought processes of the at-risk student and students of all levels is crucial in this fast-changing social, education, and economic order.

ANACHRONISTIC SCHOOLS

In the August 22, 1995, edition of *USA Today*, Louis V. Gerstner, chairman and CEO of IBM Corporation, wrote:

Information technology revolutionizes business, streamlines government and enables instant communication around the world. Yet information technology has had little impact on most public schools. Before we can get the education revolution rolling, we need to recognize our public schools are low-tech institutions in a high-tech society. The same forces that have brought cataclysmic change to every facet of business can improve the way we teach students and teachers. They also can improve the efficiency of how we run our schools.

Schools in the 1990s are referred to as anachronistic factory era products of the Industrial Revolution. Only 14 percent (Snyder 1995) have a basic telephone connection to the outside world. The 84,000 schools in the United States contain 4.1 million computers, nearly one-third of them Apple IIE machines, which are dinosaurs in today's multimedia marketplace. In a survey published in *USA Today* (June 5, 1996), South Dakota had the best ratio of computers per student, six students for every computer. However, the ratio of computers with multimedia capabilities that are capable of CD-ROM, sound, video, or Internet access, rises to 15.4 students per computer. California is number fifty in the survey with 16.2 computers per student. However, students in California who need multimedia access will have to share one multimedia computer with fifty-two other students.

Schools need to move to a different beat and adopt the pulse of this decade. The challenges of the twenty-first century are manifesting themselves in the job market, in the skills that will be needed by this generation in the new academic and social orders that are beginning to permeate education and society. Pedagogies that actively make use of the technology to teach and help students learn must be incorporated into in-service sessions and in the classroom. The pace of electronic global change is moving too quickly to accommodate "technophobic educators who like school more than they like learning" (Mageau 1995, 16).

Technology is not a new contraption that faculty and students must use. The question is how will the technology make what the school library media specialist, faculty member, and/or student want to accomplish better? What is technology's value to the project, to solving the problem, or in achieving the desired plan of action?

The school library media specialist should be at the forefront of the electronic world of information and the use of educational technology in his/her school. It is the proactive library media specialist who should be leading the team-teaching environments and learning communities of multiple disciplines in the integration of text, video, CD-ROM, videodisks, and online telecommunications to provide multidimensional learning and multisensory education to meet the needs of a variety of learning styles. As our experience with telecommunications instruction increases, it is becoming clear that information is a verb rather than a noun. It is interactive. Digital technology does not change the nature of information, it simply changes the nature of information users. Digitization makes all information data—sound, video—malleable, fluid, combinable, and changeable (Gehl 1995).

In 1994, Secretary of Education Richard Riley stated that 75 percent of high school youth did not complete a four-year college education. He said: "We are the only major industrialized nation with no formal system for helping our young people—particularly the high school youth who don't go on to finish a four-year college—make the transition from the classroom to the workplace. That translates to lost productivity and wasted human potential" (Couch 1994).

In Germany, major corporations such as Mercedes Benz have worked cooperatively in schools to forge partnerships to provide updated technological skills to high school students not planning to go to college. The dual system allows students to learn skills in school while serving as apprentices to gain experience. This has saved the corporation both time and considerable money in corporate training and has provided the technologically trained work force necessary for global competition.

The unemployment rate in the United States for students who do not complete high school is twice as high (11.9%) as for those who do complete high school (6.9%). There are many studies that show that students with higher degrees earn more money and are more likely to be employed (Couch 1994).

One of the main goals of our educational system should be to assist those individuals in the population who do not complete a four-year degree in making the transition from the classroom to the changing technology-oriented workplace. Wisconsin's state superintendent calls this group the "neglected majority"—America's "mid-kids" who are needed to provide the human resources for every business from high tech electronics to manufacturing and banking. Depending on our success, they will be the backbone of our future work force or a drag on the economy and doomed to lower living standards (Couch 1994).

Another educational goal is to reach those (25% of the student population) who may not have the confidence after high school graduation to attend a four-year college. Many high schools direct their resources and outstanding teachers toward working with college-bound students, neglecting the talents and potential of America's mid-kids.

There is another learner, the adult learner, who is also at risk. A new type of education program is needed, one focusing on learning rather than education, on technology rather than institutions, and on private competition rather than public administration. The Information Age economy focuses less on expertise and more on "flexpertise." This is not in the realm of the school library media specialist unless the library media center and its technology are available for use by the community.

The study from the National Center on the Educational Quality of the Work Force emphasized that schools and businesses must—but at present do not—have a direct relationship with work-related education and training. Even with wide-scale downsizing, employers continue to invest in the skill requirements of their nonsupervisory personnel. Eighty percent of the 4,000 managers surveyed offer formal or structured training throughout the workplace, and 57 percent increased that training over the last three years. The three major areas for training by corporations include: safer use of equipment and tools; attitudinal and behavior skills that include teamwork efforts and problem-solving skills; and training in sales and customer service. What is of significance is that higher education, adult education, and public schools are not likely to be leading the training. The preferred providers of training include equipment suppliers or buyers, private consultants, and private industry councils. When choosing job applicants, the study found, teacher recommendations and educational performance are rarely considered. Business leaders have stated a strong disappointment in the caliber of graduating students and the lack of skills that are needed for success in the real world. One can infer from this study that there is not a strong correlation between success in school and success in employment. The corporations surveyed appeared to have a negative view of the impact of school on job performance (Change 1995, 39).

SCHOOL CULTURE

How should we use these new technologies to improve learning, enhance economic competition, and strengthen citizen participation?

It is interesting to note that one-quarter of the national economy evolves around some educational activity—$200 billion on teachers' salaries, $4.2 billion on school curriculum, and $600–$800 million on electronic materials. Lack of familiarity with the technology is an obstacle in education. The successful integration of technology into the curriculum is also inhibited by the school culture, which does not support collaboration among teachers, students, and parents. Another concern is that educational practice has not changed significantly from the time of the Industrial Revolution. Meaningful interactivity among students and teachers is often missing, as teachers deliver passive lecture-oriented sessions. The culture of the information technology revolution is interactive with networks enabling users to link in real time to the world of remote information, people, and projects.

Energetic information-technology explorers who are committed to change have to be aware of their threat to other faculty and administrators as they reflect on and question the structure that has been in place since the nineteenth century. An MIT Sloan Business School study found that a number of ambitious information technology projects fell far short of expectations because they did not invest in human resource development and cultural cultivation to take full advantage of the new systems. The K–12, community college, and university environments are isolating. Teachers and library media specialists in many schools rarely interact and often are unfamiliar with the changing business technological environment outside of their schools.

Technology transforms organizational structures into flexible, looser groupings of people who use communication to learn and work collaboratively. The insights into how to learn and manage information and the ability to create new knowledge are part of a framework that stresses sharing of information. Instructional models are being developed where the distinction between school, home, and the world are blurred as students are networked, and the scheduling concerns of an industrial age philosophy are dimmed. Learning can happen anywhere and at anytime not just during school hours.

THE CURRICULUM IN TRANSITION

Microcomputer manufacturers are hoping that from now on computers will be as commonplace as television sets in our homes. This trend has been verified in recent studies. However, the computer is not only the box, the gadget; it is how one uses it that empowers growth, power, and success. This empowerment needs to begin at the elementary level. If we are in the midst of the information technology revolution, then the school library media specialist should lead this revolution within the school! School library media specialists and educators have the responsibility to reexamine the curriculum in light of what services and multimedia formats are needed to support currency and relevancy in the 1990s and the coming century.

The curriculum should be in transition. It is the curriculum that drives the technology. The technology is a necessary tool that expands the possibilities for student success. Technology is not only a tool; its use also promotes the critical need for parallel-thinking skills, for definitive and flexible search strategies, and for the ability to navigate in an increasingly electronic global village. Without this commitment, students of all levels are at risk, and those who do not have even the basic skills are becoming part of the growing underclass.

Walt Haney of Boston College's Center for Educational Testing stated in an August 25, 1995, National Public Radio broadcast that the nation's SAT scores have increased. The higher scores were due to the fact that the students taking the test were from affluent socioeconomic levels and that these students tended to score higher. His concern was that there was a drop in the number of students taking the college-bound test from lower socioeconomic levels.

Magnet schools are being created in science and technology and are well funded in many parts of the country. Access is only for the gifted and talented and competition is tough. In the 1990s, there appears to be a growing division not only in what access the students have to technology at home but also within the same school or within the same school district. There is an increasing class of students who are being disenfranchised from the technological educational system and, thus, from the changing job market and, ultimately, from the American system of success.

THE DIVIDED SOCIETY

The reality of a divided society has alarmed U.S. technology-oriented educators since the advent of microcomputers in the 1980s. Denmark's government published its plan to meet the demands of the information technology revolution in education, labor, and industry over the Internet. Its report stated, "The winners are those with a higher education who are able to master the new technology, who know the possibilities of the Info-Society and are able to learn and develop the qualifications necessary to cope with jobs of the future" (Information Society 1996).

One of the students in my telecommunications class is a fifty-year-old Silicon Valley engineer who was forced into early retirement and is now working as a consultant. He wrote,

Electronic communication is changing the way we interact with each other. How we do business. It is even changing the core underpinnings including education, business and even our monetary system and what little security, privacy and anonymity we still possess.

Today we are drowning in a sea of data. Information processing is the buoy that allows us to stay afloat. How many of us truly know how to use this life raft? All of us MUST become information engineers.

If you need further proof, look no further. Ask yourself, "why am I in this class?" Did you note the average age of students? Or how many students are displaced workers recently laid off, participating in programs such as OTI, ProMatch, Potential Unlimited, or forced into early retirement? Have you ever asked what displaced the displaced worker? A euphemism that is closer to the truth than many realize. Displaced by Information because you did not have the microcomputer and Internet skills?

Take a look at an average business workday and how you use the microcomputer, phone, pager, network and Internet services. . . . I think you get the picture. WORK is electronic communication and Internet and e-mail access.

The job market is changing radically. Students graduating from college are given Internet addresses on the World Wide Web to access new jobs. There are entry level, low-paying jobs available that may lead to higher more professional jobs requiring more education. One student of mine who is in his late thirties to early forties sent out résumés by mail and received an 18 percent response rate to his inquiries; by fax, he received a 22 percent response rate; and via the Internet, he received an overnight response including an offer to interview. This demonstrates the power of technology and the expanding gap between those that have the technological tools and those who do not.

Donald Norman, a cognitive scientist, stated, "The failure to predict the computer revolution was a failure to understand how society would modify the original notion as a computational device into a useful tool for everyday activities. Progress required a different, more enlightened view of the computer as an information processor and controller where information includes words, sounds and pictures" (Heterick and Gehl 1995).

What will education look like in the next five years? We may not be users anymore, and the computer may not be considered a tool. The information technology revolution is moving toward becoming an environment, and one does not use an environment, one lives in an environment.

A recent report by the U.S. Committee for Economic Development (Henry 1995, D1) stated, "When technology is effectively integrated into mathematics and science education, it can raise the quality of teaching and the level of student understanding and achievement just as it has made the high performance workplace possible." For $200 to $300 per pupil, or less than 5 percent of the typical annual school budget, students can have classrooms equipped with CD-ROM, modems, and online communications. The report recommended one computer for every five students. At present the ratio is one computer for every nine to twelve students.

The report strongly advocated the integration of technology into the curriculum of schools in lower socioeconomic levels. The report continued that schools serving poor students tend to have little access to computers and online resources. The computer work for these students, if available, is typically low-level drill and practice exercises.

Three tiers are becoming evident in this decade. The first tier are those adults and children who understand how the technology can assist them in solving problems, in searching for information, and in communicating worldwide. This tier is empowered.

The second tier are adults, those with advanced degrees, those with a high school degree, and K–12 students who share a commonality in their determined fear, lack of interest, and/or self-imposed isolation from the technological revolution that is taking place around them. They can participate in their choice of courses at schools and universities or in training and retraining programs in adult education or at the community college. If this second tier includes educators at any level—elementary, secondary, or higher education—whose refusal to participate in this turn-of-this-century's revolution will have a profound effect on the educational foundation in our schools and in the restructuring and reform movements.

Educators including library media specialists can no longer remain in this tier of society. Several studies have found that technology integrated within the curriculum can only succeed if teachers receive adequate training before its implementation and if the administration offers words of support and financial commitment. It is of critical importance that our graduate library schools and teacher-education institutions, both graduate and undergraduate, include mandatory training in the instructional uses of educational technology in the curriculum and in successful pedagogical approaches. All public schools should provide in-service training in curriculum development and technology integration. David Thornburg of the Thornburg Center for Professional Development stated, "Unless we make serious investments in our educators to help them learn new paradigms of education (using technology or not), all this high-tech stuff will simply be a new bottle for a wine that long ago turned to vinegar" (Mageau 1995, 16).

Without a true understanding of the linkages between technology, the curriculum, the job market, and society, educators cannot be leaders for their institutions in the latter part of this decade or in the coming century. Louis Gerstner (1995), chairman and CEO of IBM, stated:

I'd invest . . . in moving teacher training out of the horse and buggy era. We expect doctors to do their training in teaching hospitals. We would not send an NBA player onto the court if his only training consisted of lectures on the theory of the jump shot, case studies of the fast break and films of games played years ago. Why then, do we entrust our children to teachers who have only listened to lectures, written essays on classroom management and read textbooks on the theory of child development? Though some schools have student-teacher programs, it's time more teachers learned their craft in real schools, side by side with expert teachers. It's time they got the kind of hands-on experience most other professions consider vital for certification.

At a recent gathering of Silicon Valley business leaders, a young woman confided in me that throughout high school and college she received excellent grades. Her courses did not contain any computer integration. She did not understand the value of telecommunications, electronic searching, or the importance of computer knowledge in business applications. Her courses were basically theoretical. She had a difficult time finding a good job. It took her five years in the business world, working with computers and being trained through the corporation, to feel that she was employable. The thoughts, decisions, and directions in education, in training the work force, and in excelling in a global economy are of concern to every U.S. citizen.

The third tier of adults and children have less choice in their ability to be involved with the technological revolution. They have been excluded because of the educational courses offered them and/or through their social and economic life outside of the classroom. In my study (1992), the use of CD-ROM technology for vocational purposes was advocated by less than half of the school library media specialists surveyed. In addition, even with state funding of CD-ROM technology, there was a significant difference between schools at the above-average socioeconomic level and schools at the below-average socioeconomic level with respect to the number of computers and CD-ROM laser disks available for faculty and students. The third tier is a growing underclass of adults and children who are disenfranchised.

In California, a Pacific Telesis employee who is involved in the latest telecommunications infrastructure of fiber optics shared the experiences of two of her children. One student excelled in school. His classes ended at 3:30 in the afternoon, and he had access to computers and multimedia software in many curriculum areas. Her daughter, on the other hand, was recently diagnosed as a dyslexic in her sophomore year in high school. Her grades, self-confidence, and achievement had suffered all through school. She did not listen or write well. Access to computers during the day was not part of her educational program. Her school-to-work experience, which was part of the school day, consisted of working at a local fast food establishment. Her formal classes ended at 12:30, early afternoon.

TECHNOLOGY AND HOW WE USE IT

Dynamic school library media specialists are redefining their curriculum by integrating a variety of technologies, including CD-ROM, videodisks, the Internet, online databases, and utilities, to achieve the instructional goals of their institutions. They are doing so by using the tools of the twenty-first century.

Lisa has multiple sclerosis, which kept her out of school on a regular basis. She was encouraged by her school library media specialist to take an introduction to telecommunications to learn how to use electronic mail, teleconferencing, online utilities, and the Internet through a computer and a modem. Having this technology available at home enabled her to participate actively in telecommunicating with her teachers and her classmates and to create and research electronically to complete her projects. Being part of this school experience has enabled her to keep pace with this changing technological world instead of being disenfranchised. In Lisa's case, the isolation that could have come from her disability was overcome in some respects to allow her to participate in an active social and educational environment through telecommunications.

For Chin Li, a recent Asian immigrant, English is a second language. Her library media center is connected to the Internet. The Public Access Catalog includes full-text magazine articles as well as citations, access to other large school, public library, and university library collections, and twenty-four-hour document delivery services. Dial-in access via a modem, through Telnet, and from any campus networked computer is possible. Remote access to the virtual library from anywhere at anytime is a reality.

Chin Li accompanied her English as a Second Language (ESL) class to the library media center for an introduction to the library's services. A teaching classroom with twenty-one networked microcomputers is available for library instruction, as is a full screen computer projection system. The library media specialist did not make use of the teaching classroom. She had the class come into the library and gather around a small twelve-inch monitor. She lectured to the students for approximately fifteen minutes on what was available in the library media center. This was Chin Li's introduction to an enormously powerful tool. Hands-on experiences and large screen demonstrations were missing. Is it a wonder that the English as a Second Language students left the school library media center bewildered, not fully comprehending the potential of the virtual library in this Information Age. They exited the school library media center questioning its significance to their education.

The problems with integrating educational technology into the curriculum and providing student access and retrieval of electronic information are not always in the availability of the technological software and hardware. In 1995, sales of multimedia software to U.S. public schools totaled $115 million and will triple by 1998. Online services, child-safe World Wide Web browsers, and multimedia high-end computers will account for the sales. In 1994 sales of stand-alone computer systems totaled $1.2 billion, and this is expected to accelerate 11 percent. Textbook publishers are including software in their products, and electronic "edutainment" vendors are converging on the classroom (Snyder 1995, A1).

In Chin Li's situation, the technology was available, powerful, and in place with tremendous potential for curriculum integration and student interaction. Unfortunately, the library media specialist did not explore the technology or the keys to unlock its power with the students. The power of the electronic catalog and the online database is in the thinking process that is necessary to access and retrieve relevant information. This information literacy process provides the stimulus for analysis and evaluation of the overload of information that sometimes accompanies electronic retrieval. It is this process of defining and linking multiple access points, relating terms, and moving from one layer to another vertically and horizontally to acquire, analyze, evaluate, and apply the information that is the critical tool for navigating the super information highway.

A visual presentation, with handouts the students could follow, and hands-on exercises would have been a more compelling educational experience for these ESL students. The faculty member would also be more inclined to pursue additional library instruction and curriculum development if the session had been more meaningful to his students.

No longer are paper and pencil the way employees handle information. Business presentations do not use chalk and a blackboard. Presentation computer tools such as PowerPoint and Persuasion add color, graphics, and multiple fonts and formats to increase comprehension and hold interest in a multimedia, information rich society. Imagine how much more meaningful Chin Li's understanding of the virtual library would have been if she had a colorful PowerPoint presentation emphasizing the important points of the library tools available, with the handouts of the overhead materials, and online demonstrations of the electronic public access catalog's potential.

FACULTY TRAINING

In my study (1992a, 1994), I found that 78 percent of school library media specialists provided formal training in the use of CD-ROM technology and most library media specialists instructed first-time users between fifteen and thirty minutes. Two factors strongly influenced the use of the technology among faculty and students in their classes: (1) in-service training, and (2) formal classroom instruction. Only 53 percent of the school library media specialists conducted in-service training. There is definitely a connection between in-service training and curriculum use—similar to that seen with the domino effect. Faculty who are part of the in-service training are more likely to have the school library media specialist conduct formal training for their classes. Students who receive formal training in class are more likely to use the CD-ROM technology for class assignments, personal research, and leisure interests.

Understanding and mastering search strategies are critical not only in retrieving information from the Internet but also in marketing your school and courses on the Internet. Training and instruction go beyond the mechanics of the hardware or a superficial introduction to the library catalog and reference area. Key word, title, subject, and Boolean searching techniques are central components of using the electronic world of information successfully. The need for faculty training within the context of the curriculum to promote relevancy cannot be overstated!

The prospect of introducing technology opens avenues of interactivity. Faculty in-service should extend beyond a designated time for a specific training workshop. It should also include project and curriculum planning and implementation. Regardless of the educator's lack of computer knowledge, the interactive and interdisciplinary environment needs to be awakened both before and while training faculty in technology within the context of the curriculum.

To develop an environment that supports collaboration, library media specialists can foster special weekly meeting times. Working with the administration and faculty, they can schedule team-planning sessions to problem solve ways that multimedia and technology tools can be integrated within the curriculum. Goals should include increasing productivity, broadening learning environments, and increasing the resources available to students.

Library media specialists should provide faculty access to print and electronic journals, bulletin boards, the Internet, and teleconferencing. In-service training is a *must* if the tools are to be used appropriately within the context of the curriculum and if faculty are to have a comfort level that makes them feel empowered to create, imagine, and explore. A 1990 study by the Center for Technology (Fulton 1993) found that it can take as much as five or six years for teachers to effectively use the technology in their classrooms. Reflection should be encouraged continuously during the workday. The importance of adaptation, imagination, and responsiveness to innovation should be stressed by the library media specialist, and this atmosphere should be communicated to the administration for its full support.

Senge (1994) states in *The Fifth Discipline* that organizations suffer from adversarial exchanges and closedness at meetings. The resistance in the

1980s to technology integration throughout all the restructuring and re-form movements is amazing considering business's dramatic transition. Educators cannot bury themselves with this same obstinacy in the 1990s; the information technology revolution is here and we are in its midst.

Senge (1994) stated that in dialogue, individuals gain insights that could not be achieved individually. A new kind of mind comes into being, one based on the development of a common meaning. In dialogue a group explores complex issues from many points of view. Dialogue is especially good for generating possibilities and enhancing understanding. Library media specialists need to stimulate this dialogue if telecommunications, multimedia, and technology tools are to be put to good use within the curriculum in their schools.

McKenzie (1993) paralleled the stages of the hero's journey with the six stages of the creative process:

- preparation
- frustration
- incubation
- strategizing
- illumination
- verification

As a paradigm shifter, remember you are a hero, and with perseverance, determination, and teamwork, you can succeed!

Many proactive library media specialists are leading the way in partnerships with teaching faculty to train students to acquire information from multiple electronic environments. They are leading interdisciplinary teams and learning communities in utilizing new forms of electronic communication and in developing logical, scientific, and critical thinking strategies. School library media specialists are assisting students and teachers in connecting to electronic libraries and museums, capturing video images, music, and simulations, and researching primary historical documents. They are creating and actively participating in learner-centered environments. They are the instructional coaches managing the activities of diverse learners at different rates of progress but affording each a wide range of information resources from which to explore.

CHALLENGES IN USING TECHNOLOGY

What are the challenges to using technology in the classroom or the library media center? The challenges in using the new technologies are:

- to provide the hardware, software, and infrastructure networks to make technology integration possible

- to train teachers and librarians in the use of information technology
- to utilize the technology to actively improve instruction in order to accomplish and surpass curriculum goals and increase student achievement
- to make its applications relevant to the job market
- to empower and motivate at-risk students to complete high school and succeed in the job market and/or continue their education

Currently, the United States has the widest rich-poor gap since the Census Bureau began keeping track of the economy in 1947. The top 20 percent of American families have 44.6 percent of the country's income, while the bottom fifth have only 4.4 percent. The Clinton administration is hoping that the new telecommunications and information technologies can bridge this gulf between America's rich and poor (Irving 1995).

In June 1995, the Clinton administration advocated a new program to target low-income households, minorities, and Americans living in rural areas and give them access to computers and training on how to use them. By September 1995, the president was calling for a superhighway Internet connection for all schools in the United States. Commerce Secretary Ron Brown said, "If we do not act, the next generation of American workers may divide between those who have used computers—at home and at school—for their entire lives, and those for whom merely logging on is an arcane and intimidating ritual." He added that the administration hopes to preclude creating a work force split between "those with vast opportunities for well-paying jobs, and those without" (*Investor's Business Daily* 1995).

The At-Risk Student

2

PURPOSE OF THIS BOOK

In writing this book, my goal is to address some of these challenges cited in chapter 1 by looking at research and outstanding case studies and lesson plans of school library media specialists and faculty. These information technology explorers have met the challenges of integrating technological tools into the curriculum, surpassed expectations, and created and implemented the learning environment of the twenty-first century.

Given the context of the information technology revolution this book has a dual purpose:

- to present the research using educational technology within the disciplines that meet the needs of the diverse learning styles of all students including those most at risk of dropping out of school
- to showcase the teaching styles and strategies of dynamic library media specialists who bring the wealth of the information technology revolution to their students within the context of the curriculum

WHO IS THE AT-RISK STUDENT?

For the purposes of this book, the definition of the at-risk student will include the average and below-average student who is in danger of dropping out, or who does not have the skills to enter and succeed in the information technology job market of today. According to the National Center for Educational Statistics (1992), the national dropout rate for the sixteen to twenty-four age group is 12.5 percent. By the year 2000, 50 percent of all new jobs will require a degree beyond high school, 30 percent will require a college degree. By the year 2010, almost constant retraining will be necessary to keep jobs or obtain new ones (Citroen 1988).

It is difficult to define who is at risk because it is not related to a simple cause but rather to what Mann (1986) refers to as a "nesting of student problems." It is interesting to note that 70 percent of the at-risk students nationwide who drop out of school score average or above average on standardized tests (Gastright 1989). Students from lower-economic status are more at risk to drop out of school (Young-Hawkins 1993).

Results from a Virginia Department of Education survey (1993) of technology teachers' perceptions of at-risk students listed low achievement on standardized tests, failure to pass the literacy Passport test, and overall poor academic performance as indications of at-risk students. In addition to academic performance, 98 percent of the schools used the following behavior criteria:

- students that were frequently absent or truant
- student behavior that resulted in suspension or expulsion

Schools also used the following outcome criteria to determine the at-risk student:

- students who are average or who have been retained in grade
- students who have dropped out

The following instructional techniques were used in Virginia to provide assistance and address the needs of the educationally at-risk student at a cost of $47 million to the state:

- staff development related to the instruction of at-risk students (93%)
- developmentally appropriate practice in grades K–3 (88%)
- peer tutoring (75%)
- accelerated classroom schools (60%)
- cooperative learning (60%)
- mentor programs (59%)
- computer-assisted instruction (7%)

It is interesting and important to note the low level of computer usage and the drill and practice nature of the use of computers when available for at-risk students. Individualized programs were most beneficial.

CASE STUDY: USING WORD PROCESSING IN THE CONTEXT OF SOCIAL STUDIES

In the mid-1980s as a library director for a junior high school, I worked closely with all teachers in integrating library research skills, critical-thinking tools, online databases, CD-ROM, videodisks, computer applications, and telecommunications into the curriculum of various disciplines. I interacted on a daily basis with students with severe and moderate learning disabilities who were either mainstreamed in regular classes or segregated in a special teaching resource room.

I observed that students who could not write more than a few sentences using the static, linear tools of the pencil and paper were able to move text, rewrite, and delete with ease, in addition to composing more lengthy passages using the computer word-processing program. These passages did not lack depth. On the contrary, their perceptions and experiences prompted me to comment to the special needs instructor my surprise at the remarkable intelligence of many of the students. They were not purely aural-and lecture-oriented learners. They liked searching for information on a CD-ROM laser disk once they learned how to define the problem and narrow their key words. Their success with the electronic resources and their newly acquired understanding of the information search provided them with the link to use all the reference print resources that they had previously shunned. Online databases, videodisks, and filmstrips provided a rich resource-based environment to acquire and retrieve information that would satisfy the learning styles of a diverse group of learners.

The students created databases from the information gathered—for example, one for Third World countries—for subsequent classes. They communicated their research in dialogues with students across the country through an online newspaper, through a teleconference, through a video cable show with a neighboring town, as well as through reports, journals, and letters to their congressmen, using the word processor and desktop publishing. The students came in early and stayed during lunch and after school to be part of this electronic revolution.

David, a thirteen-year old with dark penetrating eyes, was classified as a special needs student. He struggled with emotional problems, lack of motivation, and poor academic performance. David came into the library with his social studies teacher. The social studies teacher, English teacher, and the library media specialist were team teaching a unit on Early Man. The social studies teacher was looking for new ways of having her students experience the logic, reasoning, search strategies, and format involved in developing a content rich outline. Students, using the traditional pencil and paper and lecture format, had problems in creating an outline. The social studies teacher took the outline from her static paper worksheet and transferred it to the word processor. Each student received a disk that he or she could work off of, adding new information, moving, and deleting text as necessary.

When David was introduced to the outline on a word processor, another dimension was opened to him. He was able to scroll up and down, add and delete information with ease. His handwriting and the confines of the paper were not an obstacle. The computer display was always legible. David brought the library media center's reference books to the computer and added short phrases of important concepts. He used the library media center's CD-ROM encyclopedia to search for terms he defined as important and then included that information in his outline.

Previously, David was overwhelmed by his handwriting. Trying to fit too much into small spaces and working in a sloppy work space caused him anxiety. The sense of disorder disturbed him. His mind would drift, and he would become disinterested. The computer was clear. It was easy to organize his work and his thoughts. He was motivated to find more information. David began to enjoy writing. From the outline, he neatly began the paragraphs for his research. He was able to easily synthesize his information. He was successful at organizing his thoughts and releasing them legibly through the use of the word processor. He enjoyed searching the CD-ROM and later moved to online databases. David, the library media specialist, and the social studies, special needs, and English teachers realized that he had a gift for writing that blossomed throughout junior high. He became a leader in the development of the student-produced online newspaper centered in the library media center—a great place for cooperative learning and team interaction as well.

David still had to cope with the dark conflict of a family living with an alcoholic father. He overcame its negative influence on his academic performance by being an active hands-on learner, motivated by his success in overcoming some of his disabilities through the use of technology integrated into a classroom project. His self-image and self-esteem increased.

CONTEXTUAL LEARNING

In a study of 133 technology teachers and their perceptions of at-risk students, 40 percent of the respondents felt that their students had the full range of variability of intelligences (Young-Hawkins 1993). One-third of the teachers thought the students lacked motivation. In another study (Gastright 1989), 70 percent of the students who dropped out of school scored average or above average on standardized tests.

There are many Davids. David was immersed in information literacy, the process of acquiring, retrieving, analyzing, evaluating, and applying information to solve a problem. This is an individual process that synthesizes the information within the student to become knowledge. The library media specialist, working with teachers on curriculum, treats each student as an individual learner. Regardless of the age of the student, topics for research are usually personalized, prompting individual investigation of multimedia and print resources.

Internet classes can be effective examples. The Net is worldwide and much too large to be able to address everyone's specific topics in a lesson. The importance of the instruction is to empower the students and the teachers with search strategy skills and an understanding of which tools are most successful for retrieving relevant information for particular information needs. The library media specialist cannot and should not retrieve the information for the students or the faculty. He or she must provide familiarity with the electronic learning environment, competence with the physical tools of the browser software for the World Wide Web, and the cognitive tools necessary to define the problem and key words for information retrieval. Simple exercises can reinforce the use of available search strategies, searching tools, and subject indexes after which the students are free to explore, searching for information specific to their interests.

The library media specialist is the guide, creating a context of relevant rationale and placing the navigational tools in the hands of the learner. This is in contrast to many of the instructional strategies utilized with the at-risk students that are generally remedial and focus on transferring information in the form of facts and procedures.

"Unfortunately, information presented as facts is then stored as facts, and for most students it is not recognized as knowledge to be used to solve problems. The consequence is that the facts remain inert and often are not spontaneously used in problem solving situations" (Bransford, Sherwood, Kinzer, Hasselbing, and Williams in press). Indeed, findings from the National Assessment of Educational Progress (Dossey, Mullis, Lindquist, and Chambers 1988) indicate that American students have significant difficulties in reasoning and in putting what they have learned in school to use in solving problems. "It appears that our present system of formal education is doing a rather poor job of attaining this goal, especially with students who are at risk for school failure" (Barron et al. 1989).

Teacher and library media specialist partnerships promote learning within a contextualized environment. The lifelong strategies of information literacy are easily transferred from one situation to another if the critical thinking and search strategies are taught and not isolated from the mechanics of the hardware and software.

In the electronic world as one is thinking, one is doing, one is concretely visualizing the thinking process. Learning is an active process. The student is engaged, interacting with the screen display. It is the visual integration and conception of ideas, key words, graphics, images, videos, and sounds that are critical learning stimuli for the students. Electronic tools allow the student to map concepts, ideas, to outline terms visually as well as abstractly while still being in control of the tactile manipulation of the data. The student is the navigator in the electronic world of information. This navigation breaks the mold of the linear and straight course. It promotes divergent thinking, branching, promoting the adventure of searching for connections, exploring and creating new constructs, forming a bridge to a new knowledge path. The minority, the at-risk, the special needs, the learning disabled, and even the average student may not be exposed to these tools of information literacy thereby restricting their growth in the continuum of lifelong learning. Library media specialists remarked that "CD-ROM helps those students to think in concrete terms, which is usually beneficial for a lower level student" (Mendrinos 1992b).

"Special education students and staff have higher expectations using the CD-ROM technology. Mainstreamed and special education students use it by themselves (on their own), accessing the information they need, and are stimulated to learn and form written and mental linkages between topics. CD-ROM technology is a great equalizer bringing success to all students regardless of their prescribed ability levels. It overcomes previous learning barriers opening up a world of information to this group of former library non-users" (Mendrinos 1992b).

Hypertext formats whether on the Internet or on CD-ROM motivate and assist students of all ages to participate and benefit from parallel-thinking strategies. Students can click on highlighted text, images, sounds, or graphics and branch and explore related information. The student is in control of the hypertext environment and he or she is empowered to make the linkages to expand and explore the new knowledge paths.

Electronic tools such as CD-ROM technology do not present information as being fixed and stagnant. Information is fluid and easily manipulated through the information literacy process. The student visually and concretely views the search and the results on the screen. The abstract becomes the concrete. The reasoning powers of the intellect interact with the sense of touch, sight, and possibly hearing for a holistic learning experience.

The research states that children often learn well when they and a mediator share a context or event that can be mutually explored (Feurestein et al. 1980). Library media specialists have a rich environment of multisensory learning tools that can be utilized to explore the specific context of the curriculum. The library media center is the treasure chest of the school containing CD-ROM, videodisks, books, audio-visual, media, and video tapes. It is the center of resource-based learning.

Sherwood et al. (1987) found that mediators can arrange the environment so that learners will encounter certain experiences. The experiences can help learners separate relevant from unrelated information. Finally, the mediators can monitor the performance of learners to encourage as much independent performance as possible. This is the role of the proactive library media specialist—to provide students with active experiences in the information literacy process. These are the critical lifelong skills, especially necessary in this information technology revolution.

Findings on the use of computers in chapter 1 programs are consistent with those on the use of computers with low socioeconomic students, including the survey results from Virginia. Computers in the schools are minor additions to the materials at some schools. If computers are available, they are used primarily for computer-assisted instruction (CAI) and drill and practice (Tucker 1987).

Drill and practice and isolated fact acquisition permeate the teaching of low socioeconomic students. This results in less instruction in comprehension and meaning than advantaged students receive and severely curtails the low socioeconomic students' chances for learning. Strickland et al. (1987) offered the following guidelines for meaningful use of computers in reading for low socioeconomic students:

- focus on meaning and reading comprehension
- foster active involvement and stimulate thinking
- support and extend knowledge of text structures
- make use of content from a wide range of subject areas
- link reading to writing

The separation of literacy skills—examples include reading and writing—from their context strings renders them meaningless and dull. Reading and writing skills are best learned within a meaningful context through the creation of interesting topical frameworks. The library media center should be the resource-based learning environment, providing the context for meaningful discovery, exploration, critical thinking, and learning.

CD-ROM–BASED LEARNING

In my research study of 381 secondary school library media specialists (Mendrinos 1992a), many library media specialists stated that if they did not have the budget for the technology they would use their book budgets. Why? The most profound educational outcome of my survey was that special education, learning disabled, and average students are not only more motivated but more productive using the CD-ROM technology.

Perceivable outcomes mentioned by the library media specialists in the use of the technology include the improvement of the student's research skills, productivity, and critical-thinking abilities. Students are becoming more specific in what they are looking for after using CD-ROM technology for reference. They are motivated to use more sources because they have the knowledge of which sources contain the information they need to fulfill their information quest and which subject headings can produce similar results in other indexes or catalogs. CD-ROM expands the students' thinking about the availability of different resources. Their productivity has increased because of CD-ROM's ease of use and their research products have improved due to efficiency in accessing and retrieving a larger, relevant number of information sources.

Library media specialists believe students are much more responsive to CD-ROM indexes than to print sources. Their observations illustrate that all levels of students are increasing their use of the library media center, not just the exemplary students. The division of topics into subtopics helps all students, especially average students and those with special needs and learning disabilities, in their search for information and in defining and re-defining their research question. These students use CD-ROM for reference purposes and prefer to use it by themselves.

The following passages from interviews capture the impact of CD-ROM technology on different ability level students.

All levels, are helped . . . not just your stellar students. . . . Kids have been here in the past but have not really used the library to its potential and I think they are a little bit more . . .

I think that it is so important 9th and 10th graders or middle of the road students that are not going to be doing a degree at Harvard have the ability to find the material they want with a minimum of fuss and bother . . . and they can do it by them-selves. . . . I think that someone is so excited anyway that the slower students would more readily use CD-ROM.

My question before and after my study is, "Why does CD-ROM and other technologies integrated within the context of the curriculum have a bene-ficial effect on the at-risk learner?"

COGNITIVE SCIENCE

Cognitive science studies the interface between the student, the mind, information processing, and technology. It reflects aspects of both the user and the system. It is cross-disciplinary in nature. Cognitive science ex-plains the psychology of why technology used within the context of the curriculum can meet the needs and the learning styles of the at-risk stu-dent. "When it comes to the abstract, scientific principles of information processing, there are general rules that will apply, regardless of what de-vice is being spoken of. So the science of information processing is relevant to us, if the engineering may not always be. This science by the way, is now being called cognitive science" (Lindsay and Norman 1977).

Cognitive science can be characterized as an approach that is:

- "Eclectic, using concepts from psychology, philosophy, linguistics, and artificial intelligence.
- Synthetic, putting these concepts together to form a connected system of theory.
- Analytic, employing the computational approach to formalize the basic pro-cesses of cognition" (Scaife 1989).

Education and psychology have contributed to and are considered ben-eficiaries of cognitive science. Educational psychology is concerned with thinking skills, metacognition, critical judgment, and self-reflective questioning. Learning and research sets are participatory in nature. Within this context of learning, there is a strong need in all disciplines to develop methods of exploration and analysis that provide a means of discovery and addressing relevant information.

Technology has changed the nature of business dramatically within the past ten years. Library media specialists who have integrated technology within the curriculum can relate to the changing nature of education.

In a symposium at Oregon State University Pea (1989) delineated some of these changes as follows:

- shifts in emphasis from subject emphasis to emphasis on learner to teacher
  - The student is an active learner in a social context, with self-constructing ideas based on previous experience. Diagnosis of the learner is critical in forming a bridge from experiential informal knowledge to formal knowledge.
- shifts from fact-driven to model-driven understanding
  - The stress is on an interconnection of knowledge across subject matter disciplines rather than on isolated fragmented facts. General and discipline-specific strategies assist learners in prediction and qualitative reasoning. This is at the center of information literacy and emphasizes the importance of proactive learners.
- shifts from curriculum-centered to learner-centered curriculums
  - Students' preconceptions are engaged, requiring students to examine their own knowledge to solve problems. It recognizes that what we need to learn is being challenged by technological and social change. It acknowledges the different learning modalities and the multiple representations of knowledge.
- shifts to more recognition of the potency of the social context in the learning process, and to utilizing contemporary research in motivation, attribution, and collaboration.

The library media center provides the resources for electronic, online, print, and media to stimulate learner-centered problem solving. Memorization of facts from a textbook is stagnant in an ever-changing technologically advancing society. The question is, "How do I gather, retrieve, analyze, evaluate, and apply the information to solve the problem and how does this process engage the student?"

Classrooms or the library media center become the intentional learning center where the students explore their own patterns of metacognition and learn from each other. Relevant research in educational technology on student participation in the creation of meaning for the purpose of transfer speaks directly to the library media specialist and to the goals of information literacy. Wittrock (1988) stated, "Students must learn to organize new information in integrated and organized units for later use, i.e., transfer and generalization. Students must take an active role in learning information for future use and for integrating other topics and problems." This research underlines what library media specialists have known through experience, "that students do not spontaneously learn with the intent of using information; however, they can be assisted acquiring skills in organization and directed inquiry" (Wittrock 1988).

Students will not transfer facts but they will transfer problem-solving strategies that arise later. The findings of Wittrock's research study indicate:

- teach information for later use
- develop study strategies for using information
- teach when, how, and where to use these strategies

If the library media specialist introduces CD-ROM, online databases, and the Internet, he or she should include searching as an electronic tool to find information on a variety of subjects as well as introduce the strategies of defining the problem and using the process of information literacy. The students will have the benefit of lifelong learning skills that can be transferred to other problems throughout life.

Donald Meichanbaum (1981) stated that students learn without self-questioning, without self-monitoring, and without the intent of using the information later. Put simply, they do not think about their own thinking unless instructed to do so. This is the potential of information literacy within the teaching process.

Based on research, Wittrock (1988) stated that several factors contributed to a variety of tasks and problems:

- "Knowledge should be well-organized into units that can be assembled and re-assembled for application to a variety of tasks and problems.
    - This could explain the popularity of CD-ROM search engines such as those used by Information Access and Ebsco.
- Information should be learned with the intent of relating it and applying it both to other school subjects and to interpretation of life events and situations.
- Students' awareness of their own thinking strategies is a key component in achieving improved learning, transfer and generalization."

When Wittrock taught these metacognitive strategies, students' attitudes changed from learned helplessness to autonomy and taking on responsibility. This is confirmed in my study.

Keogh and Hall (1983) summarized the characteristics of training that produce transfer:

- present well-organized, categorized information
- give strategy training across different tasks
- build upon the background knowledge of the students

In developing an information-processing model within a context that is learner related, several studies have found that metacognition that includes thinking skills, with a subjective student response to the individual problems, produced related belief and valuing processes within the student.

What does this mean? It means that students develop increased productivity, increased motivation, positive self-image, and increased self-esteem. Several comments from library media specialists in my study (Mendrinos 1992a) confirm this:

I had lower 8th grade students studying pollution . . . they were successful in their searching and had their articles in hand . . . they were reading, writing and analyzing their articles.

Special education students and staff have higher expectations using the CD-ROM technology . . . special education and mainstreamed students use it by themselves on their own. . . . They get all their information . . . they love computers . . . they are stimulated to learn and connect other topics.

Everybody uses it. . . . CD-ROM is a great equalizer. . . . Mainstreamed Special Ed kids come in with other classes and use it . . . then they come on their own.

"The goal of multimedia education is to provide a stimulating, tailored nonjudgmental environment in which children can explore their creativity and develop individual learning strategies" (Menn 1993b). Students can search for images of space in a science class, students can rotate the images, focus in on specific aspects of a moon or planet, using raw scientific data found on the Internet. Some students have made discoveries in the confines of the classroom. There is a sense of exploration, discovery, and empowerment.

When thinking is embedded in disciplines, reasoning and judgment improve along with increased knowledge in a particular domain. The research in educational psychology, cognitive science, and library science has direct implications for special education, average, and at-risk students. It explains some of the reasons why these students benefit so greatly from educational technology integrated within the context of the curriculum as well as the importance of teaching the information literacy process.

The advantages of multimedia educational tools include:

- patience on the computer
- tailored to one-on-one teaching

- instant feedback
- absence of other students that could slow learning
- ability to teach information that would be otherwise difficult and expensive to communicate
- promotes team learning and cooperation

Limitations include:

- overhyped tools
- boredom from using a slow microcomputer
- need for teachers to learn a new technology
- software is not appropriate for all applications
- entertainment (Menn 1993c, 62)

Numerous educators have found that when technology is integrated into the curriculum:

- standardized test scores have improved
- school attendance increases
- social skills improve
- self-esteem increases (Menn 1993c)

For educational technology to have a substantial impact on the instructional process, schools should:

- clarify the role of computers as a pedagogical tool
- define its relationship to existing curriculum
- establish the level of human and financial investment they are willing to make (Burnett 1994)

Strong technology programs have the following characteristics according to the study by Jordan and Follman (1993). The following recommendations arose from my personal observations over a period of twelve years in integrating technology in the curriculum from middle school through graduate school:

- emphasize cooperative learning models and allow heterogeneous groupings of students to work together collaboratively
- emphasize higher-level problem-solving skills while also reinforcing basic skills
- support interactions between students and teachers rather than use computers as "teaching machines" to supplant the teacher
- create interactive learning environments built around real-world problems
- be adaptable to a variety of learning styles

TELECOMMUNICATIONS

The use of telecommunications through the Internet provides high-ways to the world. Technology applications within the curriculum have exploded exponentially with the advent of the Internet, specifically with the ease of using a World Wide Web browser, such as the Netscape Navigator. Many elementary, middle, and high school library media specialists are partnering with faculty in interdisciplinary curriculum development using worldwide telecommunications. Students use telecommunications with peers worldwide on a variety of topics ranging from pen pals to scientific analysis. Asynchronous computer teleconferencing, using a modem and a computer or a networked computer connected to an online service or the Internet, is providing instantaneous communication across geographic boundaries. It is being integrated within courses to enhance and promote local, national, and international studies and communication and to enroll students internationally in programs and degrees offered by schools in remote sites. The strengths of asynchronous computer teleconferencing are:

- it is a student-centered medium
- it promotes active learning
- it promotes "faceless intimacy" among students
- it encourages less aggressive students to participate
- it requires more organization than face-to-face instruction
- it reduces student isolation irrespective of location
- it encourages instructors to transform their teaching (Eastern Oregon State College 1995)

This type of distance learning and interaction will be explored through the case studies and lesson plans highlighted in the following sections.

MULTIMEDIA AND COMPUTER APPLICATIONS

Technology, thinking, and teamwork are critical elements for successful achievement as evidenced by the following study. The Stoddard Bosnick (1995) study focused on how the computer and multimedia were used to motivate at-risk students, encourage participation, and develop their higher order thinking skills.

The study addressed four major objectives:

- improving critical-thinking, problem-solving, and decision-making skills
- integrating mathematics, reading, writing, science concepts, and skills
- developing social skills in cooperative learning situations

- encouraging practice and demonstrating the use of the computer as an instructional tool

Studies have shown that people retain 20 percent of what they hear, 40 percent of what they see and hear, and 75 percent of what they see, hear, and do.

Reports have shown that the use of the computer focuses attention and directs impulsive behavior. Multimedia instruction is defined in the Stoddard Bosnick study as using video, sound, and graphics to foster interactivity. Using the technology within the context of the curriculum improved student learning by an average of 38 percent over more conventional instruction, for example, reducing time to competency by 31 percent. It also provided the best means for superior retention.

Multimedia provided a rich source of information with opportunities to notice various images, features, issues, and problems. It helped students acquire the pattern recognition skills that are related to visual and auditory skills. It assisted students in developing higher order thinking and decision-making skills. The study included forty elementary school teachers with substantial teaching experience. Ninety-five percent of the students were considered at risk. The control group received training on computers—word processing, graphics, desktop publishing, databases, and spreadsheets.

Instructional strategies included problem-solving techniques, cooperative learning, and the use of instructional technology to alter attitudes that students had about school. School attendance increased 5 percent in grades two through five. By the fifth grade, attendance increased by 10 percent. The level of content acquisition rose as measured by the students' achievement, which increased from the C- to D range to the B through C+ range.

Teacher performance also increased significantly. Teachers involved in the project used the computer at least once per day for instructional purposes. Teacher and student learning behavior was positively affected:

- it stimulated exploration and discovery
- it provided more flexibility and openness for teachers
- it produced more student-oriented lessons that addressed critical-thinking and problem-solving strategies

Teachers stated that they developed more leadership skills, became more assertive, and visualized instruction in an integrated manner across the curriculum after being trained in multimedia technologies. The outcomes of the study indicated increased sophistication among student portfolios and more positive teacher attitudes toward at-risk student achievement levels and computer integration. The teacher attitudes had a direct and significant effect on students' attitudes toward school, on student academic achievement, and on the students' personal growth. Teachers who stated that computer integration was successful had students who achieved more academically and acquired a sense of competence and pride in the work produced.

At-risk student participants in this study are viewed as motivated to perform and on-task when using the nontraditional instructional systems. Multimedia instruction is more student oriented and fosters a more hands-on approach to training. Students function more independently and share in the responsibility for their own learning. One teacher stated, "It has been so rewarding to see the change in my students' attitudes. They are enthusiastic and look forward to using the computer daily. They are working cooperatively and have been much more tolerant of each other" (Stoddard and Bosnick 1995). Self-consciousness and stereotypes are often dissolved as students exchange assistance and share successes; disabilities are minimized.

VIDEO-BASED CONTEXTS FOR AT-RISK STUDENTS

My research cited important productivity gains among at-risk learners using CD-ROM technology. The Stoddard and Bosnick (1995) study confirmed achievement gains using multimedia and technology applications. Studies using video-based contexts also demonstrated positive learning strategies for the at-risk learner.

Before David and his classmates could grasp the world of Early Man and learn new concepts, it was important for the library media specialist and the teacher to find a bridge or an anchor that would link the new concepts learned to concepts that were already understood by the students. This is called an Advanced Organizer. Brighter students who are more attuned to an aural mode of instructional delivery can relate a new concept to one they already know through a lecture. Most average and at-risk learners do not listen and learn well and the connection is rarely solidified. The use of video technology such as a videotape or random access videodisk can be very valuable in this situation. The teachers and the library media specialist can create the context in which to share and immerse the students.

Three advantages noted by Bransford et al. (in press) in the use of video-based contexts provide a research foundation as to why visual context clues are important anchors in linking previously stored knowledge with new knowledge. Many at-risk and average students are visual learners. Visual context clues help students in a number of ways:

First, they provide rich sources of information with opportunities to notice sensory images, dynamic features, relevant issues and inherent problems. Second, they give students the ability to perceive dynamic moving events and to more easily form rich mental models. This advantage is particularly important for lower achieving students and for students with low knowledge in the domain of interest. Third, video allows students to develop skills of pattern recognition which are related to visual and auditory cues rather than to events labeled by the teacher. In sum, video images are ideal for creating a common experience for the teacher and learner that can be used for "anchoring" new knowledge. (Barron et al. 1989)

Two projects coordinated at Vanderbilt University's Learning Technology Center illustrate that visual technologies offer definite advantages for at-risk learners. The first was a 1987 study of preschoolers who were considered at risk. The students were divided into two groups. The library media specialist began reading a simplified version of *Swiss Family Robinson* and showed the other group a videodisk of the same part of the story. Both groups learned from the story. However, the videodisk group learned and experienced the storm and the waves, the fright and the sounds. The library media specialist could only describe waves and storms to the text-based group who were too young to have those concepts in their knowledge bank. The sense of the storm and the trials of the sailing ships could be replayed to anchor the new concepts securely for the videodisk group.

Fifth-grade classes in an interdisciplinary project involving language arts and social studies content introduced the Young Sherlock Holmes project. In this study, the experiential group included average and at-risk learners. The Young Sherlock Holmes video series was used as an anchor. The comparison group received the same information but without the benefit of the video anchor.

The video anchor produced these results, which were not reflected in the comparison group:

- students who viewed the video anchor were more likely to use the targeted vocabulary
- stories written by students who had the video anchor were more likely to use the historical references and make inferences from the motives of the turn-of-the-century stories they read and saw
- story elements and plots were more likely to link character actions to goal statements and goal resolution (Kinzer and Risko 1988)

The use of the video technology in the form of the videodisk and the videotape was in the context of the desired learning mandated by the curriculum. It was not extemporaneous. The video images were an integral part of the curriculum, creating mental models with visual and auditory cues necessary to understand and anchor the new concepts to be learned. They also could be reviewed and replayed, bringing to light images that may have eluded the first-time viewer. Barron et al. (1989) rightly emphasizes that it is the merging of the information from these disciplines with the technology that can make a difference, not the technology itself.

Library Media Centers: An Environment of Equity and Access

3

The library media center, information literacy, and the need for staff development in integrating educational technology in the curriculum will be discussed in this chapter. Case studies of proactive and technology savvy library media specialists will paint a picture of those meeting the challenges of the twenty-first century later in the book.

Harvard Law School professor Charles Oglethorpe strongly stated at the Annual American Library Association Meeting in the summer of 1996:

The more connected some of us become, the more disconnected most of us become. . . . There are millions who, because of poverty or race cannot even fathom the dimensions of the information age. . . . The consequences are staggering. Many of the most basic necessities are unavailable to many Americans stuck in poverty. If it is not possible to obtain a job, or to receive an education, or health care, we certainly can't expect this underserved population to meet today's technological challenge without a telephone or a computer (Galst 1996).

It is our duty as library media specialists to make sure that all students have exposure to the same information literacy and critical-thinking skills. Combine this with inquiry learning and the integration of educational technology available to all in our library media centers, and we can positively affect the lives of our students. Oglethorpe discussed the importance of the library in opening his eyes to the opportunities available: "The public library in my hometown literally saved my life and made a new life of opportunity possible" (Galst 1996). We can do the same as school library media specialists.

The U.S. 1995 National Assessment of Educational Progress (NAEP) had some very grim news in *two* significant areas. First, 57 percent of the high school students tested nationally failed to demonstrate a "basic" knowledge of history. Maintaining our democracy depends on the understanding of the United States as one country, its ways of governing, and its history as it relates to the past and as the past relates to the present. Second, only one-third of the graduating seniors in 1994 were proficient readers at the level set by the National Assessment Governing Board for all students. Thirty percent of the students were "below basic." "Below basic" is the term for nonfunctional readers. These students were to graduate within weeks. This meant that 750,000 semiliterate 18 year olds entered the work force with high school diplomas. "Out of 2.5 million graduates, only about 100,000 were reading at 'advanced' or 'world class' levels" (Finn 1995). Only 12 percent of blacks were "proficient" readers. Fifty-four percent were "below basic." Forty-eight percent of all Hispanics were "below basic," and 18 percent were proficient readers. Only 1 percent of blacks and Hispanics were advanced readers (Finn 1995).

California had the worst showing in the 1995 NAEP. The white population in California scored the lowest in reading among the white population in the nation. The Hispanic population in California also scored the lowest among the Hispanic population in the nation. Only 23 percent of fourth graders who took the California Learning Assessment System, which is now defunct, were reading at a satisfactory level. Just 28 percent were proficient in math. In the summer of 1996, the national news agencies stated that the largest national gap between rich and poor existed in California. It is not that the rich are getting richer, rather the poor are growing poorer. The middle class is disappearing.

Given the national test scores, especially those in California, and given the enormous and swift technological changes that are taking place in the workplace, the need for an educated populace is critical for maintaining a democracy. Reading is the essence of empowerment in an information society. Information literacy, which is the ability to access, retrieve, analyze, synthesize, and evaluate information to solve problems, can only happen if students can first read the material.

The California scores are not surprising. Studies have demonstrated the correlation between student achievement and excellent school library media centers. The library media specialist is in the best position to teach students and faculty the skills needed to access the Internet. The library media center is the center of equity and access for all students to experience and to work with educational technology to meet their curricula information needs.

The 1996 Status Report to the Chancellor's Office for California Community Colleges on the need for an Information Competency General Education Requirement cited the crisis in K–12 libraries (Norman 1996). Norman stated:

The lack of K–12 libraries with professional certified personnel has created a serious problem for community college libraries. Information literacy skills are almost non-existent among entering students . . . that the State's K–12 schools are not in a position to certify that students are skilled in the information search process or retrieval of information, especially utilizing new and emerging information retrieval technologies. It is evident that the majority of students in existing K–12 institutions, whether they drop out or graduate, lack the information retrieval skills necessary for a successful collegiate, vocational experience and or lifelong learning.

High schools in Montgomery County, Maryland, graduate almost all of their high school seniors with 86 percent going on to higher education. Local community colleges reported that 71 percent of entering students were deficient in math, and 50 percent did not meet the English standards (Finn 1995). Considering the results of the NAEP, this is probably more the rule than the exception. According to a survey conducted by the NAEP, levels of literacy among young Americans between the ages of twenty-one and twenty-five were considered "not adequate on average, for maintaining world leadership in a changing technological society." Literacy was defined as the ability to "do" something, versus knowledge "of" something.

These statistics underline the importance of a meaningful, self-directed, self-involved, action-oriented educational experience that leads to success. A Nation at Risk (National Commission on Excellence in Education 1983) reported a twenty-year decline in educational achievement and called for the creation of the "Learning Society." The Learning Society extends beyond the boundaries of the traditional institution, reaches out to libraries, "and indeed, into every place where the individual can develop and mature, work, and live."

The Internet encourages the growth of the Learning Society. It can make it a reality. One is no longer confined to the boundaries of the home without access to a virtual library of information. Lifelong learning can occur anywhere and at anytime.

Richard is a sophomore in high school and is researching the rain forest. He has access to the World Wide Web browser, Netscape. The library media specialist is working with the students and teacher in Richard's class. She has demonstrated the Netscape search engines and how to use them successfully to retrieve information on the World Wide Web.

Richard uses SavvySearch (http://www.cs.colostate.edu), a metaindexing tool, to search the Internet on the rain forest, successfully retrieving information from several different search engines, including full-text articles. Richard also accesses discussions posted on newsgroups by scientists and loggers, as well as videos, photographs, and graphics on this subject. Utilizing his home computer's modem, Richard can also dial into his public and school library to scan the catalogs for relevant books that he can check out. His school and public libraries also make available magazine and newspaper indexes that have full-text articles. Richard can dial each library and search for the rain forest. The number of articles available is too large, so Richard narrows his selection by a specific geographic location and date. He wants to know what has happened within the last two years. Richard captures the information using his telecommunications software. He prints the articles from the Internet. Richard then prints the articles from the school and public libraries at home on his laser printer. After reading and outlining the articles, Richard begins to write his report. Richard is fortunate to have access from home. He does not have to leave his home. His ability to telecommunicate and access these resources allows him to be a part of the Learning Society.

New technology threatens to widen the gap between the "information rich" and the "information poor" even as it promises to revolutionize how we live, learn, work, and govern. The statistics below underscore the need for policies to ensure equal access to electronic information:

- "Fewer than one in three U.S. households own a computer. Those living in rural areas and central cities are the least likely to be connected.
- Families with incomes over $50,000 are five times more likely to have access to computers and ten times more likely to have access to online services.
- African American and Latino school children are less likely to have access to computers, both at home and at school, than other children" (American Library Association 1996).

More and more businesses and educators are communicating instantaneously through electronic mail. They may have desktop video conferencing where they talk with their colleagues from remote locations. At the same time, they can share word-processing documents, spreadsheets, or visuals and work on them together at their microcomputers regardless of distance. On their desktop, they also have access to the Internet and can get financial information and research important company topics for the most up-to-date information. The picture I am drawing is one of literacy in action. The workplace of the twenty-first century will not tolerate illiteracy, especially in well-paying jobs. A polarization is occurring.

Carol is disturbed by the noise of the classroom. She has to work at least twenty hours a week to pay for her clothes, her food, and her car. She wants to concentrate, but the lack of discipline in her classroom is making it difficult. There is no library media center in her school. She does not have access to computers except through one of her classes. Her science teacher does not like to teach. Every week Carol receives a packet of materials, which she reads, for her science class. Carol is scheduled to go to the computer lab to word process the answers to the science questions. Carol enjoys word processing—it is one of her first introductions to computers even though she is a junior in high school. She has used computers in math class to solve problems using computer-assisted instruction, which was the extent of her computer usage before now.

Carol often changes jobs. She has worked for Burger King and McDonald's. She is not competent in computers, so she cannot even try for a data entry position. Carol has never been exposed to the Internet, CD-ROM technology, and video laser disks. She has never researched any of her reports using resources other than print. She is bored with school and has asked to take her remaining courses as Home Study. She is bright, disenfranchised from the learning environment, and in danger of dropping out. Carol does not live in a low-income community. She lives in the heart of Silicon Valley, California. The average per capita income according to a 1996 study in the San Francisco Bay area is $63,000.

Library media specialists and faculty can work together to bring equity and access to the learning environment of all students—possibly not in the home because of financial restraints but in the schools and most likely in the library media center.

One author has noted: "Technology is not by itself socially unjust. It is, however, inextricably intertwined with the distribution of wealth, race, and gender relations. Since technologies are a product of the existing structure of opportunities, and constraints in society, they are likely to extend, shape, rework or reproduce this structure" (Maddaus 1994). Studies have indicated that the use of computers with low socioeconomic students consists primarily of computer-assisted instruction (Tucker 1987). This concern was widespread in the federal Chapter 1 reading program in 1992. A dominant pattern appeared in suburban schools: Students with outstanding math abilities were introduced to computers while computer-assisted instruction was for "disabled" students. This encouraged the more affluent students to "tell the computer what to do," and the less affluent students to learn "to do what the computer tells them" (Watt 1982).

Richard Riley, secretary of education, reiterates a concern that research in several disciplines has revealed: If students are not challenged, their level of achievement remains low. It points to a bias that has been part of American education and is most visible in the pattern of tracking students:

Social scientists attribute much of the white-minority differences in achievement to the higher incidence of poverty in the families of minority children and the lower average educational levels of their parents. It is difficult for schools to compensate for such disadvantages. However, there is evidence that extraordinary schools and teachers make a difference in how all students perform. For example, research on early intervention and on one-to-one tutoring demonstrates that at-risk students can achieve at far higher levels than they have in the past. There is also some evidence, particularly in math and science, that taking more challenging courses is related to higher performance and achievement. (Riley 1995)

This concern is being addressed in the latest national science standards, which emphasize the importance of science to all Americans.

The U.S. Department of Labor's Secretary's Commission on Achieving Necessary Skills (SCANS) report *What Work Requires of Schools* (1991) outlines the changes in the American workplace and recommends the necessary skills all students should have for success in an information-based society. The following competencies are very much the essence of information literacy:

- acquiring and evaluating information
- organizing and maintaining information
- interpreting and communicating information
- using computers to process information

The national standards in math, social studies, and science were restructured in the early part of the 1990s to reflect the needs of inquiry learning. This type of learning fosters problem solving, reasoning, investigating, communication, and notions of context and decision making. Within these frameworks, library media specialists can work with instructors to utilize the full range of information resources and educational technology and relate them to curriculum goals and objectives.

The National Council for the Teachers of Mathematics (NCTM) advocates that the assessment of mathematics be based on using information in meaningful ways to demonstrate understanding. The National Council for the Social Studies (NCSS 1993) has stated that "it is important that students be able to connect knowledge, skills, and values to action as they engage in social inquiry." The National Committee on Science Education Standards and Assessment (NCSESA) is recommending science for all. There should not be differences of content—in science, math, or social studies experiences—between different levels of students. Science should foster inquiry, which includes investigation, critical thinking, habits of the mind, and positive attitudes toward learning. These disciplines should reflect real-world problems in their curriculums.

In all three disciplines learning is extended from textbook and multiple choice learning. The teaching of science offers a useful example. Scientists research in order to form a hypothesis; then they conduct investigations. There is a substantial link to the information resources of the library that knows no bounds. In the surveys of library media specialists, it is evident that science has discovered the rich resources of the library media center and beyond.

WHICH INFORMATION LITERACY SKILLS ARE REQUIRED IN THE WORKPLACE?

The library at City College of San Francisco surveyed the business community in order to discover which information literacy skills were required by the employer for their employees in the workplace. The responses include the following:

- "broad awareness of information sources, relative value of information; basic skills in formulating questions"
- "skills in communicating research requests"
- "knowledge of when to use the library's services for their research; ability to focus their research queries to get more precise information"
- "working knowledge of using hard copy reference materials, searching proprietary on-line databases, navigating the Internet and installing and using CD-ROM products at their workstations"
- "Internet skills"
- "Boolean searching"
- "analytical skills"
- "computer skills-searching databases"
- "skill in using indexes and making their own files and indexes"

Several of the comments from business follow:

- "Scientists rely on 'searching for information before researching.' Business staff needs information in order to remain competitive."
- "Research determines both the company's product line and the internal culture."
- "You cannot be a manager without competent research skills."
- "Writers must know where to go, what to ask for" (Cohen and Elmer 1995).

The development of these skills is not the purview alone of the community colleges or the university. Their development needs to occur at the elementary school level and continue through high school. Information-processing strategies need to be developed. Regardless of the format, print, electronic, or online, the thinking strategies for accessing and retrieving information are similar.

Electronic and online indexes and databases are not linear. They are relational. Parallel and branching critical-thinking strategies are needed to connect to related terms, and to navigate through a web of information. Recorded knowledge and information is no longer separate and isolated. However, it is the navigator who seeks out the connections and travels the path to information success. It is the library media specialist who provides the navigational tools and strategies for a successful journey. Information literacy is the ability to access, evaluate, and use information from a variety of sources. The study of reading, writing, math, science, and social studies needs to be coupled with practice in communication, critical thinking, and problem solving.

The steps to successful navigating include:

- Being able to define the problem
  - This could be in the form of a question or a statement

- Brainstorm the key terms and concepts that are related to the topic
  - Use Boolean logic, if possible
    - use "and," "or," "not"
- Identify the resources that will be on the information quest
  - For example, books, CD-ROMs, videodisks, the Internet
- Locate, and find the information
  - Are there any key terms or concepts that will enable one to find more information?
  - Is there too much information?
  - Which terms can narrow or expand the search?
- Analyze and evaluate the information
  - Relevancy
  - Audience
  - Authenticity
    - Is it up to date?
    - What are the credentials of the author?
    - Is there bias?
- Synthesize the information from multiple sources
  - Relate the information retrieved, analyzed, and evaluated to the problem
  - Avoid duplication
- Evaluate the information
  - Is it coherent?
  - Is it convincing?
  - Is it cogent?
  - Is it accurate?
- Apply the information to solve the problem
  - What conclusions can be made?

An *information literate* person is one who:

- recognizes the need for information
- formulates questions based on information needs
- identifies potential sources of information
- develops successful search strategies
- accesses sources of information including computer-based and other technologies
- analyzes information critically
- evaluates information
- organizes and manipulates information for practical application

- makes decisions based on accurate and complete information (Washington State Library/Media Director's Council 1994).

Language arts teachers, resistant to technology, began to appreciate the value of the World Wide Web when it was presented in the context of information literacy. It was a context that was important to them. They no longer viewed the Internet as alien but as another substantial way for accessing and retrieving information. They also realized that by not exposing their students to this information highway, they were widening the gap between socioeconomic levels and contributing to inequities in access and discernment.

Information technologies can dramatically change the ways in which knowledge and information are obtained. The instructional process is being transformed in our midst. Those who are part of this learning environment are developing new ways of thinking. The "Learning Society" is real. Telecommunications and the ease of using the World Wide Web have given everyone who is trained the ability to retrieve, display, and manipulate the vast array of recorded worldwide information and knowledge.

DEVELOPING INFORMATION COMPETENCY

The role of the library media specialist is changing and expanding. It is increasing in importance. Telecommunications, distance learning, and the Internet are and will continue to profoundly affect our profession. Administrators should be made aware that the major goals of each of the disciplines and the SCANS' report relate to information literacy. For a library media specialist to be effective, educational technology must be another format of access and retrieval that is second nature, similar to retrieving a book from a print collection:

The library, whose traditional mission as a place where physical collection, storage and access of recorded knowledge was coupled with professional expertise in the effective use of new and emerging information and knowledge, will be able to carry out this mission in both a "real" or physical space, and "virtual" (or electronic) space. By taking advantage of technological capabilities being developed worldwide—creating networks linking students, faculty and other users on and off campus and integrating this technology with other academic and instructional activities—the library of the 21st century will be at the center. (CSU Council of Library Directors 1994)

One library media specialist shared these insights in an electronic discussion group:

Thanks to some recent time devouring nightmares (a WASC accreditation self study and a new technology plan), we were forced to take the time to meet together and sort out our mission and goals.

About half way through the year, it dawned on us that we were beginning to develop some interesting insights, namely that our jobs and the role of the library had drastically been changed. In essence, we had moved from a "traditional" library where we were the storehouse of knowledge and we patiently waited for our customers to a "TECH/LIBRARY/MEDIA" program that serves as the information center for resource based learning.

Simply put, we no longer had the room to be the study hall, the social center, the lunch time gaming area . . . because the facility was constantly being used by classes and individuals for information based learning. (Daulton 1996)

Several state accrediting associations such as the Middle States Association on Higher Education and the Northwest Association for Schools and Colleges have included information literacy as one of the conditions for accreditation. It is a survival skill for life, enhancing one's personal life, citizenship, and career. It opens doors for the student allowing him or her to participate fully in the learning environment regardless of race, gender, or ethnicity.

With the general shift in curriculum standards, library media specialists are in an outstanding position to partner with the subject disciplines to integrate information literacy and information technology into these disciplines. Studies indicate that in the fields of social studies and science inquiry-based learning using educational technology increases achievement among all groups of students including those most at risk.

There are several different models for incorporating information literacy into the curriculum. The library media specialist in planning with the subject specialist(s) can decide which model is best suited for the project being planned. Models include the following:

- Resource-based learning
  - Incorporates a library research component into the curriculum, utilizing print, electronic, video, media, and online resources.

- Inquiry-based instruction
  - Discovery models of teaching emphasize the student as the learner. Students seek out and use information-based discoveries to predict, reason, forecast, and problem solve.

- Small group instruction
  - Small groups are introduced to information literacy competencies within the subject discipline, or as requested.

- Course-integrated instruction
  - The library media specialist can work with the teacher to integrate information literacy, teaching the classes several times during the unit or project.

- Linked courses
  - The library media specialist can be teaching a research course that complements the course work and projects of a course in another discipline. Students will take both courses simultaneously. The teacher and the library media specialist will plan the courses together.
- Team teaching
  - Information literacy strategies and resources are integrated into the curriculum of a course.
- Curriculum design consultation
  - Library media specialists work together in designing units, projects, and courses to include information literacy and a wide variety of resource materials and formats. (Washington State Library/Media Directors' Council 1994)

LIBRARY MEDIA/TEACHER PARTNERSHIPS

There is a psychology to working with teachers, the understanding of which may assist the library media specialist in understanding how teachers plan. It is important to work with the teacher in a nonthreatening manner. Schon (1983) referred to "knowing-in-action" as an underlying tenet of what we do as professional educators:

Our knowing is ordinarily tacit, implicit in our patterns of action and in our feel for the stuff with which we are dealing. It seems right to say that our knowing is in our action.

Similarly, the workaday life of the professional depends on tacit knowing-in-action. Every competent practitioner can recognize phenomena . . . for which he cannot give a reasonably accurate or complete description. In his day-to-day practice, he makes innumerable judgments of quality for which he cannot give a reasonably accurate or complete description. In his day-to-day practice, he makes innumerable judgments of quality for which he cannot state rules and procedures. Even when he makes conscious use of research-based theories and techniques, he is dependent on tacit recognition, judgments and skillful performance.

Planning is a mental activity. According to Yinger (Wolcott 1994), teacher's planning is nonlinear. Subject matter and activities are more prominent than evaluation. Teacher's planning also centers around published curriculum materials, teacher's guides, and methods.

The library media specialist and faculty member can reflect on the content and goals the students are to achieve. The library media specialist can encourage the faculty member to explain the issues that are important in the unit or project. Activities that were successful and those that were not as successful are also discussed. This provides an understanding of what the faculty member wants to accomplish. One can then evaluate and describe the educational technology resources that are available and can meet the needs of the teacher. A demonstration of the technology may be helpful.

The teacher is the key to the content. It is a partnership. The library media specialist can assist in developing the critical thinking and information literacy skills and strategies necessary for the students to succeed in accomplishing or exceeding the teacher's expectations. Together they can reflect on the planning process from the teacher's perspective. They decide what role the library media specialist and media center will play. It is very helpful to begin to develop daily lesson plans outlining the discussions and topics that will be covered, the technology resources that will be used, the part each will play, and the physical environment, be it the classroom or the library media center, that will house the lesson. Understanding the outcomes and expectations of the students will keep the partnerships focused and cooperative.

STAFF DEVELOPMENT

One of the major barriers toward the successful integration of educational technology in the classroom is the lack of or limited support provided to teachers. In April 1995 the Office of Technology Assessment (OTA) stated that helping teachers use technology effectively is the most important step in assuring the maximum benefit from investments in educational technologies. Many teachers have not had training in working with the technology and do not feel comfortable with it. Their lack of comfort and expertise also limits their creative uses of the technology to complement and extend the goals of the curriculum. If the teachers are not comfortable, they are less likely to work with students who are at-risk learners.

Many district computer coordinators and administrators underestimate the importance of staff development programs' achieving their goals. According to the OTA study, an average of only 15 percent of the technology budget is allocated for staff development and teacher support. In addition, the technology is not always available for the teacher to use. Although one-third of the public schools had access to the Internet, only 3 percent of the instructional rooms, including classrooms, media centers, and technology labs, were connected.

TEACHER INCENTIVES

The greatest barrier to technology cited in the OTA study was the lack of teacher time to attend training or workshops, or to experiment with machines and explore software. Time was also needed to talk to other teachers about what was working and what did not work. Planning for lessons using new materials and methods requires a substantial investment of teacher time. Incentives, release time, and an honest discussion of ways to overcome this significant problem will ensure the success of the technology implementation.

At the Hueneme School District in Southern California, staff development programs include training to integrate technology, teaching strategies, and instructional management. Hands-on instruction in a laboratory setting includes coaching, cooperative learning, and a staff orientation about the operation of all technology in the model technology classroom. Teacher visitations are also encouraged to view technology projects within and outside the district. Teachers are given a reduced workload to plan, develop, and implement the technology in the classroom and library media center. Teachers designing technology classrooms have been relieved of all teaching duties for extended periods of time to research and complete the projects.

The OTA study finds that technology offers teachers the ability to perform many teaching tasks efficiently and quickly. This was also confirmed in the Library Media Survey. Library media specialists believe that technology increased their workload but also made it possible for them to work more efficiently. Teachers in the OTA study stated that they were able to update student profiles with electronic software, assemble current materials for the following week's lesson through an electronic database, and use videotapes for student performance assessment.

Teachers in the OTA study believe that technology can help them improve student learning and motivation, for average students as well as students with different learning styles or special needs. Technology exposed their students to a wider world of information and experts. It encouraged student initiative and collaboration.

STAFF DEVELOPMENT GUIDELINES

Computer use in the general content areas is the most neglected and underdeveloped of computer skills. Computer classes unrelated to the curriculum teach computer skills in isolation. These classes are not as effective as when students use the technology to solve real problems related to the curriculum. The application and transparency of the educational technology within the curriculum teach students to apply computer skills in meaningful ways (Eisenberg and Johnson 1996).

The Mankato Public Schools (1995) have delineated teacher technology proficiencies. These guidelines may serve to inspire similar guidelines at your school and/or district. They begin with the assumption that we cannot ask teachers to integrate technologies into the curriculum if their skills in this area are lacking.

Doug Johnson, district media supervisor, shared a more complete list with worldwide library media specialists through the LM_NET listserv. Sections of the message follow:

VII. Suggested Professional Staff Technology Competencies:

This list is to assist the district and building staff development committees in identifying essential technology skills for teachers, and to provide information relating technology competencies to student achievement, the graduation rule, and the Minnesota Graduation Rule, on which all staff development plans must be based.

A. Basic Beliefs:

1. Teachers should not be expected to teach skills they have not mastered themselves, therefore technology goals deemed as essential to students are appropriate goals for teacher staff development efforts as well.

2. Technology skills should be integrated throughout the curriculum and at all grade levels, requiring mastery by all staff members.

3. Technology can assist teachers in record keeping, student assessment, home-school communications, and lesson presentation.

4. Effective information accessing, processing, and communication depends on technology.

5. Technology skills are essential in business and education for both the district's students and staff.

6. Effective technology skill acquisition by teachers requires adequate resources:
   - equipment
   - software
   - training
   - time
   - incentives

The following are the Competency Goals of the program. These goals may provide impetus for your staff development program.

D. Mankato Schools Professional Staff Technology Competency Goals:

Adopted from the International Society for Technology in Education Teacher Technology Competencies. Essential Competencies are boldfaced.

Professional staff will be able to:

1. Demonstrate the ability to operate information technology and use software successfully.
   - **use card catalog and CD-ROM encyclopedia**
   - **use a modem to access the university and public library catalogs**
   - **operate a video camera, and use a video recorder to record and play programs**

2. Evaluate and use computers and related technologies to support instruction.

3. Apply current instructional principles, research and appropriate assessment practice to the use of computers and related technologies.

4. Explore, evaluate and use computer and other technology-based materials, including educational software and associated documentation.

5. Demonstrate knowledge of uses of computers for problem-solving, data collection, information management, communications, presentations, and decision making.

   - **use a computerized student record keeping system**
   - **use building and Internet networks to communicate with electronic mail and transmit data**

6. Design and develop student learning activities that integrate computing and technology for a variety of student grouping strategies and for diverse student populations.

7. **Evaluate, select and integrate computer and other technology-based instruction in the curriculum of their subject areas and grade levels.**

8. Demonstrate knowledge of the uses of multimedia, hypermedia, and telecommunications to support instruction.

9. Demonstrate skill in using productivity tools for professional and personal use, including word processing, data base and spreadsheet programs, and use print and graphic utilities.

   - **use a word processing program**

10. Demonstrate knowledge of equity, ethical, legal and human issues of computing and technology use as they relate to society and demonstrate appropriate behaviors.

    - understand and apply copyright guidelines to all media, including computer software
    - know and teach the district's Internet Acceptable Use Guidelines

11. Identify resources for staying current in applications of computing and related technologies.

12. Use computer-based technologies to obtain information to enhance personal professional productivity.

13. Apply computers and related technologies to encourage the personal development of the learner and educator.

Developed by the District Staff Development and District Media/Technology subcommittee on teacher technology competencies: Dennis Jeske, Barbara Green, Patricia Stoffel, and Doug Johnson. (Johnson et al. 1995)

STAFF DEVELOPMENT SUCCESS

Successful staff development programs have certain commonalities. Staff development training should foster the educational goals of the district. The Mankato plan delineates the goals of the district and then details how the staff development program will support these goals. Student achievement and success is the foundation for most educational programs. Acting on it will produce buy in from the teaching staff. Studies show that it can take teachers as long as five or six years to become sufficiently comfortable with the computers to use them effectively in their classrooms (Burnett 1994).

Classroom teachers who have used technology successfully are very willing to share their experiences. They can share their trials and how they overcame them. Lesson plans they developed can be distributed. They can also form the drive for interdisciplinary team instruction. Teaching colleagues respect the work of their peers and many times are stimulated to join in. They can create a multimedia production highlighting the teaching faculty's use of technology in the classroom with interviews from the students and the teachers. This can be used to share philosophies and successes both within the district and outside the district. Teachers involved in the project will feel appreciated for their hard work, creativity, and innovation.

Training should be continuous and build on competencies developed in previous workshops. One session in technology training is not enough. Depending on the topic, a sequence of sessions within a workshop promotes competency. In conducting staff development workshops, it is important to have teachers produce a product, lesson, or unit that they can use after the workshop in their classes. In this way their learning experience is directed and focused, and they feel successful. They are encouraged to continue their learning experience.

Staff development workshops should focus on teaching and learning. Teachers should be able to answer the following questions: How will this apply to my teaching? How can I integrate this in my curriculum? How will this help me to be more productive? How can this help my students achieve more? If the teachers are directed and have a purpose, the staff development workshop will be more likely to meet their needs.

Staff development workshops should be open to everyone. Sometimes it is the faculty you least expect who come up with the most original and innovative curriculum project.

Once teachers complete the staff development workshops, they need support. This may include equipment, either software or hardware. It may include setting up the electronic mail accounts for the students, or troubleshooting network problems. If the support is not there, teachers will become frustrated. Remember their time is limited. Establishing mentoring relationships among faculty is a positive way of problem solving and continues the learning process. Computer literate volunteers can assist teachers in each building. As sophistication with the Internet, routers, networks, and data lines increases, technology support specialists will be needed to maintain and update the programs. The technology specialists can provide overall support and continuous training during staff development sessions as well. Success stimulates growth.

A sophisticated infrastructure needs technical support. As more teachers want to integrate the technology within the curriculum, equity and access will become issues. A dynamic technology committee composed of teachers, administrators, and library media specialists can plan, implement, and update the technology plan. It can identify needs, seek out funds, develop a budget, and allocate funds for additional personnel, phone lines, or whatever is needed to keep the technology plan moving positively with the faculty behind it. If faculty needs are not met after the staff development sessions, faculty will become discouraged and resentful of the time and energy they expended.

Outside consultants can be brought in to introduce technologies that are new to faculty. The state may have regional training centers. Outstanding conference speakers who have worked in the classroom may bring additional expertise to the staff development sessions. Vendors also provide workshops and may not charge for them. However, their workshops may be strictly focused on their products and do not reach out to general applications and concepts. They also may be interested in selling their products. Some vendors will send previews of software for the school to examine for several weeks. The library media center is an excellent location for these materials. Faculty in the respective disciplines should be notified so they may take advantage of the preview time. The most successful staff development workshops include teachers training teachers.

Language Arts, Educational Technology, and the Library Media Center

4

The remaining four chapters will highlight:

- the research integrating educational technology within the discipline
- model instructional programs
- the library media specialist's role in developing discipline specific and multi-disciplinary faculty partnerships

WRITING AND THE THINKING PROCESS

The best way to integrate computers into the language arts curriculum is to focus on the student and curriculum—not on the computer . . . the key to using the microcomputer is to consider it in relation to the teachers' and students' goals and needs. (Daiute, 1985)

The language arts classroom focus in the 1990s integrates learning, thinking, and language as processes and as one inseparable process. The duality of process and integration recommends and promotes instruction that

- crosses different subject matter
- combines various kinds of thinking
- integrates different language behaviors (Farr and Tone 1994b; Herman et al. 1992)

This contemporary theory of language emphasizes "thinking" or problem solving as a major focus of instruction. Involving students in real and meaningful situations promotes performance-application of the strategies and information needed to reach solutions. These meaning-constructing processes can integrate reading, listening, comprehension, effective speaking, and writing (Wiggins 1993).

Literacy skills for the twenty-first century embrace the following:

- Accessing
    - reading—text both in print and digital forms
    - listening—in person, videoconferences, and on the phone
    - researching—print, media, and online
- Thinking
    - discriminating, analyzing, and interpreting textual, numeric, audio, and visual information
- Communicating
    - writing—on paper and online
    - speaking—English and at least one other language
    - presenting—orally and with multimedia (Turned on to Reading and Writing 1992)

Information literacy in the resource-based environment can be an alternative learning environment for the language arts program, offering a background of resources in multimedia formats for real-life problem solving whether it be a discussion on global warming, literary achievement in a multicultural framework, or environmental pollution. Assessment of students' writing abilities is refocused from multiple choice and fill in the blanks to applying the rules of grammar, spelling, and description through writing as a response. The problem is defined and analyzed, and the resources are evaluated to develop a solution.

Portfolio assessment that endorses a reliance on teacher and student judgment raises the question of standardized accountability. The library media specialist and the teacher(s) in a department can establish criteria for assessing:

- the number and types of resources used
- the research skills developed and utilized
- the information gathered
- analysis skills
- evaluation skills
- skills in applying the information to solve problems
- skills of inference

The language arts teacher can create criteria for scoring how students organize and develop their responses. Examples of student responses can be provided that match different scores.

With authors and publishers creating textbooks and instructional materials that integrate various disciplines, it is important to be able to measure construction of meaning and problem solving and to encourage collaboration. The library media center lends itself to this type of learning.

Carol Gallagher, a seventh-grade social studies teacher, stated:

Resource-based learning has increased the demands on the classroom teacher for researching and networking. I discovered that our library media specialist was willing to share the information skills with students, to empower teachers with up-to-date technology and information, and to network curriculum ideas with the staff. Our partnership in curriculum development and in resource-based learning enabled me to focus more on the learning that was occurring in my classroom among my self-directed students than on the teaching. (Mendrinos 1994)

A partnership with the library media center can foster an integration of all aspects of the language arts curriculum, including reading, writing, listening, and speaking. These include:

- the use of literature that inspires and motivates reading
- information literacy in a resource-based learning environment
- the use of collaboration and group work as an essential component of learning

Language arts instruction will be more meaningful if students are required to construct responses rather than merely recognize correct answers; to apply their knowledge rather than write a report; to identify the problem, and put the writer within the context of the solution. For example, the students can be the medical doctor seeking drugs to combat the century's major illnesses or the pharmaceutical researcher confronted with the elimination of the rain forest as a major source of new drugs.

Teachers should present students with tasks that have a realistic focus—for example, the study of the impact on the area's major water supply of a possible new golf course with its attendant water pollution. What are the political and environmental implications of the location of the golf course? Learning that is both personal and collaborative encourages critical thinking. Students who are reading, writing, discussing, and interacting with a variety of learning materials in multiple ways are more likely to become critical thinkers.

WRITING ACROSS THE CURRICULUM

Writing Across the Curriculum (WAC) encourages this type of learning. Three positive benefits include:

- It is a resource for better understanding the context of the discipline.
- It is a technique that aids retention.
- Students begin to write better (Sorenson 1991; Walker 1988; Kurfiss 1985).

Teachers and library media specialists can link writing-across-the-curriculum projects with library research, CD-ROM, online databases, and Internet searches. Students can share their knowledge, opinions, and inquiry with peers, scientists, and business professionals through electronic mail and electronic conferencing.

Research supports the fact that writing to learn improves higher order reasoning skills (Gere 1985). "Assuming that students gain new knowledge by making associations with prior knowlege, the writing activities commonly used across the curriculum give students the opportunity to make those connections" (quoted in Sorenson 1991; see also Walker 1988; Self 1989; Barr and Healy 1988; Kurfiss 1985; Steffens 1988). "With the hectic pace of back-to-back fifty-minute classes all day, students need the chance to assimilate information, make connections, and face whatever may still confuse them" (Sorenson 1991). Hamilton-Wieler (1988) calls this kind of writing "a way into or means of learning, a way into understanding through articulating."

"Ammon (1990) advocates using Writing Across the Curriculum in a content area, arguing that writing can be a rich source of information for science teachers who wish to take their students' present understandings into account as they plan and carry out instruction" (Sensenbaugh 1993). Fifth-grade students' cognitive behavior was examined (Winograd 1990) as they wrote, solved, and then, in small groups, shared original math story problems. The students' story problems provided an outstanding alternative to teacher-generated and textbook story problems.

EXPRESSIVE WRITING AND PRODUCT WRITING

Two types of cross-curricula activities that have gained popularity and have had positive results are expressive writing and product writing. Learning logs, journals, problem analysis, and peer dialogues are forms of expressive writing. They stimulate a form of freedom of expression for students.

In studying the Third World, social studies students were exposed to speakers, slides, videos, CD-ROM, video laser disks, online databases, and research through the library on their particular country of study and on the entire region. The social studies teacher in concert with the English teacher gave the students five to ten minutes at the end of each class/library session to capture their thoughts, impressions, fears, and hopes. The English teacher would meet with the students and discuss their learning logs individually. In another example, the growing divisions occurring on the American economic and social scene can be studied through magazine articles, movies, and television reports. Too many times students are passive vessels filled with images that have not penetrated their core. They are not asked to think, problem solve, analyze, and reflect.

Idea processors can capture their reflections. The students' notes can be used to generate outlines that become the substance of product writing: "The student cuts and pastes key ideas and passages from the readings into a note taking software program, which is more an idea machine than a stack of cards. The software permits dynamic searching, and sorting, the actual synthesis of puzzle pieces in new arrangements that ultimately flow into an outlining program, which supports the students in creating a report" (McKenzie 1993).

Product writing is the development of more formal products, essays, tests, questions, responses, library papers, and lab reports. Expressive writing can be the background for product writing, creating meaningful thought-provoking works without the fear of plagiarism.

Student letters written to senators on behalf of pending legislation provide one example of this approach. The Internet can facilitate communication between government officials and students. After research, reflection, and coming to an understanding of the issues, the students were able to develop cohesive arguments in support of the bill. The following is an excerpt of the letter sent to the congressman from Kaitlin May, one of the students in the class.

I am writing to you about the Bill 5153 because in social studies and English we are learning about water pollution in Massachusetts and what we can do to prevent it and clean up the areas that are already polluted.

I think that the Bill 5153 should be passed because I am worried about water pollution. In school we watch videos, read articles and have guest speakers come in and talk to us about water pollution. There is already a shortage of water in Metropolitan Boston. We are going to lose even more water if we don't protect certain areas from becoming polluted that are important to us because they supply certain places with water. Wachusett Reservoir is one of these places. It is located in Worcester and Leominster and it is very important because it supplies one third of Boston's water.

Schools with computer video capabilities and scanners, and teachers and library media specialists who are familiar with this equipment can work with students to create visual, multimedia text-oriented products to capture the students' work. However, the glitz of technology should not obscure the cogency of student thinking.

"Students should do research on questions that matter to them, questions that require original thought and inspire a degree of passion. Questions that touch the core issues of what it means to be alive—what the Coalition of Essential schools calls 'essential questions' (Sizer 1992)—drive student research with such power that parents sometimes must unplug computers, set curfews and hold students back" (McKenzie 1993). This was an outcome as all students in my library media center including those with special needs and learning disabilities became involved in research, analysis, evaluation, and synthesis on questions that mattered to them and to the world they are living in and and will inherit.

As Barr and Healy (1988) summarize the research, they state that a "study of writing achievement across the curriculum attests to the fact that writing improves higher-order reasoning abilities. WAC programs are ideally suited to achieve these ends for they provide the theoretical base for teachers and the instructional strategies that enable students to reformulate ideas from text."

COMPUTER-ASSISTED WRITING

Computer-assisted writing instruction can stimulate at-risk students to share their reflections without the fear of rejection because of poor handwriting. The word processor is at the center of an effective writing curriculum as it encourages and fosters connections between reading and writing and early language production. Computer-assisted writing instruction has a strong positive impact on the achievement of the at-risk student. The process of writing with the microcomputer has increased productivity and positive attitudes toward writing according to several studies (Simic 1994) with at-risk students. Many times the average and special needs student may have excellent ideas that do not reach the intended audience. Handwriting difficulties become overwhelming with pen and paper. Revising, crossing out, and recopying can create confusion, messiness, frustration, and despair for many of these students with hidden talents. Anxiety develops with apprehension as repeated erasures create holes in the paper.

The microcomputer and word-processing software integrated properly in the curriculum can encourage writing and positive attitudes among these same students. Thirty-four students (Phillips 1992) from eighteen school districts in Connecticut who were associated with academic failure and disruptive behavior were involved in a study to research the effects of process writing using computers on written expression and self-esteem. Process writing was taught in a computer lab setting between November 1990 and May 1991. The students' written language abilities increased, especially among the younger students. There was a significant correlation between measures of written language and self-perception, particularly in the area of reading. The teachers' perceived a strong positive impact on written language and self-esteem. Unexpected outcomes included:

- students use their writing at educational planning meetings and in therapy sessions
- strong positive social interaction in the writing process
- total lack of behavioral problems

- sustained attention to the task when writing in the computer lab setting
- increased awareness by teachers of the academic potential of their students
- positive impact on the total school curriculum (Phillips 1992)

Research has found that many teachers do not have an understanding of the process of writing and the creative process of successful writers (Hansen 1987; Harste et al. 1988). Teachers traditionally ask students to write papers without providing instructions or guidance on the steps needed to produce quality writing. The writing process requires multiple stages. The two keys to fluent writing, according to writing research, is to write as much as possible and to revise repeatedly. As a fifth-grade elementary schoolteacher, writing was a critical ingredient for all aspects of my curriculum. My students were required to write three drafts, with the last being the final draft. They wrote continuously each day—stimulated by Newbury Award authors—writing reflections of experiences, or motivated to finish a story I had begun. Sometimes I would play a classical or ethnic piece of music and have them write their thoughts or create a fairy tale or science fiction adventure. A piece of art could also provoke their thoughts. When these students were in high school, the freshman English teacher approached me and shared that she could tell every student who had been in my fifth-grade class because of his or her writing ability. The class was a heterogeneous mix of bright, average, and disabled students but their writing abilities stretched their potential. This experience served me well; as a library media specialist, I utilized an interdisciplinary curriculum, combining writing, reading and research in productive teacher partnerships.

In the library media center, students created a student newspaper and wrote their diaries as immigrants from the perspective of diverse eras in American history. They researched topics and defended in writing their views on pollution and nuclear energy. The word processor stimulated the revision process, making it easier and faster for students of all levels to rewrite, rethink, and expand their thoughts. Most students can experience success in writing through the use of a word processor with instruction and support from the teachers and their peers (Bright 1990).

One of the important issues discussed by Newman (1984) included recent research in using the word processor in the writing process. Newman stated, "Writing improves more by mastering many aspects of the process at the same time." Word processing assists writers in sustaining the mental images, capturing them while experimenting with language through the rapid manipulation and alteration of the text. The search/replace capability encourages the use of synonyms and substitutions, and the use of the thesaurus. The clean screen display encourages revision and thoughtful discussion of ideas and creativity.

Newman further delineated the difference between using the computer for drill and practice and using it for word processing. Drill and practice controls what is learned by telling the user what to do. With the word processor, the learner exerts control in using the computer and learning to write. This requires teachers and library media specialists to provide students with time for prewriting, rewriting, and rethinking on the word processor.

Proofreading is easier. Complex changes involving moving sections or cutting and pasting from two different documents or notes are possible. Creating an outline and adding and deleting sections to preorganize a paper are much easier. It is clean and neat and makes outlining achievable for the average and special needs student.

"Free writing" can also be done at the computer, engaging students to focus on learning and self-discovery and encouraging them to take risks. They can always change their minds and with a few keystrokes rewrite.

If too few computers are available or if students feel more comfortable first writing with pencil and paper, students can enter their first drafts in the word processor. They can print their work, after saving it on a disk. Simic (1994) states that before word processing, many teachers were hesitant to expect revisions and students were more apprehensive about putting their thoughts on paper. When a computer is used, revisions and rewriting are allowed to be cognitive processes rather than the mechanical drudge and confusion of crossing out and erasing, squeezing new thoughts into tiny spaces and around the margins of the paper. Word processing promotes the integration of active research and writing in the library media center, adding new sources to old to deepen the theme and purpose of students' papers. Analysis, evaluation, and synthesis should be the goals of processed writing and information literacy. Data is gathered. It becomes information related to the topic. After analysis, evaluation, and synthesis, it becomes insight.

Multiple copies of the students' works can be printed for peer editing and reading. The students' final copies can be part of a published book, a newsletter, letters to their congressman, an interactive electronic bulletin board, or a collection of writing. Handwriting does not undermine one's presentation or thoughts.

Seventh-grade at-risk students were participants in a university practicum (Zoni 1992) specifically designed to improve their process-writing skills by increasing interest through the use of the microcomputer and word-processing software and telecommunications technology. Sixteen students wrote eight basic, handwritten essays as part of the regular language arts classes. Then they completed their assignments on the word processor and printer. They transmitted their final draft using a phone line, modem, and special software to a local bulletin board service (BBS) for distribution through a national "preteen conference network."

Imagine the students' excitement as they contacted the BBS on a daily basis to check for responses. Weekly brainstorming sessions involving each student, the classroom teacher, and the university professor produced new writing ideas, suggestions, sharing, and a means of responding to the writings of other students and reporting on messages downloaded from the BBS. Analysis of pre- and posthandwritten and computer-written essays showed an increase in process-writing skills. They were scored using a holistic scoring approach. The evaluation of a daily journal, the analysis of pre- and postattitudinal surveys, observations by the classroom teacher, group counselor, and the university professor revealed a substantial increase in the number of students with a positive attitude toward writing. The preteen conferences could have centered on any number of social ethics or global themes that can be researched in the library to develop or justify a position. Telecommunications offers a broad, regional, national, and international audience for student-to-student communication.

Simic (1994) stated, "The word processor offers great advantages but also makes great demands." Flexible scheduling, or the ability for a teacher and library media specialist to work together in a media center lab or computer lab to provide the computers for word processing, is necessary for success. Teacher commitment to word processing is crucial if it is to be successful. This commitment includes the time the students will need to learn how to use the word processor. The library media specialist may provide this instruction. The teacher and the library media specialists can decide when and how it is best to give instruction.

Having students learn word-processing skills while they are writing or revising is an intrusion on the writing process and may reduce the effect of technology on the learning outcomes. It is best to instruct before the project begins (Snyder 1993). Word processing was found to be more effective and beneficial for writers who planned minimally and revised extensively. This also relates to the situation where the students are in the process of doing research and continuously adding, deleting, and revising.

The most uniformly positive results of the study underlie the importance of teaching writing skills while the word processor was being used. The critical point is that we "should not expect the technology alone to improve writing but that when students are concerned about the quality of their writing for other reasons, the processors are great" ("Word Processing, Multimedia and Literacy" 1993).

The teacher and library media specialist must become familiar with the word processor before it can be used in the classroom. If all the students have access to a word processor, the teacher-library media specialist can instruct the students using an LCD panel at the head of the classroom before the project begins. A short cheat sheet of word-processing commands can also be beneficial. An arrangement of computers that I have found promotes learning is to have the computers networked around the perimeter of the room. The center of the room has chairs and can be used for lecture or video viewing. One could also have large tables or areas of desks in the center for collaborative projects, depending on the room's intended use. Students can turn their chairs to listen to instructions rather than playing on the computer, which is a temptation if the students are lined up in neat rows in front of the computers. In a networked lab, it is important to have the capability to display any one of the student's computer screens through the LCD player or computer projector for comments, questions, and peer review. Timbuktu software can facilitate this process. Electronic blackboards also make it possible to send notes from the blackboard to the students' computers, and vice versa, in order to have an interactive conversation. The information, if valuable to student learning, can be saved on a disk by the students.

A peer system can also be set up. A group of students can be taught the program and they can teach one or more of their peers. The important point is that students need hands-on activity. The teacher becomes the guide and must feel comfortable relinquishing the lecture format. For composition to become as natural on the computer as it is when handwritten, students must have sufficient computer time to write. Computers can also be clustered in groups of four to stimulate problem solving and collaboration.

If every student does not have access to a word processor, students can work together and interact with each other on their writing. The class can be divided so that some students can research while others write. Writing shared with others is interactive and can provide an immediate audience for emerging writers. Students can also brainstorm their research to formulate problem-solving stategies for complex issues.

Janet, a sandy blonde-haired seventh grader with large blue eyes had difficulty with researching, note taking, and outlining. The task was to research a city-civilization in the Bronze Age, describing its lifestyle, culture, and religion. Index cards were given to each student by the social studies teacher. Students were to gather information and record it on the index cards. Students were to use reference books, nonfiction books, the CD-ROM encyclopedia, videodisks, video, and audiovisual materials related to ancient civilizations in this era.

Janet located some facts and recorded them on the index cards. She researched the subject headings in the encyclopedia and the public access catalog to come up with synonyms for her civilization, for example, Mesopotamia instead of Babylonia. She was successful in searching the CD-ROM encyclopedia and securing a list of related terms and articles that appeared to have relevance.

Her next task was to take the information and enter it in an outline that would precede her report. The social studies teacher had prepared an outline and the students were to research the information, create the note cards, and then transfer the appropriate information under the headings of the outline. Janet stared blankly at the static sheet of paper with the outline of her topic. Her handwriting was large and incomprehensible and could easily take over the entire paper with only a few sentences. The outline on the static, linear sheet was creating inner anxiety. Janet began to tremble and look awkwardly into space. Where could she write all her thoughts and how could she erase without making her work more confusing.

Observing the anxious, stumbling, unfocused students before them, the teacher and the library media specialist looked at the computer and brainstormed a simple idea—"Place the outline on the word processor!!" Involve the English teacher in process writing and work with the students on transferring their notes to the outline. Precede the task with a discussion of the outlining process. An idea processor could also have been used from the onset, capturing the students' notes and assisting in the outlining process.

The teacher typed her static outline worksheet on the word processor making it fluid, manageable, and more easily manipulated by the students. The library media specialist gave a lesson on the word-processing program and distributed a sheet of instructions and a disk to each student. Janet was excited and began to feel competent, even looking forward to the task. She could add three thoughts under a heading without running out of space. Janet could bring her research materials to the word processor to fill in missing links. She could delete incorrect or poorly written information, replacing it with greater insights.

The word processor was not added as an external mechanical device to bring glitz to the curriculum. It was integrated into the program to solve a problem, to foster clarity, to facilitate thoughtful expression and flexibility in writing and revising. Students could share their insights with their peers. They could be grouped by a particular civilization. Working in a group makes writing an interactive activity. Receiving feedback from others made Janet aware of the importance of clarity—so that her ideas could be understood by others. Interactivity fosters growth during the process of revision. It also provides each writer with the experience of helping others revise their work.

Word processing is revolutionizing writing. Students are no longer beleaguered by the mechanics, messiness, and pain of revising. Students invest in their writing their thoughts and expression and want to revise to create their masterpieces. Extensive writing leads to better writing in the elementary grades.

Imagine using the Internet to connect with students in foreign cultures to share research and insights and seek out primary sources. Video desktop conferencing is becoming more affordable. Video desktop cameras can be connected to a computer that is networked using an ethernet TCP/IP connection or an ISDN line to transfer images of your classroom and the students to any remote location that has a similar set up. Utilizing video desktop conferencing software, that is, CU-SEE-ME, students are no longer limited to text communication but can communicate remotely via audio, video, and text. Students can see each other, speak to each other, and exchange research. Ethernet TCP/IP connections and ISDN high speed lines are needed to transfer the video. Improved video transfer, the availability of high speed networks and data lines, and the decreasing cost of video-conferencing cameras and software will make this technology more available in the classroom.

Access to telecommunications can increase library media specialists' ability to have an audience for students' writing. Library media specialists invite authors to speak to the students about their books and inspiration and conduct writers' workshops online. Students can focus on a theme to write an essay and send their work by telecommunications to the author for feedback.

WRITING USING ELECTRONIC MAIL

Twenty students in the fourth through seventh grades telecommunicated with an English professor (Jenkinson 1992) from the University of Indiana during the summer of 1990. Over a four-week period, the professor received 263 pieces of writing. Drafts were written on Microsoft Works and transmitted on the modem using CCMAIL, an electronic mail program. Students wrote everything from three-line haikus to fifteen- to twenty-computer screen stories, reports, poems, monologues, and letters.

Students were first instructed in the writing process. The professor was introduced to the class via e-mail and finally met the students the last day of school. Real-time computer conferencing was encouraged in order to comment on the students' work. The project produced the following results:

- The quality of the writing was impressive.
- Students were encouraged to use the word processor.
- The students were encouraged and understood that the professor could put samples of their writing in a publication and would use them for articles in journals.
- Each student received personal feedback electronically, including encouragement, short lessons on specific problems, and suggestions for other types of topic writing.

The professor concluded that students write more and write better when they use a computer and when they have an interested audience in addition to the classroom teacher and the library media specialist.

WRITING FOR THE REAL WORLD

The purpose of another study (Estrin 1993) was to motivate at-risk urban youth to write a composition effectively, dispel the fear of writing, and focus on topics that would encourage the students to write with success. Topics were selected that would stimulate self-confidence, dignity, and a sense of self-worth. The library media specialist can be a very effective partner to the language arts instructor and assist in the selection of well-written and thought-provoking materials. This teacher focused on black culture. Students were encouraged to use the anthology *Black Culture: Reading and Writing Black*, edited by Gloria M. Simmons and Helena Hutchinson (Holt, Rinehart and Winston 1972).

Provocative, realistic selections captured the students' interest. Several of the essays covered the following topics:

- the beauty of black
- language and revolution
- self-hate
- the why of violence
- separation, integration, violence
- black heritage

Theme writing assignments stimulate pro and con views of each selection as well as oral interpretations of the poetry and prose. Using the word processor students can print multiple copies for feedback, discussion, and debate with their peers. Class discussion of the papers can focus on improving writing techniques—grammar, usage, organization of sentence structure, punctuation, and vocabulary. Peers, the library media specialist, and the instructor can comment, raise questions, and stimulate the student to further thought and recommend a relevant text, article, CD-ROM, or video. Students can share other resources in all formats that can expand understanding. Students should be encouraged to look for positive aspects in ideas and writing approaches. Reading well-written selections can motivate students to become better writers.

The use of the word processor removes the obstacles of poor handwriting, the lack of time, and the need to recopy. It encourages revision by pointing out redundancies. Estrin (1993) stated, "When the students see the words, sentences and the paragraphs which they and their peers, have written, the study of how to rephrase becomes a more meaningful experience in both language and composition."

Frisk (1989), along with Estrin (1993), underscored the importance of instilling self-confidence while presenting a knowledge of the self-identity of each student and the dignity of each student's personality.

One student wrote after reading and writing about the essays in the anthology:

It [the book] helps attain the desire to say that you are proud of being a Black person, a desire to say that you are someone valuable to the society, and the desire to say that you are someone—someone who cares, shares, feels, thinks, talks, and handles himself like a true person should—with dignity and pride. The book is a practical experience because you learn to experience the different emotions that the book contains, such as fear, hate, love, pride, courage, and an entire mixture of emotions shared by a mistreated society for a hundred years. This itself is Black culture, an assortment of emotions and values that the Black man must read to be a person to whom everyone can look up. When you say, "I am proud 'cause I'm Black" then you are truly a Black person in the best of possible ways—in soul and in heart. (Estrin 1993)

In these examples the library media specialist is working with the language arts teacher to promote the process of writing by integrating the technology to overcome the mechanics of writing and facilitating ideas, revision, and research.

REVISION

Revision is at the center of the writing process (Lehr 1995)—it is a means by which ideas emerge and evolve and meanings are clarified. The writing process includes three stages, prewriting, writing, and revision. Revising, according to an NAEP study (1977), included attention to spelling, punctuation, and grammar. Changes such as starting over, adding or deleting parts of a paper, or adding and deleting ideas seldom occurred (Applebee et al. 1986). Yoder (1993) studied journalism students and found that surface level changes predominated over meaningful changes.

What does improve the writing process? Direct library media specialist and teacher intervention seems to produce positive results (Hillocks 1982). If the students begin to research and take notes on the resources and enter them into an outline, the teacher's and library media specialist's comments can focus on the fluidity, substance, analysis, and insights thereby helping students achieve their purpose. Students can contemplate the teacher's and librarian's comments, which are focused on specific skills and goals, as well as utilize the process of revision to improve the quality of their writing.

Students in grades two to six produced better stories after they revised their work in response to teacher questions directed at specific content (Robinson 1985). Collaborative writing helped ninth graders move toward more thoughtful, sophisticated writing (Lehr 1995). At the college level teacher comments were too text specific and took students' attention away from their own purposes and focused it on those of the teacher. Students need to establish purpose in their writing and should be allowed to do that at any age.

Calkins (1986) suggests asking students to find bits of their writings—words, lines, passages that seem essential—and then having them explore why these sections are so significant. Balajthy (1987) recommends providing students with class time for revision and allowing flexibility in due dates as a way to encourage students to engage in more extensive revision. Following personal observation of interdisciplinary units involving the library, social studies, and language arts, I provided class time for research and in-class revision, and had students working furiously on the computer, not only in class but before and after school. I made due dates flexible because the revisions sometimes reached the seventh draft with students adding, deleting, and revising. These were not only the brightest students but those with special needs and learning disabilities.

The library media specialist and the language arts teacher can publish the students' writings, thereby sharing them with a larger audience. Products can include hardback books, newspapers, newsletters, electronic communications, or oral presentations.

Computers and Revision

Studies investigating the use of the computer as a tool to manipulate text and promote revision offer a variety of perspectives. Kurth (1986) reported that word processing motivated students to write but that computer use did not affect the length of the papers or the amount and quality of the revisions made.

Flinn (1986) found that sixth graders using computers to revise compositions wrote longer papers and received slightly higher holistic scores than those using pen and paper. The most striking difference she found was that the group that used the computer put greater writing emphasis on fluency, word choice, and mechanics. Tone and Winchester (1988) agreed, noting that the computer offers real facilitation of revision "to writers who know how to compose on one."

Owston et al. (1991) confirmed this. A study of eighth graders found that papers written on the computer were graded significantly higher than those written by hand. Student data indicated that revision was continuous at all stages of the writing process, specifically in the initial drafting session.

Womble (1984) observed that students using word processors tended to work longer on their work, make more changes to text, and develop a sense of audience. Teachers and library media specialists should emphasize the whole text over its parts to increase the power of writing.

Students could be instructed in using the word processor and then introduced to the CD-ROM, videodisk, and videos, which stimulate thought and anchor preexisting ideas with new thoughts. The library media specialist can introduce search strategies using the Internet's World Wide Web browser, if available, CD-ROM, videodisks, and print resources on the topic to be researched. Students can be taught how to cite the different resources, including electronic, print, and media, and can be provided with written examples.

After being introduced to the word processor, students can receive an introduction to process writing, resources, and research. They can:

- select an appropriate subject and limit it
- consider the purpose of the writing
- develop the central idea of the composition
- develop a working outline of the idea before beginning the composition to help structure their writing
- use the outline as a tool in writing

REMEDY A FLOUNDERING TECHNOLOGY PROBLEM

Several school districts that have installed technology-based process-writing programs have been less than satisfied. The new technology is doing less for faculty and staff than expected. It is not the technology that presents the problems but rather how the schools planned and implemented the technology. Major problems occur if the technology has not been integrated realistically within the curriculum. This can create obstacles for success. Schools, however, can provide a midcourse correction to overhaul a floundering technology program.

Eliot Levinson (1994) provided these excellent insights.

Faculty and staff should all be involved in the decision to move into computer technology and should also be involved in choosing the products. This keeps enthusiasm and support for the system high and motivates people to learn the system. Schools moving into new technology-based programs should also establish goals that they hope to meet by installing a system. These goals should not only provide for visible achievements along the way but should also detect when the program is not doing what is expected. The system should be installed long before the class begins so the faculty has an opportunity to learn it comfortably.

As the technology is implemented, it is important to assess how it is being used and determine its effect on student achievement. The goal is not to justify the purchase, but to collect reliable data to affect the most positive and beneficial use for faculty and students.

A small group of elementary teachers in a Baltimore school chose the technology for a process-writing course that would be implemented through the eighth grade. Only the small group had enthusiasm for the project. No measurable set of goals was established to enable educators to find out if the program was meeting its objectives. Finally, the writing program was taught in the computer lab by the lab manager. The process-writing program was extraneous to the language arts curriculum and the curriculum of other disciplines. There was little follow-up in the classroom. The integration of technology in the process-writing program should help improve writing through frequent revisions and creative thought. The goal is not to simply master the mechanics of a word-processing program.

The principal of the Baltimore school analyzed the disappointments and attacked the program on three fronts: curricular, technological, and organizational. Her plan for success is applicable to all programs. In-service training was vital. Teachers were paid for two weeks in the summer to attend workshops in process writing and plan the curriculum for the year. Administration and faculty worked together to establish achievable milestones and define specific writing objectives for the students. The principal and the teachers agreed to close the lab and place five computers in each classroom. Another possibility would have been for the teachers to schedule the computer room and teach process writing there or to move the computers to the library media center for access to a resource-based learning environment. The library media center provides an alternative learning environment, combining literature, videos, media, CD-ROM, videodisks, and telecommunications to stimulate deeper subject exploration and discovery in the writing process.

The money allocated for the lab manager was used to pay an expert in computer-based process writing and give teachers ongoing training and coaching. As one author noted:

Staff development should be conducted with the word processor to demonstrate how ideas may be constructed, broken down, reconstructed, elaborated, extended, condensed and amplified. As teachers of writing see their own thinking pass through stages of development in the fluidity of the screen, they will grasp the challenge of today's writing teacher—how best to lead students through similar stages of development. (McKenzie 1993)

Release time for the teachers to meet regularly to discuss how the program was working was provided. This is critical for library media specialist and teacher partnerships. Time is needed to meet, discuss, plan, and implement the program using the technology and the resources for the project.

It is neither the technology nor the hardware and the software alone but rather the creative integration of the technology within the discipline—designed to reach and exceed the goals of the curriculum and improve student achievement—that provides substance to the use of technology for the at-risk student.

CRITICAL READING—THE MEANING MAKERS

In order to compose in a process-writing learning environment, one must be able to read critically. Critical reading is essential in the electronic information age. Only those who have developed these skills will be able to sift through volumes of unrelated information and focus on and determine what is relevant. Understanding the underlying themes of critical reading will assist the library media specialist in working more successfully with students in reading text, both electronically and in hard copy. In addition it will provide a common foundation between the library media specialist and the reading teacher that can lead to meaningful curriculum development.

In the 1980s the concept of critical thinking became an essential part of the teaching of reading. It stimulated the need for the reader to develop the ability to relate new information to what is known in order to find answers to cognitive questions. According to the 1981 National Assessment of Education Progress (NAEP) study, 85 percent of 13 year olds could complete a multiple choice test of reading comprehension. However, only 15 percent could write an acceptable sentence summarizing the paragraph read. The study found that students were rarely encouraged to support evaluative interpretation (Collins 1993). Reading lacked critical analysis. Reading programs must go beyond drill and practice.

Critical reading begins with reading, leading the reader to comprehension, inference, and decision making (Carr 1988). Library media specialists, working closely with subject specialists and/or the reading teacher, can develop topics to support inquiry-based learning to challenge and motivate students to be critical readers. Ideas, values, and ethical questions can create an atmosphere that fosters inquiry; examples include environmental concerns, nuclear issues, biotechnology gene manipulation, and ethnic issues, both national and international. Teachers should be encouraged to focus on topics that stimulate students to question, make predictions, problem solve, and learn to reason through reading. Paulo Freire (1985) stated, "Those who share in the learning process are empowered by a critical consciousness of themselves as meaning makers."

CRITICAL READING AND METACOGNITION

Metacognition (Collins 1994) plays an important role in reading. Metacognition is the understanding that fosters conscious control over one's learning (Tei and Stewart 1985). Four variables are important in a metacognitive approach that enables the reader to be in control of his or her learning. These four variables are: texts, tasks, strategies, and learner characteristics.

Text relates to the factors that influence comprehension and memory in the reading materials. These factors include the arrangement of ideas in the text, the vocabulary, the syntax, the reader's interest, and the reader's familiarity with the text. Research on the features of the text reveal that:

- the structure of the text influences learning
- knowledge of the effect of the structure of the text on learning is dependent on the age and the ability of the reader
- if the learner becomes aware of the text structures, learning is optimized

Cognitive processing (Harris 1990; DiGisi and Yore 1992) is slowed by ambiguous words or confusion within the text. Older and more fluent readers are more aware of text inconsistencies and can judge whether or not their comprehension is altered because of such inconsistencies.

Being aware of the text structures assists the reader in detecting patterns of organization, the arrangement of the author's ideas, and the kinds of structures used to interrelate ideas. The reader becomes more efficient. Muth (1987) presents three strategies to help the reader understand the text structure. These include:

- hierarchical summaries
- conceptual maps
- thematic organizers

Reading taught within this framework forms a strong bridge interrelating the knowledge and skills of the library media specialist with those of the reading teacher to assist students in becoming critical readers and tackling investigative research in the disciplines. Developing methods of understanding text structures through the three strategies outlined can assist students in defining the problem, determining key words and terms for expanding research, and developing a working outline of their topic.

The importance of critical reading and its relationship with electronic resources is very often overlooked. Successful access and retrieval using electronic means depend on a conceptual map of the topic so as to properly identify the problems and associated terms that will retrieve the appropriate information from a databank of literally millions of sources. Arguments over the book in hand versus the electronic form of the information are arcane.

I can clearly remember a reading teacher stating that students were not reading in the library media center, even though they were immersed in researching topics, analyzing information, developing positions on controversial issues based on their analyses, and applying the information to solve problems. Concern over literature versus nonfiction research or electronic versus the book in hand disguised the real problem of forty-five minute reading periods that lacked thinking processes and were possibly increasing the students' probability of becoming more at risk. All reading whether in literature or in nonfiction requires analysis, synthesis, and evaluation. The purpose of reading is to construct meaning. It is very important for the reader to adapt reading behavior to specific texts. This is especially critical in a resource-based environment. Utilizing metacognition strategies, the reader should develop ways of knowing when he or she does not comprehend the text. Self-regulation is important; this includes forming a mental image, rereading, searching the text to identify unknown words, and predicting meaning that lies ahead.

Good readers use the most effective and efficient method to obtain comprehension. Self-awareness and control of learning can be taught through underlining, outlining, note taking, summarizing, and self-questioning. Improved performance was noted in studies with middle school and junior high students using these strategies (Gertz 1994; Langer and Neal 1987). Reader self-knowledge would include his or her background knowledge, degree of interest, skills and deficiencies, and how these affect learning. Awareness of these areas should stimulate a change in reading behavior. Successful students relate information in texts to previous knowledge. An active role in reading should advocate an awareness of the structure of the text, knowledge of the task, and an awareness of the characteristics of the reader.

READING AND TECHNOLOGY

Lynn Rutter, a Chapter 1 reading specialist, uses technology to inspire students to innovate and create within a critical reading environment. Working with learning disabled students, she pushes them beyond their limits. For two days students read a variety of materials, and then they have two days of writing with close integration. Reading allows students to capture new vocabulary, including adjectives that conjure visual images. For example, students first read science fiction, then students create science fiction. They are the heroes and heroines of their stories. Using a folder of their writing on the computer, students capture ideas, phrases, and clip art as they outline their first draft. Students, generally, write three to four drafts before they are satisfied with their work. Achievement has soared for these at-risk students, moving them from the 40th percentile to the 80th percentile in reading ("The New Literacy" 1992).

A comfortable and nonthreatening learning space was created for the students, incorporating computers in the classroom. The library media center can create this interactive learning space by surrounding students with a multitude of accessible resources, including books, CD-ROM, online formats, and computers.

Students can create multimedia stories or interactive book reviews by using the video camera and digitizing video or by using a digital camera or by scanning in photographs. Students can showcase their stories or books they have read through an electronic slide show or through video, text, and photographs using a variety of computer multimedia, presentation, and desktop publishing software. PowerPoint, Astound, Hyperstudio, and Page-maker are programs that can be used. An interdisciplinary learning community involving the library media specialist and the teachers of reading, language arts, music, and art can add several dimensions in advocating students' concepts and ideas through a multisensory experience. Stories and book reviews can be published or sent electronically to peers at other schools for discussion.

Creating a message in a multisensory format forces the creator to decide which visuals, sounds, graphics, or animations convey the message. One has to succinctly identify the problem. When using presentation software, such as PowerPoint or Astound, the student cannot become verbose or wander around the true points of discussion. An electronic slide presentation is one impetus to energize the student to critically think and delineate the major points of contention. The challenge of "less is more" is demonstrated through action. Reading, writing, and thinking skills are tested for clarity and cause and effect. Using presentation or multimedia software to communicate ideas simulates the skills needed to be successful in the workplace. Multimedia software is commonly being used to present ideas in business, medicine, and the educational community.

ELECTRONIC BOOKS

Learningsmith, an educational sales center in Palo Alto, California, sells reading software targeted for the home market. Many of these software programs are referred to as "edutainment," combining games and activities to teach students skills and information in an engaging environment of fun. CD-ROM electronic books such as Broderbund's release of Mercer Mayer's *Just Grandma and Me* or Discis Book's version of the *Tale of Peter Rabbit* beckons parents and young readers to point and click on the beautifully animated characters, listen to the entire book or just the highlighted text being read aloud. Electronic books, according to the manager of Learningsmith, sell well. Excellent interactive CD-ROMs are replicas of best-selling children's books illustrated by the same outstanding artists. Repetition, dramatic readings, clever animations, and pleasing graphics assist students in developing excitement toward reading.

Michael Mellin, publisher of Random House's electronic book division, believes electronic books give the reader more value. According to Mellin, text has more navigability, allowing the reader to search phrases or vocabulary words, look up specific themes, make bookmarks, and take notes (*Turned on to Reading and Writing* 1992). Parents call these electronic books "cute." When they are very seriously concerned about promoting their child's reading abilities, parents purchase more "heavy duty" reading programs such as the *Interactive Journey of Peter Rabbit* or *Baily's Book House* according to Learningsmith management.

COMPUTER-ASSISTED READING

Computer-assisted reading programs reinforce reading skills that involve identifying letters, letter sounds, vowel sounds, words, compound words, and rhymes as well as comprehension. The best programs combine educational pedagogy with an engagingly simple interface to develop reading ability and logical writing style.

Research indicates that learning is more profound when several of the senses are used. This is known as multisensory learning. In many of these software programs when a student is using the computer, he or she is seeing, hearing, and touching all at once. He or she is in control, initiating the action and directing the agenda by pressing the computer key or clicking the mouse.

The best programs reward curiosity and allow the student to compete in the absence of peer pressure while reinforcing cognitive and language development through repetition. Students also gain automaticity—the ability to treat certain tasks as routine while "freeing up the brain's higher centers for more complicated tasks" (McCormick 1995).

Computer-assisted reading instruction was part of a study in reading achievement in a rural system that included 142 students randomly selected in grades three through eight. Seventy of the students were designated as the experimental group and were involved in the Take Home Computer Program (THC). The experimental group and their parents participated in a workshop that trained parents to work with their children on the computer to reinforce reading skills. For a six-week period, students and their parents had access to appropriate grade level software. The seventy-two students who were part of the control group did not have access to the computer software or the computers. The California Achievement Test (CAT) was used to measure reading achievement gains. The major results of the study concluded that:

- "students who participated in the THC groups made greater achievement gains in reading on the CAT than the comparison group.
- parents reported that their children's interest in reading increased, their grades improved and they read more.
- students reported that their involvement with the THC Program increased their understanding of reading skills, improved their grades, and they enjoyed having their parents work with them on the computer.
- teachers observed positive changes in students' reading habits and skills performance" (Everhart 1991).

GUIDELINES FOR COMPUTER-ASSISTED
READING INSTRUCTION

What are the guidelines for computer-assisted reading instruction programs in a critical reading environment? Programs should focus on meaning and stress reading comprehension. They should provide students with opportunities to work with word recognition programs that stress the use of word meaning in conjunction with phonics and structural analysis. They should foster active involvement and stimulate thinking. Student decisions should exert influence and control over the computer tasks. They should be encouraged to make predictions and experiment with text in creative ways within a contextual environment. Evaluation of the software should demonstate that it is not strictly drill and practice.

Computer usage should not be exclusive. It is important for students to use all the resources in a variety of formats in the library media center, learning additional means of sharing and retrieving information and linking reading with writing. When working with computer-assisted instruction, it is critical to keep in mind the importance of a positive attitude (Simic 1993b).

The following criteria can be applied to evaluate computer-assisted reading software by the library media specialist and/or the reading teacher:

- Interactivity—Interactive functions should enhance reading comprehension and instruction not detract students with slick but unrelated graphics, videos, and/or animations.
- Speed—Consistent speed and response time in turning a page and sorting and selecting terms or passages are critical for keeping the reader engaged.
- Clarity—The design of the program should be clear and intuitive for the young reader.
- Speech/Sound—If speech and sound are done well, they can positively affect the student's comprehension. In some programs, the young reader can input his/her own voice as a complement to reading, writing, and vocabulary activities.
- Graphics—Clear and colorful illustrations should be based on those in the previously published book. Videos, animation, and the graphics should stimulate the student's interest in reading and promote literacy skills.
- Writing—Reading programs that integrate writing activities as a response promote a critical reading environment.
- Management and Assessment—Management and control in reporting performance and tracking certain aspects of the student's interaction with the software are useful features for parents, teachers, and library media specialists. Some software allows for programming of class needs or tailoring lessons to the students' needs, for example, by determining the percent of correct answers required to advance to the next level.
- Auxiliary Materials—Print versions of books and a teacher's manual should be included with the reading software program if relevant. Second language support is

especially helpful for students who have English as a second language (Simic 1993b).

Book publishers are developing CD-ROM and videodisks to complement their readers. Lessons are bar-coded so they can be customized and selected by the teacher and library media specialist. In one of the selections from the Houghton Mifflin's Channel R.E.A.D. videodisk, in the *Adventure of the Ordinary Princess*, students must stop the princess from destroying all the books in the universe by predicting her next move. Students must reflect on what they already know about the princess; they must compare her to characters they read about in a previous story to make critical connections that can lead to an accurate prediction. The videodisks are designed to be used by the whole class, a small group, and/or individual instruction. This particular videodisk is correlated with *Houghton Mifflin Reading: The Literature Experience*.

Videodisks should be evaluated in terms of their relation to the curriculum and goals of the reading or library media program, as well as their cost. Strategies for critical reading, including a meaningful context for language as well as skills for reading and writing development, should be incorporated in the selections. These multimedia programs should not simply emulate television or a video arcade environment. Hypertext that allows terms and concepts to be linked through multilevel, branching connections within the text should be present to stimulate parallel modes of thinking. Video, sound, and animations should be consistent in creating an active reading environment for the student.

RETHINKING READING INSTRUCTION

For active critical reading to occur teachers must foster an atmosphere of inquiry. Students are encouraged to question, make predictions, organize ideas that support value judgments, problem solve, and learn to reason through reading. Teaching students to read, write, and think critically is a dramatic shift from what has generally taken place in most classrooms.

In 1988, Wilson stated that the educational community should rethink the way it teaches reading. In a longitudinal study that followed economically disadvantaged students from preschool through high school, results indicated that students whose classes had an academic focus rather than a remedial one had higher reading scores in high school. Students should be encouraged to formulate questions prior to, during, and after reading. They should be encouraged to analyze passages in terms of their own values and to respond to the text through a variety of writing activities. The critical-thinking reader is actively and constructively engaged in the process of writing. The role of background knowledge and the student's ability to draw upon it are essential to critical thinking/learning.

Students should be exposed to reading in a variety of formats, including online, CD-ROM, and hard copy. The instructional model for problem solving (Flynn 1989) promotes:

- analysis, synthesis, and evaluation of ideas
- clarification of information by examining component parts
- synthesis by combining relevant parts into a coherent whole
- setting up standards and judging against them to verify reasonableness of ideas

This is not only a college or high school model. It is a model to be used in preschool, elementary school, and through the graduate level. Using fairy tales for young children can place reasoning at the center of their reading experience. Results of reading studies indicate that students who began formal reading instruction at kindergarten had higher reading achievement scores as seniors in high school (Hanson and Siegel 1988, 1991). Beginning reading instruction in preschool and kindergarten is critical to adult literacy. Parental involvement in encouraging reading and library trips promote reading achievement. Preschool activities—learning nursery rhymes and stories, watching "Sesame Street," playing word and number games, being read to while attending nursery/preschool, and participating in special lessons such as swimming, dance, or music—were all positively related to students' reading ability in high school (Siegel 1994). Smith and Sensenbaugh (1992) point out that these activities are not widely partaken of: "Today, however, the vast majority of preschool children are not provided with these kinds of early educational experiences yet amazingly educational leaders and national policy makers seem puzzled as to why so many students graduate from high school as functional illiterates."

There are many problem-solving contexts in which to involve students at any age. Life, itself, requires one to be an excellent problem solver—one who can read to comprehend, evaluate evidence, draw conclusions, make inferences, and develop a line of thinking. Instead of passively reading from the textbook, have the students question, analyze, and use the resources of the library media center to read critically. Critical reading and information literacy fit together like puzzle pieces that can complete the whole and help to solve the problem of illiteracy.

Student-centered classroom and library media center environments that are both personal and collaborative encourage critical thinking. Students who are reading, writing, and discussing in a variety of ways are more inclined to become critical thinkers.

Educational Technology, Library Science, and Social Studies

5

The study of social studies in an inquiry-learning environment utilizes critical reading, process writing, and information literacy. Integrating educational technology within this context increases student interest and achievement especially among at-risk learners.

Social studies lends itself to the investigation and critical analysis of the past and its implications for the present and future. It can be one of the most exciting, thought-provoking disciplines. It can have a pervasive impact on citizenship and democracy. Inquiry learning can stimulate investigation, analysis, and reflection. Too often rote learning, memorization of unrelated facts, and lecture classes create an atmosphere of boredom and learning is passive.

Social studies should be interactive, stimulating the active participation of the student. It is an outstanding discipline for partnering with the library media specialist. It lends itself to utilizing the most current Internet technology, CD-ROMs, videodisks, and computer software.

The Nebraska Department of Education's Strategic Plan for Social Studies in Nebraska (1993) can easily move the belief statements to action in developing information competency. The interactive use of the Internet, educational technology, library science, and social studies can propel a dynamic, inquiry-based curriculum. Several of the belief statements follow:

- Social studies provides the opportunity to understand global cultures, past and present, and promotes respect for individual and cultural diversity.
- Social studies links the past, present, and future.
- Social studies develops an understanding of the individual's role in a family, community, state, and national and global society.

- Social studies promotes responsible management of global resources.
- Social studies provides knowledge and skills important for lifelong learning.
- Social studies develops knowledge, skills, and attitudes enabling individuals to make informed personal and social decisions.
- Social studies develops responsible, active citizens in a democratic society.

SCIENCE, TECHNOLOGY, AND SOCIETY (STS)

One of the major themes in social studies education is the effect of science and technology on the development, growth, and change in society. Library media specialists can train students and teachers in developing competent, information-seeking behaviors to investigate, hypothesize, problem solve, and evaluate forms of information from a multitude of resources in print, online, and electronic formats. They can work compatibly with social studies teachers in political science, geography, history, and social science, presenting an alternative learning environment in which one can think and learn about the influences of science and technology on society. Trends in social studies education relate science and technology to human societies in the past and present. Science and technology not only affect but are also affected by the institutions and values of a society. The major STS themes (Heath 1988) include:

1. *Critical Public Issues that Affect the Well-Being of Individuals and Societies throughout the World.* Bybee and Mau conducted a study in 1986 that indicated that science educators perceived the most important science and technology problems to be worldwide hunger, unchecked population growth, declining air quality, depletion of water resources, and the destructive capacity of modern weapons systems. A decade later, these issues are more critical with the instability of the Third World, the Arab world, China, Russia, the Balkans, and Eastern Europe.

2. *Processes and Skills in Thinking about Critical Public Issues Associated with Science and Technology.* Decision-making, problem-solving, and critical-thinking processes related to students' ability to gather, analyze, synthesize, and apply information can create strong partnerships between social studies teachers and library media specialists. Students should "inquire about alternatives and their consequences in the process of making rational and defensible choices" (Heath 1988). This type of thinking requires information literacy. It requires more information and judgment than a chapter in a textbook.

3. *The Utility of Trade-Offs in Decision Making on STS Issues.* These issues are viewed in shades of gray. Environmental decisions and concerns are prime examples. They are related to economic and possibly technological progress including corporate and individual greed and/or financial success. Limiting types of progress and protecting the environment, may be necessary for humankind's ultimate welfare, benefit, and existence. The trade-offs are not clearly defined. The limits of each issue and the decision-making process involve compromise that may occur in a matrix of negotiation.

4. *Knowledge and Skills in Civic Action*. Simulations, role playing, and investigation stress the responsibilities and the importance of the vote in a democracy. They promote a lifelong civic understanding that will stay with the students. Library media specialists can work with the social studies teachers to investigate local issues that come up before the population. There are also excellent CD-ROMs and videodisks that explore the election process and promote role playing. World Wide Web sites are being used for presidential campaigning. Students can participate in conferencing and electronic mail exchanges.

5. *Interrelationship and Integration of Knowledge and Cognitive Process Skills from Several Academic Disciplines*. Interdisciplinary studies between several disciplines can occur. One example would be to develop a unit on the environment that involves biology, geology, language arts, history, science, and political science. The library media specialist can be the glue that coordinates the projects, assisting in the research, providing training in electronic resources including CD-ROM, video laser disks, online databases, and the Internet. The computer teacher can assist students who are interested in scanning videos, photographs, and texts into multimedia projects. Astound, PowerPoint, Macromedia Director, and Hyperstudio are multimedia authoring programs that can facilitate some of the projects.

The library media specialist can work with the teacher to examine the powerful and pervasive effects, both positive and negative, of human actions in society. A holistic view can investigate their interconnectedness and their effect on society and the living world. The thought-provoking reality of a disappearing rain forest—hastened by the availability of technology to enter lands once inhospitable to widespread human existence— is an example. The rain forest provides plants that are used for developing medicines as well as many yet undiscovered plants one of which can be a future vaccination for the AIDS virus. The rain forest also balances the oxygen-carbon dioxide cycles on the earth. In Siberia, on the other side of the world, another one of the earth's richest remaining forests is being logged feverishly.

A profound understanding of how the changes in technology and science are influencing culture, ethics, and ideals is important for an educated citizenry. As the global village becomes smaller through the information superhighway, citizenry takes on a broader meaning.

The ability of citizens to make informed, rational decisions is a fundamental goal of American education, which is directly linked to understanding public issues related to societal applications of science and technology. If the social studies curriculum includes an emphasis on the interactions of science, technology and society and the decisions that citizens make in their social and personal lives in terms of these interactions, then students are likely to develop capabilities that enable them to act responsibly and effectively as members of local, national and global communities. (Heath 1988)

One example of a technological advance that can have both positive and negative effects on society and the individual is DNA testing. The discovery of the gene that causes breast cancer appears to be very beneficial. It will promote early detection of the cancer for those with a predisposition to the disease. But DNA testing for a predisposition for breast cancer or heart disease is being used by the insurance companies as a means for mandatory exclusion from coverage for persons demonstrating the predisposition, even though they have never had the disease. The posture of the insurance companies is being debated in legal, medical, and political arenas including Congress.

These are topics that integrate disciplines and stimulate critical thinking. They develop the student's ability to comment, debate, discuss, and present their research and conclusions through collaborative writing, electronic mail, and forums, as well as through multimedia projects. The information students retrieve can be analyzed, evaluated, and applied to solve problems, and will become part of their cognitive knowledge much more than will data, rote facts, or unrelated information. This knowledge will lead to a high level of understanding of social reality. It is the foundation for a citizenry that can relate to and affect the complexity of a technological society. For the at-risk student, this is action-oriented learning that is not dependent on lecture. Allowing the students to explore, discover, and direct their own learning in a multimedia rich environment stimulates achievement.

Marlow (1991) suggested

that emerging adolescents in middle schools will do better in social studies if activities are encouraged that develop and maintain student interest. Goal centered, interesting learning opportunities are a must in the social studies curriculum. Middle school students need ample opportunities to engage in problem solving. Lifelike problems chosen by middle school students with teacher guidance emphasize interests of learners in ongoing lessons and units. To achieve the broad goal of developing interest in teaching-learning situations, middle school students need to achieve meaning in subject matter studied, purposes or reasons for learning, and have an experience that provides for individual differences.

The discussion of STS can be infused into existing courses of study or into units that are relevant from either a historical, present, or future perspective. Opposing views can challenge preconceptions or textbook perceptions. A course of study, for example, can include a case study on an environmental issue. Most eras in history have been influenced by technological innovations, that is, radio, television, the automobile, or computers. The development of the atomic bomb in World War II, the invention of gun powder and its effects on war among nations and peoples, the treatments of tuberculosis, polio, and heart disease and their effect on life expectancy, and population growth are other examples how science and technology affect society.

A systematic interdisciplinary course of study can be used to design a learning community composed of social studies, language arts, science, library media, and computer science teachers. The course of study can be organized around social problems and issues discussing the interrelationships of science, technology, and society. Information gathering and retrieval, investigation, analysis, evaluation and application of solutions, or the generation of more questions stimulates individual and group problem solving. Strong cooperation, time, energy, and training between and among disciplines and the library media specialist are crucial. They will need to devote time to develop the curriculum and carry out its implementation in the classroom, library, and computer lab. The library media specialist will need to train and motivate faculty and students to research through electronic, online, media, and text formats. The Internet, CD-ROM laser disks, videos, and print create a multisensory experience similar to the life that is at the center of the social issue. Content can interrelate history and the various social and natural sciences in a problem-solving, mind-expanding curriculum.

AIM LAB

The AIM Lab at the University of Illinois at Urbana is the World Wide Web development lab for the College of Agricultural, Consumer and Environmental Sciences. It is dedicated to the design and production of academic materials for the Internet's World Wide Web. The lab has created the Discovery System. It is available at this World Wide Web address: http://www.uiuc.edu. It includes an online Mind Module that can form an integral foundation of the scheme and expectations of the thinking processes to be developed by the students.

Several of the modules in the Discovery System can provide a wealth of virtual information on topics in science, technology, and society using a multidisciplinary approach to the social sciences. The Discovery System is a significant arena for the development of information competency that can be used by the library media specialist as a guide to plan and develop relevant curriculum. Information literacy is growing in importance in a technological society that is expanding its ways of knowing: from print to media to multimedia and through the Internet. The AIM Lab's Mind Module develops thinking strategies in many following areas (see Figure 5.1). Questions and the guidelines (see Figure 5.2) can be used by the library media specialist and the teacher to foster inquiry learning and information literacy. This type of thinking can be integrated into individual and multidisciplinary units in the following disciplines: social studies, language arts, science, and library science. It uses all the resources of educational technology.

Figure 5.1
Thinking Strategies of the Mind Module

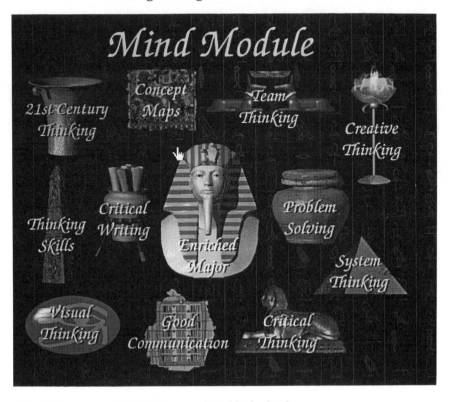

http://w3.ag.uiuc.edu/AIM/Discovery/Mind/index.html

SAMPLE PROBLEM, LOGGING IN OREGON

Before proceeding further, the problem must be defined—Should there be logging in the last ancient North American rain forest? Defining the problem stimulates a nonlinear thinking strategy. What is the problem and where and who does it reach? What are the issues and implications of logging in Oregon? Brainstorm the key concepts, key words, and related terms. Logging and Oregon are key words in the information search process.

The appropriateness of logging the last ancient forest in the United States is being discussed in Congress and the states of Oregon and Washington. The logging industry, federal and state environmental agencies, and citizen groups are continuously debating these issues. In order to adequately address the problem with a pro and con rationale the problem can be rephrased, "Should there be logging permitted in our last ancient forest?"

Figure 5.2
Questions to Ask in the Problem-Solving Process

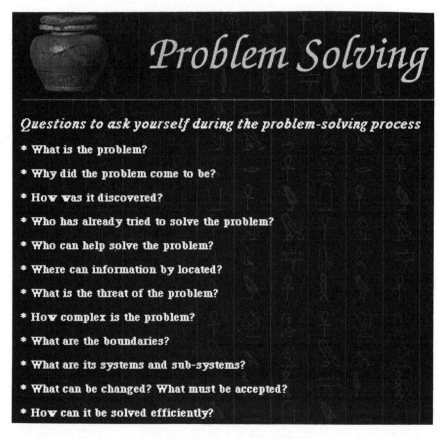

Problem Solving

Questions to ask yourself during the problem-solving process

* What is the problem?

* Why did the problem come to be?

* How was it discovered?

* Who has already tried to solve the problem?

* Who can help solve the problem?

* Where can information by located?

* What is the threat of the problem?

* How complex is the problem?

* What are the boundaries?

* What are its systems and sub-systems?

* What can be changed? What must be accepted?

* How can it be solved efficiently?

http://w3.aces.uiuc.edu/AIM/Discovery/Mind/prob-solving.html

Systems thinking and cognitive skills need to be developed in a parallel, branching, relational mode by the students. This type of thinking will enable students to succeed in accessing and retrieving information in a variety of sources—CD-ROM, online databases, videodisks, the Internet, and print. "Systems thinking" promotes holistic problem solving. Developing this type of thinking will assist students in using the technology more effectively, especially students with special needs. Systems thinking stimulates students to examine the problem within the context that surrounds it (concept mapping). Concept mapping can visually allow the student to view the problem within the whole situation, and to detail the many "systems" that are interrelated and can be affected by the problem. Visualizing the problem through the concept map can help students in their research and lead to sound decision making.

"Techniques such as . . . concept mapping have a profound role to play in analyzing processes of learning and they provide a means for understanding human knowledge with the aid of computer technology" (Bower and Hilgard 1981; De Mey 1992). Concept mapping is a metalearning strategy based on the theory of meaningful learning (Ausubel 1978; Novak 1977; Novak and Gowin 1984; Shavelson, Lang, and Lewin 1993). Several software programs exist that guide students in creating concept maps that provide the teacher with a window into the students' minds (Fisher 1990). "Concept maps are designed to find out what the learner knows about a subject and are in effect, maps of cognition" (Wandersee 1990).

Many issues can form the components of a complex problem. These components and their relationships can be visually depicted through the use of concept mapping. The conflicting components of our problem—logging in the Oregon forest—consist of the destruction of an ancient forest, biodiversity, recreational needs, economic needs, and climatic and environmental repercussions and concerns. Concept mapping can illustrate the problem (see Figure 5.3).

The visualization of the problem can promote group problem solving and multidimensional analysis. Systems thinking is holistic, integrative, and realistic. It does not allow one to view the problem so narrowly that related aspects are excluded. It also allows one to focus on one of the dimensions without losing sight of its effect on the whole. In effect, "it formulates innovative, creative and realistic solutions to complex problems" (AIM Lab 1996).

Figure 5.3
A Basic Concept Map

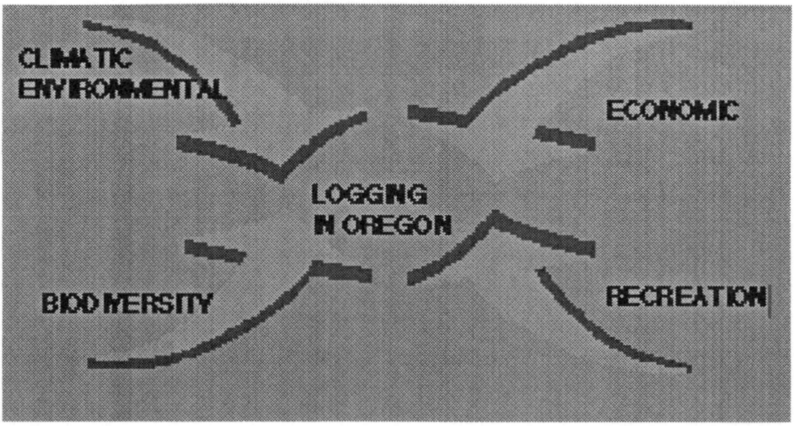

Concept maps allow the student to represent the information visually and assist in stimulating the development of information literacy.

1. Defining the problem
   - What is the question that needs to be asked?
   - What is the statement that needs to be made to distinguish pro and con arguments?
2. Brainstorming key terms, relationships, and interconnections between concepts
   - List the terms from prior knowlege of the topic
   - Develop a list of key terms from a multitude of resources (Print, Internet, CD-ROM, videodisks, online databases)
3. Locate and find resources
   - printed resources
   - video tapes
   - CD-ROM disks (electronic encyclopedia, SIRS, magazine and newspaper indexes with full text and citations, Biology Digest, etc.)
   - videodisks
   - Internet World Wide Web searches
4. Inquiry-based investigations
   - Analyze the information
     - Add terms to the concept map as the data gathering proceeds
     - Is the information authentic, relevant?
     - Does it show bias?
     - Is the author an expert in the field?
       - What are his or her credentials?
   - Synthesize the information
     - Develop a multisensory database of information
   - Evaluate the information
     - Visually seek and represent the solution
   - Apply the information to solve problems
     - Ask more questions if the solution is not easy to find

"Concept maps harness the power of our vision to understand complex information at a glance" (AIM Lab 1996). The pictures and graphical representations of the concept map energize brain power to construct meaning. Presentation tools such as PowerPoint can be used to construct concept maps.

Concept maps can also work in a hypertext environment. Students can use hypermedia programs such as Adobe's PageMill or Microsoft Assistant with Netscape to create an interactive concept map. By clicking on a link the student can connect to more specific or related information. Hypertext is used to link and relate terms from the broadest to the most specific or to branch to parallel ideas and related concepts. It is used as the interface for the Internet's graphical browsers for the World Wide Web, in CD-ROM laser disks, and videodisks.

Computer software including a word processor is preferable to creating a concept map using a static piece of paper. The computer programs allow the students to be more flexible. They can alter, add to, and expand their maps more easily on the computer than on a piece of paper.

Concept maps enable students of all levels to develop the types of thinking necessary to succeed in an increasingly electronic environment. There are different ways to create the concept map—the visual picture and evolution of the students' thinking and information literacy processes in researching their topic. As it is developed by the student, it can lead from the problem to the solution.

The design of the concept map is personal. It is dependent on the visual image the student has of the topic he or she is exploring. Different topics also lend themselves more clearly to specific designs. Some examples of the design of concept maps follow. (See Figures 5.4 through 5.6 for further visualization.)

1. Spider concept map
   - The central theme, problem, or question appears in the center of the map.
   - Subthemes, or interrelated topics, surround the problem and branch or radiate from the center. An example is the concept map on logging in Oregon. A simpler depiction is the following:

Figure 5.4
Logging in Oregon: A Simple Concept Map

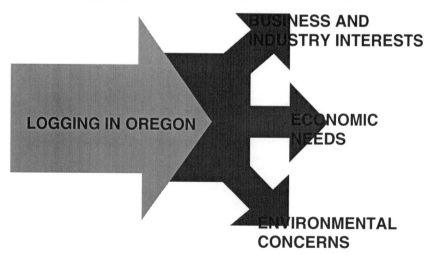

Figure 5.5
Logging in Oregon: A Hierarchical Concept Map

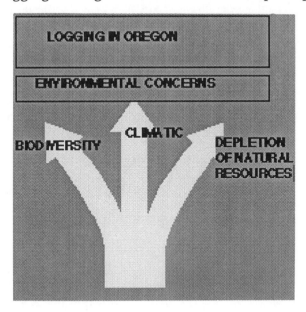

Figure 5.6
Logging in Oregon: A Final Concept Map

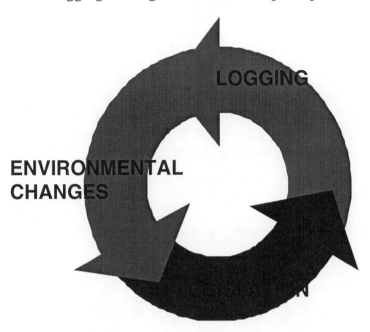

2. Hierarchical Concept Map
   • The problem, central theme, or question is located at the top of the map.
   • The information that is the most important branches from the problem in a downward trend.
   • Information is then linked from each of the topics in descending order of importance.
   • Each link may have substantial sublinks.

3. Flow chart
   • The information in a flow chart is displayed in a sequential and linear format.

4. Systems Concept Map
   • The information is organized much like that in a flow chart.
   • In a systems concept map one can add information as input and have an output as well as a feedback and evaluative loop (AIM Lab 1996).

A concept map can depict the final visual representation of solving the problem and incorporate all the major considerations. It can be as intricate or as simple as the students design it.

The library media specialist and/or teacher(s) will not know everything about every topic. They should not feel intimidated. The beauty and importance of allowing the students to do the research and investigation are that they will be the experts. They have control of their projects and receive guidance and direction from the library media specialist and/or teacher(s). The students are developing the cognitive tools to problem solve and make decisions after finding, analyzing, and evaluating the information. Concept maps are a reflection of the thinking and brainstorming process. They allow average and slow learners to visually plot and detail their thinking. By defining and adding key and related terms, they are creating visual maps to follow in their research. This is especially helpful when using electronic resources, where an overload of information can easily occur. Having a concept map in place will allow the student to more easily narrow or broaden the research with the key words and related terms from the map.

DEVELOPING METACOGNITIVE SKILLS

The library media specialist working with the teacher can develop a lesson on teaching the students to think about thinking

Lesson Plan 1: Developing the Concept Map

Objectives:

• To stimulate students to think about thinking
• To create a visual concept map illustrating the thinking processes

1. Library media specialist and/or teacher describes the problem. Oregon has one of the few remaining old growth forests in North America. The forest is home to the spotted owl, an endangered species. The teacher and/or library media specialist reads and/or provides a series of short selections to explain the pro and con issues.

CON POSITION

"Andrew Daunis sits under one of the tepees. He slides his arm inside a plastic pipe running through a 55-gallon drum filled with concrete. Inside the pipe is a metal rod. On their belt loops and bodies, the 22-year-old Massachusetts native and his fellow environmental protesters carry 8-inch-long chains with thick links. If law enforcement or U.S. Forest Service officers come to evict them from this beautiful national forest, Daunis and the others say they will chain themselves to the pipe inside the barrel. 'There is no law,' says Daunis. 'All our laws get thrown out—the Endangered Species Act, the Clean Water Act have all been nullified by other laws. That's why we're here.'"

"Radical environmentalists, who are few in number but adept at attracting media attention, are outraged by what they consider the gutting of environmental legislation by recent federal and local measures and court decisions. In recent weeks, hard-core groups such as Earth First, many of whose members have been living in their self-styled Cascadia Free State in the Willamette National Forest since last September, have begun to escalate their opposition to federal, state and private plans to log more timber on national forest acreage" (Tharp 1996)

PRO POSITION

"A number of Oregon residents are more worried about the impact of economic growth and development, than the effects of the forest products industry, to the environment and quality of life. Many Oregonians remain cognizant of the fact that wood products and other natural resources are important to the long-term economic future of the state." (Beuter, 1995)

A video, CD-ROM, or videodisk presentation can provide visual images of the problem. The video anchor is important as a powerful tool to introduce new concepts and associate them with prior knowledge.

2. Library media specialist and teacher ask students to define the problem: Should logging be permitted in the old growth forests of Oregon?

3. Library media specialist and teacher brainstorm with the students the key terms of the problem: Logging—Oregon—Old Growth.

4. Library media specialist and teacher brainstorm some of the related terms that discuss the effects of logging in Oregon

   • environmental concerns
   • economic realities—jobs
   • recreational needs
   • biodiversity—plants and animals

- governmental laws
- political realities of reelection

5. The teacher and/or the library media specialist *can* provide additional information or allow the students to research subtopics regarding:
    - information from the Sierra Club
    - congressional action
    - Supreme Court action
    - president's support in removing all environmental laws that could inhibit logging
    - federal agency positions

6. Library media specialist and teacher create a concept map with the students and/or illustrate templates developed for their use:
    - Examine photographs, graphics, and visual materials and discuss how they display and relate information.

Figure 5.7
Logging in Oregon: Descriptive Facts in the Concept Map

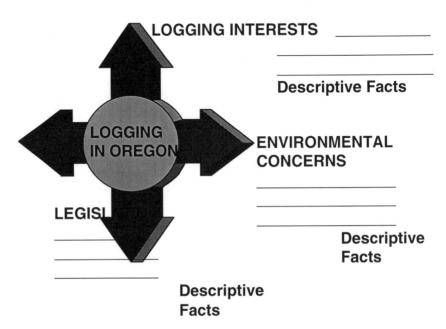

CONCEPT MAPPING

- Discuss the concept of visual language and how it differs from text.
- Have the students close their eyes and visualize terms and concept relationships. This is known as free association.
- Encourage students to experiment with a variety of visual formats.
- Encourage students to use colors, arrows, and accent words through bold face, italics, or underline for emphasis (AIM Lab 1996).

Students may want to include brief descriptive facts (e.g., July/August 1994, Social Studies) in each area of their concept map that will assist in report writing (see Figure 5.7). It will afford the flexibility to decide how to assemble the final report. Colored markers can be used to group all related topics together. Students could have a concept map template on a disk and use a software program to color and group the objects and record the descriptive facts.

It is important for average and special needs students to use the computer to develop and expand the concept map. A paper copy of the same exercise is static, limiting, and does not allow these students to easily add and revise. Handwriting is often a problem—including specific handwriting disabilities. The computer can provide a more even playing field for success. Collaboration and group problem solving will enable the students to ask questions and reach solutions in a nonthreatening team-oriented environment. Concept mapping can be used as a visual tool for note taking and outlining.

EDUCATIONAL TECHNOLOGY AND THE SOCIAL STUDIES

Online and CD-ROM Databases

Social studies as a discipline has an abundance of CD-ROM, videodisks, online databases, computer software, and Internet World Wide Web sites that complement the curriculum. Online databases are used as emancipatory tools by social scientists, faculty, and students. Numerous online and CD-ROM databases offer a wealth of information in all aspects of the social studies and social sciences. Lexis, Nexis, Magazine Index ASAP, and many of the DIALOG databases are available in some library media centers. The CD-ROM indexes, have been, however, more popular and more cost effective from the end user point of view. The CD-ROM magazine and newspaper indexes, Information Access, EBSCO, Newsbank, and SIRS are examples of well-used sources in the library media center environment. Accessing and retrieval of this information is only one step in the information literacy process; it is the user who interprets the data.

Instructional Software

Instructional software transmits facts and interrelationships and can be used by students to reinforce previously presented concepts and theories.

Tutorials, drill and practice programs, and simulations are examples of instructional software. The Carmen San Diego series is an excellent and successful example of software for special needs and average learners. It engages them in an important geographical experience and builds knowledge that is lacking in many elementary curricula. The Oregon Trail is another example.

Instructional software can be used as a supplement to classroom instruction and can be available in the library media center. Teachers can work with the library media specialist to provide instructional software that complements and enhances the curriculum.

Simulations

Simulations such as SimCity are "revelatory" software (Brady 1994) and allow students to use the inductive learning approach. The learner discovers for himself or herself the concepts and knowledge arrived at within that discipline. The student becomes the social decision maker displaying decision-based competencies. Group decision making and collaborative learning can be utilized in simulations that allow multiple players.

Hypermedia

Hypermedia contexts are used in social studies CD-ROM laser disks, videodisks, and World Wide Web sites. Hypermedia or hypertext programs are structured hierarchically to break down general concepts into more detailed and specific subconcepts. Students can find established examples of prior knowledge and link them with new and novel relationships, providing opportunities for concept exploration. Hypermedia focuses on constructing meaning through an interrelational web of information that facilitates associations (links) between and among concepts (nodes) (Horn 1989). Facts are not isolated. Language development processes are facilitated including concept formation, comprehension, remembering, retention, and retrieval (Palumbo and Bermudez 1994). For cognitive psychologists (Kumar, Helgeson, and White 1994), hypermedia is becoming the interface between technology and psychology allowing for the study of and understanding of human cognitive processes.

Hypermedia can be used to represent semantic language. Semantic language is the scientific study of the relationship between signs or symbols and what they mean or denote. Psychology also examines behavior as it is influenced by signs. "For example, concepts in the form of texts and graphics may form *nodes* and the semantic relationships between the concepts form *links*. Using this analogy, information and concepts that are related could be represented by cards, screens or video images, and linked via electronic 'buttons' in a hypermedia computer system" (Halasz 1988).

There appears to be considerable similarity between human knowledge and the "node-link" framework of the hypermedia, which utilizes a computer environment to represent and organize information as proposed by cognitive theories of learning (Jonassen 1988; Sowa 1984; Yates and Chandler 1991).

The Netscape Navigator is widely used as a World Wide Web browser on the Internet and is an example of a hypermedia environment. Its ease of use promotes relational-thinking strategies worldwide. It has stimulated the immense popularity of the Internet.

Hypermedia is designed to resemble human knowledge structures. It can also be a tool to understand human cognitive processes, such as moves and decisions made in a problem (Collins 1990; Kumar, Helgeson, and White 1994). Hypermedia creates an omnidirectional environment to assist in linear and nonlinear thinking (Jonassen 1988). Computer technology used interactively stimulates special needs and average students to exceed the teacher's expectations.

Social studies instruction should involve analyzing and solving problems. Hypermedia utilized in a computer-based, problem-solving task allows the problem solver, through various key strokes and/or mouse clicks, to document the steps used in the decision-making process. Some of the software programs and the Internet browsers will record the steps to be taken to reach the decision. The problem solver can return to one of the steps and redirect the process if necessary. This type of computer interaction provides a window into the cognitive processes of the individual and assists the teacher and library media specialist to guide the students toward success.

Palumbo and Bermudez (1994) praised the use of hypermedia:

Hypermedia enables intuitive, "how-to" learning opportunities for students in contrast to the more traditional approach which underscores teacher-generated and controlled instruction. Since hypermedia is self-paced and student-centered, it offers students unique opportunities to tap into their prior knowledge and experiences by allowing them to create their own paths through the information web presented. Levels of fluency, knowledge, motivation and interest are addressed individually; hence inclusion of culturally and linguistically diverse populations is ensured in the learning process.

MULTIMEDIA AUTHORING PROGRAMS

Students can work with and explore hypermedia software, CD-ROMs, videodisks, and the Internet World Wide Web sites already developed and/or they can create their own. Once students are familiar with developing hypermedia relationships, they can design their own project to engage others. Concept mapping can be used as the beginning of a script. Multimedia production is time consuming and mind expanding. The student not only must know the information and the relationships between broader and narrower topics, but he or she must also know how others will access the information. What cognitive processes will be used? Who is the audience? What is their frame of reference? How much information is too much? What pictures, photographs, music, and videos will excite the learning environment of the prospective end user?

This is a high cognitive stage and will utilize high order thinking skills. As the student becomes engaged in reflective inquiry, it is the student who constructs meaning. Multimedia programs such as Macromedia Director, Astound, and PowerPoint can be used to create knowledge bases that integrate photographs, video, text, audio, and graphics. An interdisciplinary team can work together to make a multimedia production a reality. Depending on the expertise in your school, it may involve the library media specialist, social studies teacher, art/graphics design teacher, and computer teacher.

One multimedia project was developed to foster teen parenting skills. It was funded by a grant for distance learning and underrepresented students in the state of California. I co-directed the multimedia program, Teens Helping Teens Become Better Parents. A team of faculty and staff created the video, CD-ROM laser disk, brochure, workbook, and electronic mail and bulletin board exercises. The team included the school's video producer, who worked at the local cable television station; a graphic designer to design the covers of the workbook and brochure; the art/multimedia instructor, who developed the CD-ROM multimedia program; the child care instructor, who facilitated the class with the teen parents; and the distance learning coordinator, who co-directed the grant.

The impetus for the grant was the need to develop good parenting skills in teen parents and the need to relieve stress in their lives. Distance learning was considered because the students could access some of the materials through broadcast television or through the use of the video and CD-ROM in independent study. When the idea of the multimedia CD-ROM was first introduced, many in the group believed that this audience would not own or have access to a CD-ROM drive or computer. I believed that many of the teens attending high school could get access to a computer with a CD-ROM drive through the library media center. I strongly believe that no group should be disenfranchised from technological and information literacy. If the multimedia CD-ROM were produced in an upbeat way that would invite its use, the parents might find and retrieve information on their own, and begin to develop computer skills.

The video can be used through cable television for distance learning or in parenting classes. It is a 1990s documentary of teens talking to teens about parenting. The first video in the series focuses on why babies cry. A pediatrician, a counselor, and the teacher, who is more of a facilitator, are part of the videotape. It is the teen parents, however, who give the video honesty and integrity, creating a vibrant, informational, and sometimes uneasy discussion.

The purpose of the multimedia CD-ROM was to provide an interactive, personal format for teens to get information on why their babies cry. What is colic? What should they do? What should they look for, and how will they know when to bring the baby to the doctor? Before developing the CD-ROM, a script had to be written. This script provides direction and the foundation for the CD-ROM production. It is similar to the concept map. In developing the plan for the CD-ROM script, the audience—their reading level and attention span—had to be considered. Research was undertaken to provide accurate information for the text portion of the CD-ROM.

Astound was the hypermedia authoring program used for developing the CD-ROM. As I read the information and created the script, I visualized the "hot buttons" that would lead the teens to the information they wanted. I also considered the nodes and the hypertext links throughout the program that would link several layers of information for efficient access and retrieval.

The CD-ROM interface for our target population needed the following characteristics:

- ease of use and navigation
- few, but meaningful, words on the page (too much text would turn off this population)
- video clips that would reinforce the information in text form
- upbeat music and colors that would relate to the target population
- authenticity and relevancy of the information presented

As a library media specialist, I wrote the grant, coordinated the project, and developed the script for the CD-ROM. The development of the script, the information to be included, a preliminary design, and the characteristics of the CD-ROM interface assisted the multimedia instructor in creating the CD-ROM. When designing multimedia programs, students should be aware of the preliminary work needed to make the final product successful. Critical, creative, visual, and information literacy skills combine with the technical skills in developing the multimedia presentation. In a K–12 environment, an interdisciplinary team of faculty can work with students to develop the final product.

COLLABORATIVE WRITING SOFTWARE

Interactive and collaborative writing creates a forum for discussions among and between classmates and the teacher. Programs such as Daedalus, Common Place, and Aspects allow the students to create a dialogue that explores their research, perceptions, and ideas. The software is available on networked computers and provides students with the opportunity to read each other's comments as they are written. Once the student begins typing he or she has the pen. His or her comments are viewed by the class immediately as they are written. This is similar to an online chat session.

Students in a class can be given a topic to research. They can share their research in an interactive collaborative writing exercise, where they present their research and have students add to it or question it. Each student can have a turn writing a response or an insight. The other members of the class view the responses instantaneously and a thoughtful written dialogue ensues. It can be accompanied by a vocal discussion that stimulates writing and thought. Students are using several parts of the brain—the tactile, the audio, the visual—by viewing, reading, analyzing, and responding to the information on the screen. Interactive writing through collaborative networking software has stimulated the immense popularity of the Internet. It allows students to brainstorm ideas for papers, have prereading discussions, share drafts of papers, and collaboratively write papers without leaving their computers.

Word-processing documents can be divided into two sections, with approximately 3.5 inch margins to facilitate an interactive post and respond experience between the student, the teacher, or other students. Students can write their essays and leave comments for their teacher or classmates. In selecting collaborative-writing networking software, it is important to test it to find out how many students can participate at one time without a serious slowdown in response time.

Videodisks

Traditional lecture/textbook strategies that present a static body of knowledge the teacher wants to impart to his or her students are not motivating to many of today's visual learners. With history, technology science, and culture changing so rapidly, students need to be trained to be independent learners. It is the wise teacher and library media specialist who learn from their students and let the students know that an information exchange is respected and encouraged. Roles can be interchangeable. The teacher and library media specialist are not threatened by the juxtaposition.

Multimedia technology related to inquiry-based learning and information competency facilitates teamwork, creative project design, and solutions. The library media specialist, teacher, and computer teacher can provide the students with the tools, the basic content, and allow them to grow and expand their knowledge level.

There are two types of videodisks: CLV extended play disks and CAV standard play disks. CLV laser disks are the ones used for movies. They can hold ninety minutes of video. CAV disks have the advantage of allowing the images to be accessed individually. Videodisk images are much sharper than those on videotape. Videodisks contain 54,000 still images on each side. They can include primary source material, videos, and text. It is how they are utilized that can make them more than a slide, a passive video presentation, or a short simulation.

Videodisks can be used to stimulate critical, creative, and visual thinking and learning. Using a bar-code reader that operates in much the same way as bar-code readers in grocery stores, students can select and sort images, videos, and text, thereby developing a sequence of knowledge for presentation to their classmates. Their presentation can illustrate opposing sides of an issue. Bar-code readers are standard equipment on certain videodisk players. Many videodisks come equipped with bar codes as an index so that selection is easy. With the swipe of a bar code a specific image, text, audio, and/or video can be accessed. The teacher or library media specialist has a choice of whether to use the remote control or the bar-code scanner.

Videodisk players and bar-code readers do not mandate the use of a computer. Using a computer, however, opens a new exploratory and creative world. On Macintosh, a Hypercard stack, and on IBM, Linkway, establish compatibility and compliance between the videodisk and the computer. The teacher or student can create a sequenced file of specific images, video, graphics, and/or text for the presentation to be used at any time, as many times as needed. An advantage of the sequenced file is that it eliminates the need to hunt for and pick out each individual image by bar-code reader or remote control. If the multimedia file is also available on the World Wide Web, the laser disk (e.g., the Louvre) is superior. It eliminates network time and hard computer disk resources to access and retrieve the file.

The file can be played back in the individual classroom/library media center using a computer, a videodisk player, and a television monitor with video input. RGB television monitors have the best reception and clearest image. An LCD panel or projection system connected to the computer and laser disk player can also project the images, many times greater, on a large screen display than the television monitor.

The computer index that complements the videodisk can contain an index with printed text to accompany the images, audio, or videos. The text is easily printed through the use of the computer. The National Gallery of Art and the Louvre laser disks are very popular and have replaced, in many instances, slide trays. The laser disk is a storage device that stores the images and facilitates their access through the computer, bar-code reader, or remote control.

Teachers and library media specialists can use the videodisk as an anchor for new information. By presenting visual images, videos, and graphics, the students can capture the essence of a time period—its dress, art and architecture, language, and music—depending on the content of the videodisk. A videodisk allows the user to create the sequence, and select, sort, or delete items. A videotape does not have the flexibility of the videodisk.

Middle school students used the Art and Civilization videodisk to explore prehistoric life. The videodisk illustrated the evolution of tools, showed cave art at Lascaux, and examined models of Paleolithic dwellings. Students created a videotape of their research and findings on the period and used videotaped images from the laser disc, adding flute music in the background for a multimedia presentation. Other groups of students illustrated the development of Buddhism in India and its spread to China. Still others focused on Japan, women and the Renaissance, life in pre-Columbian America, and the Industrial Revolution and its effects on the eighteenth and nineteenth centuries. Visual, aural, and textual images and information can enhance research (Crane 1993). Note the studies presented in chapter 1, which recommend the use of videodisks for teaching and learning.

A multisensory experience of a period in history can be developed using videodisk images, CD-ROM, print, the Internet, and online resources. When studying the Holocaust, for example, a laser disk with images, videos, and text of World War II can be used. Music from the 1940s can help establish the culture of the period along with art work selected from the laser disks of art and architecture of the period. Students can research the period through the Internet Newsgroups (soc.culture.jewish FAQ: Holocaust) and World Wide Web pages (http://remember.org, http://www.ushmm.org/education/guidelines.html/).

CREATING THE MULTISENSORY EXPERIENCE

Images are primary source documents that can stimulate discussion. Electronic search tools lead to further investigation through text, media, and online documents. As a library media specialist, I continuously discovered that when students searched the information on their topic on a CD-ROM encyclopedia, they were motivated to search their terms in online databases and in print. It is the interrelationship of these materials in a resource-based environment that encourages and fosters research.

Students can work in teams to research and develop different aspects of the projects. Students can create multimedia programs on CD-ROM using Astound or Macromedia Director. They can create a videotape of their images and text selected from the videodisk, the Internet, or reference books so long as they do not violate copyright laws.

The question/problem for student investigation should require the student's own reflective inquiry and research. It should not be a problem that can be plagiarized. A topic, for example, the Holocaust, can be divided into different areas:

- the culture of the period as reflected in the music, art, journalism, and society of the period
- the politics, media, philosophy, history, fears that contributed to the rise of Nazism and Hitler's ascent to power
- the war
- reaction of the Allies in music, film, literature, and art
- lasting effects—fifty years later

The dynamics of a period in history can be the basis for an interdisciplinary study in which experts in each area share their knowledge and stimulate important cognitive connections among students. This same context of multimedia, the living representation of the period, can be used to study modern Russia, China, or the Balkans. Multimedia can capture the time period, through the images, sounds, videos, and text, in a way that text alone cannot always bring to the audience. The videodisk on communism and the cold war, developed by ABC News and the Florida Department of Education, presents a mix of video clips, stills, and high quality graphics and provides the teacher and students with visually appealing materials designed to capture the students' interest. Sections such as "Music in the Cold War" and "Visions of a Nuclear War" stimulate creative debate.

Multimedia presentations should not be the goal of the social studies unit nor should the use of the technology. Technology is put to its poorest use when students become so involved in the mechanics of developing a multimedia program that the social essence, and significance, of the content is lost.

INTERNET AND THE SOCIAL STUDIES

The Internet is a phenomenal resource for getting a glimpse of countries worldwide. It provides insights into the way countries want to portray themselves—their music, art, society, architecture, government, politics, education, shopping, and sports. Major corporations in the United States are multinational, and a literate citizen will most likely interact with a variety of cultures at school, in the home neighborhood, or at the workplace. The Internet brings the cultures, thoughts, and needs of remote countries to the window of the personal computer. It is an "open" network to the world we live in.

When working with twenty-two Japanese students and teaching them about the Internet, through practical hands-on experiences, its potential as a bridge between cultures and societies began to be unveiled. After explaining in rather technical terms what the Internet is and what it can do, and illustrating graphs on who is using the Internet, the connection was made when I was able to search for their hometown of Toyama, Japan. Maps and photographs appeared instantly of the land they left and were three thousand miles away from.

At the end of the first session, I asked the class of mostly young Japanese women in their early twenties what was of interest to them. Almost universally, music appeared on everyone's list. I began the lesson with an Internet music video segment of a famous Japanese pop star singing a duet with Natalie Cole, thereby creating interest for searching the Web. Sony Corporation is online and headquartered in Tokyo with one of the best Web sites on the Internet (http://www.sony.com). In one visual, aural, and textual expression, the gap between two cultures was bridged and the students were stimulated to explore the Web. Students searched for information on Asian news, American and international fashion such as Louis Vuitton, in addition to astronomy, NASA, art, and specific countries. They were so intrigued with the Internet that our class sessions were extended from four sessions to five. Most of these young women had never used a computer and had no knowledge of telecommunications or the Internet before coming to class.

They were most impressed with the Internet's ability to understand, access, and become involved in another culture. These students were going to have access to the Internet at their school in Japan. They could study, interact, and conduct firsthand primary investigations of the United States, through the authentic experience on the Internet: they could discover American music, art (National Gallery of Art, the Smithsonian), NASA, and even send electronic mail to the White House (http://www.whitehouse.gov). Reality in a multimedia format of American culture, music, shopping, science, and art was at their fingertips. As I watched them discover and explore, I thought that American students could be introduced to foreign cultures in much the same way. ESL students could be welcomed to a new culture through the same connection.

Learning is most effective when it is purposeful and direct and when learners are involved in the learning process and are able to set meaningful goals for themselves. Students from Japan could continue their cultural and educational exchange through electronic mail with their American peers. Electronic mail is the most popular function of the Internet, connecting people worldwide and allowing them to share business and other communications through memos, files, graphics, videos, and programs. It is cheaper than a long distance phone call and can convey technical information in a more direct, clear, and precise manner. It is cheaper and more interactive than a fax and will arrive sooner than an overnight mail delivery. I use electronic mail daily to communicate with vendors and business and educational associates worldwide. It is the most efficient way to get responses to my queries quickly, with clarity, and with a record of what was decided upon.

ELECTRONIC MAIL AND THE SOCIAL STUDIES

Many times after an initial introduction, electronic mail and key pal correspondence lack substance in the educational arena. To be effective electronic mail needs to:

- relate to a school project
- have an immediacy to create and maintain enthusiasm
- generate real data that can be used to solve relevant problems

Using technology should not be the goal of the project. The question should be asked, Can electronic mail be used to generate solutions, data, and insights and form relationships that will assist the student in solving problems or in completing his/her task?

Obstacles encountered when using electronic mail can include the logistics of the library media environment. Is there only one computer connected to the Internet mail server? Are the computers networked to an Internet connection, thereby providing more access to more students simultaneously? Scheduling students is critical for success. Levin (1989) stated that it "takes weeks to get students organized and scheduled on the computer and all the while students at the other school are asking their teacher every day if their responses have arrived yet." The logistics on accessing and retrieving electronic mail by the students should be worked out between the teacher and the library media specialist before the curriculum project begins. Schedules for students should be defined and accepted by all those involved in the project.

Students of all levels in my library media center were intrigued to send and receive electronic mail. The electronic mail transmitted opinions from their remote peers for solutions to real life problems based on student research or to fictional stories that needed an ending or a beginning. Students came into the library media center before school, during lunch, and after school to send and receive electronic mail. Electronic mail worked best when students sent unfinished stories to their peers to complete. The completed story was published in both school newspapers. Opposing views presented as editorials such as those on nuclear energy sent and received from remote sites close to nuclear reactors also were very rewarding. Pro and con views were published in both school newspapers and were related to the curriculum in social studies, language arts, and science. Students were working and researching these topics. Publication of the electronic mail assisted in expanding their information resources as well as improving their writing and communication skills.

Lack of clear structure and purpose is another reason electronic mail exercises fail. Questions and responses are shallow and superficial and rely on process rather than content. If students are studying water pollution, possibly they can collect and analyze water and soil samples and exchange the data. They can research endangered species in their area, or write and share information on species that are now reproducing because the environment has improved. Students can research and send solutions to their problems to the other sites. They can also inform each other on political actions and measures in the state legislature that have worked. Possibly the other site can duplicate some of the actions by writing to their congressmen.

If students are studying cultures that are foreign to them such as those of the Aborigines, Native American Indians, or Asians, they can use the Internet to search for current works of art, music, and poetry. They can use electronic mail to have online discussions with the artists, writers, or school-age peers about their unique culture. Electronic mail needs to be issue driven, teacher driven, and learner driven. It should not be a technological add-on without purpose and direction. Each unit should have a start date and a completion date.

Electronic mail is one avenue of communication. Students could also send videotapes and photographs of their activities or create interactive World Wide Web sites. Regular mail delivery may take longer to receive. It does not have the one-to-one interaction of purposeful electronic mail between students. In communicating with Australia, it took three weeks to receive photos and videos through the U.S. Postal Service. By the time our students received the package, the Australian students were on their summer break while our students were still in school. Electronic mail would have been more meaningful and direct. The visual materials could have followed the online correspondence.

PLANNING FOR A SUCCESSFUL ELECTRONIC MAIL UNIT

The teacher(s) and the library media specialist should meet before the unit begins, contact the remote school(s), and develop the curriculum time table, questions, problems, and process for telecommunication. The Internet should be investigated for relevant sites of information with multimedia capabilities and for electronic mail addresses of the researchers, scientists, political and/or literary figures with whom students will telecommunicate. Online and CD-ROM databases and print resources should be identified. Teachers should become familiar with these resources before the curriculum unit begins. These resources can open up a new world of opportunity, investigation, and exploration for the teacher, enhancing and sometimes supplementing an outdated textbook environment. Library media specialists can work as curriculum coordinators and staff developers helping to train and introduce teachers to these technologies. Library media specialists should be an active part of the curriculum development process.

GEOGRAPHIC INFORMATION SYSTEMS (GIS)

An emerging technology that is relevant to the social studies is GIS. What is GIS? Geographic Information Systems is a tool that is used to explore social, economic, political, and environmental information through a geographical context. It is a way to pose practical questions and view information visually. The answers have relevance in a business decision-making context, for assessing educational facilities and programs, and for government, county, and/or town planning. Some examples include deciding where to purchase or build a home, a shopping center, or a mass transit system (see Figure 5.8). By arranging and displaying data about places on earth in a variety of ways—tables, maps, charts—GIS is a tool that uses the power of the computer to answer questions and visually relate the data to geographic locations and boundaries. It is a relational, geographic database tool that stimulates creative, critical, and visual thinking (see Figure 5.9).

Geographic Information Systems addresses another dimension of information. Before the development of desktop GIS, this type of information was extremely expensive and was utilized primarily by researchers and scientists. Geographic information can be used to understand, define, and explore spatial processes. GIS incorporates databases of information. Examples include census data, population of countries worldwide, ethnic diversity in the United States, and percent of change in the voting age by county at the time of the presidential elections. The data is broken down by sex, age group, race, and ethnicity.

GIS desktop software will allow the student to view the data visually in the context of, say, the map of the United States (see Figure 5.10). One can zoom in on a particular state and define specific parameters. For example, one can examine where the U.S. population over the age of fifty resides. This is the majority of the voting population. Data is viewed visually and spatially. The question needs to be first identified, and then the strategy for seeking the data needs to be developed. Desktop GIS means the software and data is no longer contained on huge mainframe computers only accessible by scientists and researchers, but is now available through CD-ROMs, which can be loaded on a desktop computer.

ESRI, the Environmental System Research Institute, is one company that is working closely with schools, libraries, and universities to introduce GIS technology into the curriculum. The ArcView series is an easy to use desktop Geographic Information System for storing, modifying, querying, analyzing, and displaying information about places as near as the local neighborhood or as remote as Australia or Antarctica. Human and physical geographic characteristics can be studied visually through information already prepared by GIS users in government agencies, universities, environmental and political organizations, and businesses of all types. It is a way for teachers and library media specialists to integrate real data when

Figure 5.8
Information about Your World

Information about Your World....

This map shows the types of features in the world around us that can be represented on a map. For example, the trees are grouped as vegetation, the telephone wires can be drawn as lines, and the buildings can be classified as either residential or commercial.

Graphic image reprinted courtesy of Environmental Systems Research Institute, Inc. (ESRI).

Figure 5.9
Points, Lines, and Areas

Represented by Points, Lines, and Areas...

This map shows the resulting map when the features shown in the map entitled "Information about Your World," are represented as map components: points, lines, and areas. For example, the telephone poles are points, the telephone wires are lines, and the grove of trees is an area.

Graphic image reprinted courtesy of Environmental Systems Research Institute, Inc. (ESRI).

Figure 5.10
Total Population of the United States, 1990

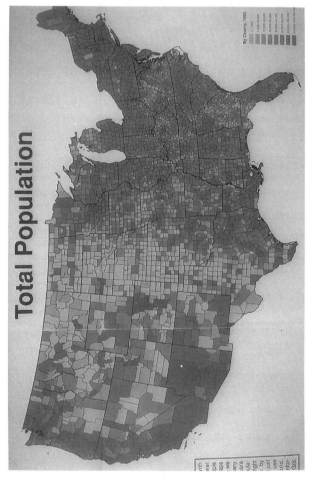

This map shows population by country for the United States based on 1990 U.S. Census figures created with ArcView® software and ArcUSA™ data set, desktop GIS software and data set from ESRI. This map provides a slightly different perspective than the population density map because it doesn't go down to the square mile scale.

Graphic image reprinted courtesy of Environmental Systems Research Institute, Inc. (ESRI).

studying problems posed by the curriculum in ways that real-world scientists, real estate agents, government employees, and business people are using it.

A library reference workstation can become a focal point for visual and geographical investigation and application of data to solve real problems. The GIS tools allow students and faculty to zoom in and out of specific data relative to countries, states, cities, and other areas (see Figure 5.11). Roads, landmarks, political regions, social questions, and/or environmental problems can be studied in detail and linked to other factors to discover and explore relationships.

Teachers and librarians can also retrieve print or download K–12 lesson plans from the ESRI World Wide Web site (http://www.esri.com). One of the modules developed with the University of Kansas through the National Geographic Alliance focuses on the depletion of ground water from a specific aquifer. What are the effects of the depletion of ground water on the human population, cropland, and the beef cattle industry in the area? The databases include information on human population, irrigated cropland, soil types, available surface water sources, and the number of beef cattle, among other variables. The database information is integrated so that students can apply five geographic themes to analyze the problem (Nellis 1994). These spatial science questions can receive more insightful consideration, understanding analyses, and predictions through GIS. Library media specialists along with faculty can introduce students to "live" information instead of simplified or made-up data for exercises.

GIS is not an electronic atlas, but rather a thematic mapping system that enables the user to create graphic displays using information stored in a spreadsheet or database. The information is not isolated and linear. Each map is based on a theme, such as population or income. Colors, patterns, shading, and symbols of various sizes show the relative value of the information for that theme at each geographic location.

As a middle school library media specialist, I worked closely with the social studies teacher to develop a database of Third World countries in Africa, including life expectancy, infant mortality rate, education, per capita income, and population density. "What if" questions were developed regarding the chances of a child surviving, receiving an adequate education, and being able to go to the university? Students researched the particular country in other resources—electronic, online, and print.

The GIS system offers the student, library media specialist, and faculty member the ability to explore real information without inputting it from the almanac. The thematic mapping tool is constantly and interactively changing. It is not strictly an abstract intellectual exercise. The student is the driver, the thinker, the manipulator. This is the essence of inquiry learning.

Average, special education, and learning disabled students want to visually see, touch, and manipulate the data. They want to be active learners.

Figure 5.11
Population Density of the United States, 1990

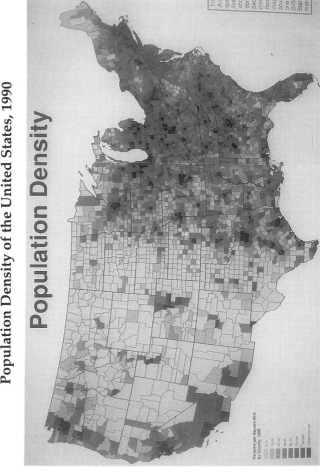

Population Density

Persons per Square Mile
by County, 1990

0–10
10–50
20–50
50–90
60–70
75–100
100–800
Greater than 800

This map displays persons per square mile by country for the United States as created with ArcView® software and ArcUSA™ Data Set, desktop GIS software and data set from ESRI. It is based on 1990 U.S. Census figures. This map specifically shows how dense the population is in each country. A quick glance at the map provides an overview of population density for the entire nation.

Graphic image reprinted courtesy of Environmental Systems Research Institute, Inc. (ESRI).

Listening to a lecture causes many of them to drift. Doing, thinking, and manipulating in color brings hard-to-understand graphs and tables to life within a context of where it is and what is happening.

Are there more divorces in California cities or in the suburbs in Massachusetts? Are there more teen pregnancies, more one parent families? Are per capita student education spending, classroom size, and standardized test results related? Are children from one parent families less likely to continue their education? Using GIS, one can zoom in on any area of the country and ask several layers of questions, with colors and charts representing the relevant data. The colors and the geographic locale make it easy to understand, relate, and draw conclusions.

Jack is a developer and wants to build a new housing tract of eight thousand homes. Are there endangered species? Where are they located? How steep are the hills? Where is the best soil located to prevent mud slides? Where are the earthquake faults and/or flood plains located? Where are the gas lines, sewer lines, aquifers? Using GIS, and looking at the data, Jack can view it geographically. The thematic map will show Jack where the water quality zone lies, where the bird habitat is, and where the steep and gentle slopes are. Through differences in color and the geographic contour of the land, the data is much more meaningful to Jack than viewing it in several difficult-to-read, static tables—each with different data presented.

Janet, a real estate agent, is working with a shopping center developer. Gary, the shopping center developer, would like to build a shopping center in a growing town. However, he does not know which part of the town would be most advantageous to his business enterprise. Janet uses a desktop GIS system in her office. She can query the geographic database to find out the per capita family income in each section of town, the number of children per family, the ages of the family members, the professions or vocations of the wage earners, and the number of competing shopping centers in each area. Gary can use the data to decide the type of stores that would thrive according to the ages and the earnings of the population. He would also consider the competition and decide on the area that would reduce duplication of retail stores.

Rain forest problems such as deforestation, population increases, and urban invasion can be looked at through data and images. Ground water contamination, incidence of cancers, and/or disease in crops, cattle, fish, or humans can be examined and questioned. Images are available that show a section of the earth over time, for example, the San Francisco Bay area, which has changed dramatically from the 1940s. Initially a sparsely populated agricultural area, it has become a center of urban growth and increasing population. By examining and interpreting remote sensing images, the colors identify indicators of change to the environment—including air quality, vegetation, and ground water depletion.

Students can research questions of pollution, population growth, and urbanization with desktop GIS. They can research the question or problem online, in print, and over the Internet. Any number of questions can be posed depending on the curriculum or course of study. The library media specialist and social studies, science, language arts, and computer teachers can form an interdisciplinary team to promote student investigations of ecological problems, their social and environmental significance, and then have students write about their hypotheses, investigations, research, and findings.

An examination of the data that is available and the curriculum can help staff decide on the problem or problems to be studied. Imagination, creativity, and preplanning by all parties involved in the curriculum is important. The planning may take three months before everyone is comfortable with the role they will have in the unit. During this period, they will have had time to develop exercises, activities, and investigate and become familiar with the GIS software, Internet sites, and online, CD-ROM, and print resources.

ARCVIEW—DESKTOP GIS

ArcView is a package that currently includes eight CD-ROM disks of geographic data containing information useful for teaching and research. The CD-ROMs include:

- ArcUSA—data about physical and human characteristics of the United States
- ArcWorld—data about physical and human characteristics of the planet
- Digital Chart of the World—global data on physical geography and human-made features
- ArcScene USA Tour—satellite images of key urban and remote areas in the United States
- ArcView Sample Data—updated country boundaries, North American data, five-digit zip code boundaries, and more

Are these skills necessary for K–12 students? Business, government, environmental agencies, and education are fields using GIS. There is a growing need for reeducation of employees who have been using paper maps and static databases to learn to use GIS. Data in all fields is being digitized for more accurate relational analysis. Visual, creative, and critical thinking skills with hands-on manipulation are the types of educational skills that will lead students to better jobs and higher education degrees. The world of the year 2000 and beyond will be more technical. It will not be a rote, machine-driven environment. It will be technical with an emphasis on the cognitive interface needed to manipulate data, think through access and retrieval strategies, using analysis, evaluation, application, and solution-oriented processes.

The study of geography becomes more exciting and visionary as it incorporates the spatial analysis techniques of modern-day technology within its courses. These techniques of analysis and thinking strategies are being utilized in business, government, and environmental agencies to solve problems. There is a need to change student learning into the year 2000 to accommodate work force needs and enhance geography education.

Users of technology must understand the basics of geographic education so they can discern and model geographic patterns and processes. A database of recent earthquake data viewed through a GIS desktop viewer can display on a world map the location and strength of the earthquakes. Moreover, the information is not one dimensional or static. By clicking on a state and changing the fields or parameters of the information requested, for example, all the earthquakes in the state of California above 4.0 in magnitude between 1996 and 1990 will appear. One can see a pattern of earthquake activity. By analyzing the data presented, students can investigate further in other library information resources causes, pressure build up, frequency, and magnitude of earthquakes. They can make predictions and forecasts based on the data. *What Work Requires of Schools* (United States Department of Labor 1991) addresses the need for competency in information processing, systems analysis, technology resources, and interpersonal skills.

LEARNING GIS

I sat in a classroom full of Macintosh 7100 computers. I was introduced to GIS and ways it could be incorporated into the curriculum. I looked at several demographics, including the number of divorces, per capita income, number of married persons, ages of the population, and births by age of mother. I could easily zoom in on a specific city in California and compare it to a specific town in Massachusetts. As I was performing the search strategies and analysis, I was surrounded by young minority women in their late teens, who were looking over my shoulder. They were intrigued and wanted to look up questions and concerns they had. The GIS data could help to answer their questions. They were at-risk minority learners, not the ones going to prominent four-year institutions. They were interested. Geography was not dull—it was happening around them—and the information on teen births, drug use, divorce rates, and education status in their area was of interest. Finding that information, using these tools, was intriguing, self-motivating, and insightful as well as fun.

Studies indicate that the integration of technology within the curriculum can increase learning. When computers are available in instruction, a University of Michigan study recorded that students gain the equivalent of three months of instruction (Elmer-Dewitt 1991). Perelmen (1990) stated that twenty years of research in computer-assisted learning found that it produces 30 percent more learning in 40 percent less time, with a 30 percent lower cost. Interactive multimedia methods of instruction raise retention 40 percent above discussion methods and 20 percent above a lecture using visual aids (Northup, Barth, and Kranze 1991).

REMOTE SENSING AND IMAGE PROCESSING

In addition to GIS, remote sensing and image processing present data collected to study world problems in a visual format. Most educators are not familiar with visual information and data collection systems. NASA is one of the national scientific organizations that uses earth observation imagery. NASA's laser disk collection of space shuttle photography includes 92,000 digitized photographs of earth recorded by shuttle astronauts since 1982 (Lulla 1993). The most traditional forms of remote sensing using satellite imagery are optical and near-infrared radiation, from about 0.4 (blue) to 2.0 (IR) micrometers. Examples include Landsat, Spot, and NOAA. These generally use a wide variety of tracking instruments.

Once the tracking instruments take the imagery through remote sensing, they are ready for basic processing. Imagery from these satellites may appear as photographs. Many times the color is manipulated to appear visually pleasing and to show interesting detail. Clouds are usually white and vegetation—where appropriate—is green. Near infrared (visual), thermal infrared (heat), and microwave (radar) are common types of imagery.

Imagery can also be three dimensional, as the World Wide Web reports: "We see the world in three dimensions by virtue of having two eyes, viewing the world at slightly different angles. It is possible to emulate this and produce 3-dimensional (stereo) satellite imagery, by superimposing images of the same ground area, viewed from different angles (and at different times). A limited number of satellites have this capability" (Satellite Imagery FAQ 1997).

In the spring of 1994, NASA initiated a series of shuttle-based multiseasonal earth observation missions to gather remote-sensing data on the earth's dynamic surface phenomena such as oceans, ecosystems, hydrology, geology, rain, and clouds. These flights also examined the state of the earth—volcanoes, earthquakes, flooding, burning, and dust storms, among others. These missions are called the Space Radar Laboratory (SRL). The laboratory includes Shuttle Imaging Radar (SIR-C/X-SAR) and the Mapping of Air Pollution from Space (MAPS) instruments. MAPS is designed to measure carbon monoxide levels from space.

Synthetic Aperture Radar (SAR) is an active microwave instrument that produces high resolution imagery of the earth's surface in all weather. Microwave radiation penetrates cloud and haze, so SAR views the earth's surface (land and sea) in all weather.

These tools have been put to important use. The remote-sensing images help fire fighters locate the fires through the dense smoke in order to extinguish them. Remote-sensing radar also penetrates the thick cloud cover. The rain forest, for example, is covered by cloud cover 95 percent of the time. Radar makes it possible to chart the rain forest through the cloud cover. It also makes it possible to take images at night. For general purpose remote sensing, this is probably the major advantage of SAR.

Radar is sensitive to texture so it is good for vegetation studies, for the study of ocean waves, winds, currents, and to record seismic activity and moisture content. Some of the questions the shuttles will try to answer include:

- Oceans—How waves move through the oceans and how the air and sea interact with each other to play a major role in determining the earth's climate. The study of sea ice will also be important.

- Ecosystems—Ecology data will be collected over tropical forests including the Amazon basin in South America, and over temperate forests in North Carolina, Michigan, and Central Europe. Images will be used to study:
  - land use
  - vegetation type and extent
  - effects of fires, flooding, and clear cutting

By studying changes in forests between missions, scientists can assess the effects that changing environmental conditions and land use have on forests and, in turn, on the global carbon cycle.

NASA's Mission to Planet Earth is making lesson plans, using the data, CD-ROMs, photographs, videos, and articles readily available on the World Wide Web. Its http address on the World Wide Web is www.hq. nasa.gov/office/mtpe. For specific information on the remote-sensing and image-processing missions the http address is southport.jpl.nasa.gov. This is an invaluable site. A CD-ROM is also available that contains two successful SIR-C/X-SAR Missions on the Space Shuttle Endeavor. Pictures, video, and lesson plans utilize the mission results to teach students about the changing earth. One can also view most of the contents of the first CD-ROM in the series on the Internet.

Real problems, real data, and the solutions are controversial. The social studies teacher can work with the science teacher to explain how imaging is used (lesson plans are included) and to examine and explain the data that have been collected. Image processing opens the door to scientific inquiry.

The social studies teacher and the library media specialist can work together to illustrate the social, economic, and political factors involved in changing the environment in the areas under study. Students can search for their specific topic using online, electronic, print, and media resources to debate their positions. Inquiry learning is involved in each stage of the problem.

Library media specialists should be introduced to GIS, remote sensing, and image processing as should their social science and science faculty. LITA (Library and Information Technology) has held workshops on GIS. The use of spatial information technologies is another way of displaying information. As library information science professionals, we need to make available data in all formats to the faculty and students we serve.

The library media specialist may not have all the scientific and technical knowledge needed to teach remote sensing, GIS, or image processing. By linking the teachers to resources in these areas through the Internet, through the videodisks and CD-ROM disks, and/or by bringing in specialists for in-service and staff development, we can make the increasing data available and their potential known in curriculum design. Limitations to the use of remote-sensing information include teacher experience, the need to interpret rather than read the imagery, and the costs involved (Weller 1993).

The emphasis for successful curriculum design should be on the geographic, social, or scientific question's impetus for problem solving, not on the technology. The technology is only one means of gathering and retrieving the data to solve the problem. Downloading images from the Web or using CD-ROM or videodisks with images that complement the curriculum will involve preplanning. To fully implement spatial technologies in the social sciences and the sciences, one must:

- Develop exemplary curriculum materials that integrate spatial technologies.
- Develop a team, interdisciplinary approach to create a "wide angle" on the problems being investigated. The team might include science, library media, computer, and language arts faculty in addition to social science faculty.
- Create a group of mentor teachers, possibly within the district or from a nearby university or college, who specialize in the applications of the technology.
- Pursue grant-writing opportunities, and be open to ideas of developing consortia with other K–12 institutions, with colleges and universities, and with private industry.
- Discuss ethics and quality standards in the use of computer-based information (Nellis 1994).

Questions to be considered in preplanning sessions include:

- Do you have Internet access?
- Are your computers capable of handling image-processing data?
- Do they have multimedia capabilities and the correct amount of RAM required for GIS and image processing?

- Do you need to order the videodisks and CD-ROMs or can they be borrowed through interlibrary loan?
- What is the role of each discipline in the unit?
- What are the goals and the objectives?
- What is the question or the problem to be addressed?
- What are the daily lesson plans for each area?
- Where will the learning take place? When will the students be in the library media center? Are computers available? Are the electronic, online, and print research tools available? Will a schedule be needed for student access?
- Are an LCD panel, computer with a CD-ROM drive, and videodisk player available for classroom presentations?
- Is the Internet available for accessing relevant information?

The potential of incorporating educational technology in the social studies curriculum through teacher/library media specialist partnerships is enormous. I hope you will further investigate and pursue some of the ideas that were put forth in this chapter.

SOURCES OF MULTIMEDIA FOR SOCIAL STUDIES, INCLUDING WWW SITES

Videodisks

Instructional Resources Corporation
1819 Bay Ridge Avenue
Annapolis, MD 21403
(800) 922–1711
   The American History Videodisk
   The Western Civilization Videodisk
   The World History Videodisk

Optical Data Corporation
30 Technology Drive/Post Office
Box 4919
Warren, NJ 07060
(201) 668–0022
   Communism and the Cold War

Scholastic, Inc.
2931 E. McCarty Street
Jefferson City, MO 65101
(800) 541–5513
   An Overview of U.S. History
   Civil War and Reconstruction
   Point of View and Community History Kit
   History in Motion: Milestones of the Twentieth Century

Struggles for Justice
Vol. 2: Women, Labor, Immigrants

Voyager Company
1351 Pacific Coast Highway
Santa Monica, CA 90401
(800) 446–2001
    Louvre Volume 1: Painting and Drawing
    Louvre Volume 2: Sculpture and Object d'art
    Louvre Volume 3: Antiquities
    Michelangelo: Self-Portrait
    Musee d'Orsay, Paris
    Regard for the Planet
    The First Emperor of China
    The National Gallery of Art
    The Power of Myth
    Van Gogh Revisited
    Vienna: The Spirit of a City

Science, Educational Technology, and the Library Media Specialist

6

The study of science provides an exceptional opportunity for the library media specialist to work closely with the science teacher in developing inquiry-based learning models. The issue-oriented approach, based on knowledge and analysis, can involve inquiry, hypothesis building, hands-on activities, and observation. Technology can assist the scientist, the student, and the library media specialist in achieving their goals in a timely, efficient, and precise manner.

According to the science report card issued by the National Assessment of Educational Progress (NAEP) in 1992, over 85 percent of participating fourth-grade students understood simple scientific principles; however, only 31 percent—or less than one-third—could apply, analyze, or integrate scientific information. By eighth grade there was little change in the students' ability to analyze or integrate information even though 64 percent could apply the information. In higher education, 85 percent of physics majors at large universities were unable to relate what they knew to real-world situations according to Champagne and Klopfer (cited in Yager, McLure, and Weld 1993).

SCIENTIFIC LITERACY

Carl Sagan rightly stated, "It is an essential aspect of the national health and well being to have a range of the population that understands science and can make informed decisions" (Brockman 1993). A definition of scientific literacy proposed by Jon Miller in a paper printed at a 1987 international conference, "Communicating Science to the Public," includes

- content knowledge
- an understanding of underlying principles and processes
- a societal impact public policy component

If this definition is accepted, it is the responsibility of our science education programs to develop scientifically literate individuals who understand the interrelationships between science, technology, and society in our everyday lives and on our environment. As responsible citizens in a democracy this literacy is crucial, especially, at a time when the resources of the earth are being harvested and polluted worldwide. Science and technology are moving rapidly in all areas including biotechnology. Science and technology are challenging ethics, morality, and the quality of life. Former New Jersey Governor James Florio stated, "Our technologically complex society demands increased understanding of mathematics, science and technology. Mathematics, science and technology play a crucial role in solving environmental problems to preserve the health and welfare of our planet" (Gluck 1993, 55).

On a recent visit to the Mojave Desert in California, many questions came to mind as I observed the increasing population growth, changing vegetation, and man-made lakes. The Mojave Desert is the smallest of the North American deserts and is situated in southeastern California, southern Nevada, a small area of northwestern Arizona, and a tiny corner of southwestern Utah. Subtropical, the Mojave is one of the hottest deserts in North America. It forms a transition zone below the Great Basin Desert to the north and the Sonora Desert to the south. Arritt (1993) defined desert as the following: "A desert is a land so wanting in water that its very essence is its aridity. Dryness is the most powerful determinant of whether or not a region of the earth is truly a desert."

Victorville is approximately one hour south of Los Angeles and is a thriving metropolis in the Mojave Desert with shopping centers, neon signs, and tract housing. When I came to California during one of its prolonged droughts, when water was scarce, questions began to emerge. What is the importance of the desert to the environment? Can man build lakes and plant sod and plants that need water to survive and not affect the balance of ecology in the rest of the state or the world? What will happen during the next drought when water is scarce and is siphoned from northern California and Colorado to help southern California?

The population of Victorville has grown to 70,000 in five years and continues to grow as residents of Los Angeles escape the city's crime and expensive housing dilemma. Are scientists and geologists involved in the state planning? Are ecological and environmental issues being discussed before public policy and city planning is allowed to go forward?

Arritt (1993) provided more insight into deserts: "In actuality, deserts are solidly linked here on earth—not necessarily by adjacent geographical borders, but by their physical inclusion in one of six arid bands that encircle the globe. The desert bands that girdle the globe run parallel to the Equator in each of the hemispheres." She added:

Deserts are integral components of earth's massive ecosystem or biosphere which comprises all the physical environments in this planet and organisms that live within them. . . . Nothing occurs within this huge system without its affecting something else along the way. . . . One tropical meteorologist likens storms over the Amazon to huge vacuum cleaners which in one year may suck up 12 million tons of atmospheric dust blown in from the Sahara and deposit nearly a pound of phosphate on every acre of the rain forest in the northeastern and central black-water regions of the Amazon basin. (Arritt 1993)

The earth's ecosystem is complex. Indestructible it is not. The more we discover about it, in fact, the more fragile it proves to be. In a study of deserts, the science teacher can link with scientists and library media specialists to investigate ecological interrelationships, human intrusion, and natural changes that alter the earth's surface. Analysis, problem solving, and scientific investigation should result in action-oriented debate, solutions, and more questions.

Utilizing a real-life problem approach when studying science mirrors some of the same questions and investigations that NASA is asking and researching in its Mission to Planet Earth (see Figure 6.1). Through the Internet World Wide Web, students and faculty can participate in the search for answers, solutions, and the discovery of new problems. NASA's mission is being shared with students, faculty, library media specialists, business, and the national and international community through NASA's Internet World Wide WEB site, http://www.hq.nasa.gov/office/mtpe.

One of the supersites for multiseason radar imagery in NASA's Mission to Planet Earth is the Sahara. Radar imagery is being used because it can penetrate the sand and view what is beneath it. According to NASA, the Sahara is riddled with river channels that dried up long ago. The SIR-C/X-SAR radar penetrates the sand and is able to detect the river channels beneath the Sahara. There is a strong possibility that civilization existed along these river channels, but due to change in the global climate the rivers dried up. Having located the river channels, archaeologists and anthropologists should be able to uncover clues of possible human life in the Sahara. Ground water and mineral resources can also be located and thus benefit the people struggling to survive in this harsh environment. This is the essence of science, technology, and society.

The American Association for the Advancement of Science's (AAAS) Project 2061 states that one of its goals is to foster an educational system that "engages students, intellectually and emotionally with the great scientific and technological adventure that dominates our culture and our

Figure 6.1

Mission to Planet Earth—from the Internet

Seeing Through Desert Sands

This image is a composite of a radar image into a visib light image. It shows the sands of the Sahara Desert. The orange parts of the image shows the sands as seen from a visible light camera. The strip through the middle shows the same area as seen through the eyes of radar. Very little detail is shown in the visible light image, whereas the radar image can see through the dese sand to the layers underneath to reveal ancient drainage patterns.

age so they can follow the world of science with interest, feel a part of it, and relate its discoveries to their own lives" (American Association for the Advancement of Science 1992).

"The capacity to take knowledge learned in one setting and apply it appropriately in a different setting is the most basic definition of understanding" (Gardner, cited in Brandt 1993). The interplay of science and technology and their interfaces with society are among the current goals and discussion in science education. Scientific/technological literacy will help the individual understand and act on science-related societal issues for the improvement of life and advancement of society (Lisowski 1993).

Throughout the 1980s, specific recommendations have been directed at grades nine to twelve in regard to science/technology and society (STS) by the National Science Foundation. These include:

- third-year elective courses to be offered in grades 11–12
- a two-year required STS sequence of courses in grades 9–10
- a science curriculum in grades 9–11 that is structured around the interaction of science and technology

Currently, science textbooks only minimally integrate these concepts. Library media specialists working together with science teachers can research these topics much more fully on the Internet and through print, CD-ROM, and online resources. If the students are to participate in the research, the teacher can introduce topics for investigation that complement the curriculum. The library media specialist can assist the teachers in researching these topics by demonstrating the thinking and search strategy processes. By introducing students to the Internet and electronic resources for research as well as print and video materials, the library media specialist will assure that students get current information on up-to-date problems. Through analysis, evaluation, and application, students may begin to develop solutions or recommendations to real-life problems.

The teacher and the library media specialist will not know all there is to know on the topics of study. Both need to be comfortable with that. The reward is to watch the students discover, uncover, hypothesize, reflect, and conclude. The Internet—through discussion groups, special chat forums, and electronic mail—provides a medium for library media specialists and science teachers to link with research scientists to explore these topics more fully.

The use of provocative questions or imagination-provoking allusion has worked well at the junior high school and high school levels. An activity approach integrating hands-on investigations, research, telecommunication, and curriculum models motivates students to investigate medicine, population growth and health, human engineering, environmental quality, utilization of natural resources, national defense and space, sociology of science, and the effects of the technological development.

The direction in science education is to move away from the rote memorization of a collection of facts. A hands-on approach emphasizes the path of exploration rather than the destination. Teachers need training and classrooms need to be wired to access this information. "The best experiment is not the one that gives you the results that you anticipated but the one that teaches you something and lights the way to the next experiment" (Finneran 1995).

New technologies increase the need for the application of science, math knowledge, and technology skills in the twenty-first-century workplace. Low-achieving and average students shy away from these courses, which they believe require technical skills and mastering of difficult concepts. Due to a lack of confidence and a failure to perceive relevance, females are greatly underrepresented in math, science, and technology (Fear-Fenn and Kapostasy 1992). A major need is to integrate science and technology in academic subjects and vocational classes because applied academic knowledge can be used to solve problems encountered in business and technical fields. Science provides the foundations for creative thinking and cognitive development that, in turn, develops the depth of understanding to allow for generalization and transfer across real-world tools (Pritz 1989).

EXEMPLARY PROGRAMS

Lankard (1993) described a recent effort to involve more students in science/technology:

The National Science Foundation (NSF) recently funded several experimental integration projects. One involved the collaborative efforts of the Illinois Board of Education, Northern Illinois University Department of Technology, five industrial partners, and five northern Illinois schools. The goal of the project was to attract average high school students who typically avoid physics by providing an integrated math, physics, and technology curriculum offered in a nontraditional learning environment through team teaching and innovative delivery models.

To initiate the project, teams of math, physics and technology teachers at each high school analyzed the existing course content for common concepts and skills, which were used to develop the integrated curriculum. Because good content and courses already existed, it was not necessary to create an entirely new curriculum for a given course. Integrated instructional delivery was essential to the project's success, and integrated teaching was made possible by nontraditional scheduling. The PHYS-MA-TECH curriculum consists of 45 instructional activities. The real-world context for the science and math content is apparent in some of the topics: laser burglar alarm, exercise machines, ultrasound, smoke alarm, programmable home thermostat, and barcoding.

The library media specialist can work with these teachers to find Internet sites and investigate current practice through online and CD-ROM databases.

INTEGRATION STRATEGIES

A collaboration between the Battelle Pacific Northwest Laboratories, Central Washington University, Northwest Regional Lab, and Rickland (Washington School District) resulted in the development of an interdisciplinary curriculum to promote math and science classes to students of varied learning styles and abilities (Materials Technology 1990):

- Academic and vocational teachers deliver this course together as students learn both theory and practice simultaneously. Their recommendations include:
  - Use the tools of the trade.
  - Community experts are highly desirable. A business and industry advisory group was developed.
  - Cooperative learning strategies for teachers in different disciplines need to be developed in order for them to work together.
    - Daugherty and Wichlein's study (1993) found that science and math teachers did not understand the scope and purpose of technology education and how to integrate the two.
- Staff had the opportunity to work with materials in industry or laboratory settings before they began teaching the courses.

Integrative efforts require open communication behavior between science/math and nonscience teachers. The faculty needs to practice interprofessional collaboration and interaction to address the needs of special needs learners. These students have varied learning styles and characteristics. In this project the strategies to teach difficult science concepts need to be more action oriented. Equipment and multimedia and research resources were also available. The lab facilities were shared by several disciplines.

The outcomes of the project were extremely positive. Each discipline involved became stronger on its own merit. There was an increase in mutual respect among teachers of various disciplines. The teachers improved their teaching skills and expanded their repertoire, strategies, and knowledge of technologies. Enthusiasm and motivation for teaching increased. The students benefited through a combination of academic disciplines and vocation- or practical-applied knowledge in science, math, and technology. Library media specialists should be part of these teams.

The Center for Occupational Research and Development (CORD) is a leader in integrated curriculum development. CORD's experience is in developing principles of technology—applied physics, applied math, applied biology and chemistry. CORD utilizes a systems approach to learning. Instead of teaching a series of discrete topics, the curriculum integrates math with problem solving, biology, and chemistry in the context of personal, work-related, and societal issues (Hull 1990). This type of learning has worked very well with the average and special needs population. By illustrating relevance with the workplace and the legitimate need for acquiring and succeeding with problem-solving strategies, students are motivated to learn science and math.

Ground water pollution, toxic waste, and chemical waste from factories are some of the nationwide issues that confront us. The Science Education for Public Understanding Program (SEPUP), created at the University of California at Berkeley, developed a middle school curriculum in science that addresses the issues of relating science and technology to society. Located at the Lawrence Hall of Science, "SEPUP develops instructional materials that highlight the scientific concepts and processes associated with current societal issues, as well as activity-based instructional strategies and materials for secondary school use. The materials are in modular form and highlight chemical and other science concepts and processes associated with current societal issues" (www.lhs.berkeley.edu WWW page).

One study of students who used these materials showed that they were more likely to elect science classes than their non-SEPUP peers. The SEPUP students' perceptions also illustrated that what they learned in science class is useful to everyday life. Students came to the conclusion that knowledge of science will be necessary in their adult lives (Ognes and Koker 1995).

SEPUP has a World Wide Web site that includes information on its programs, workshops, and publications, http://www.lhs.berkeley.edu. The SEPUP activities are in modules and are designed to be conducted in sequence. The modules utilize an inquiry-based problem-solving approach, allowing students to collect and process scientific evidence and use it to make decisions. Focus is on important issues in today's society such as toxic waste, paper versus plastic, recycling, waste management, and the presence of chemicals in the home.

With the involvement of the library media specialist, students can research the area of ground water pollution or toxic waste, for example, write about it in language arts class and discuss its political implication in social studies class.

TRACKING

Tracking and the discouraging of students who are not above average from taking courses in math and science are contributing to a growing gap in the skills and level of the technological work force in the United States. In the summer of 1996, a newscast announced that California had the

largest division between its rich and its poor. The news program emphasized that it was not that the rich are growing richer but that the poor are
growing more poor. Without the skills, understanding, and motivation
needed to work and live in a technological society, average and special
needs students find it difficult to work and advance, thereby creating a
greater problem for society.

Results of the International Assessment of Educational Progress (Science), as reported in *USA Today* ("Riskline" 1993), show that U.S. students
are near the bottom of the list of participating countries:

Korea	78%
Taiwan	76%
Switzerland	74%
Hungary	73%
Soviet Union	71%
Slovenia	70%
Italy	70%
Israel	70%
Canada	69%
France	69%
Scotland	68%
Spain	68%
United States	**67%**
Ireland	63%
Jordan	57%

As of 1994 the national assessments of science have shown a ten-point
improvement since the Nation at Risk report was released in 1983. But, even
when scores have improved, there is almost always a flip side. The NAEP
science scores in 1994 were better than in 1982, but still worse than in 1972.
"There has been a steady decline in science achievement scores of the United
States' 17 year olds as measured by national assessments of science in 1969,
1973, and 1977" (National Commission on Excellence in Education 1983). Integrating science, math, and technology with vocational education is one
way that has had success in motivating the at-risk and average students.

INQUIRY SCIENCE

Student investigation is the backbone of the inquiry curriculum. Inquiry
learning is the active search for knowledge or understanding to satisfy a curiosity (Osborne and Freyberg 1985). Inquiry learning is a process that focus
the science content on developing scientific thinking skills and conceptual
understanding. Problem solving and decision making are the foundation of

the science, technology, and society curriculum that is aimed at creating citizens who understand science. Students are able to participate intelligently, develop critical-thinking, problem-solving, and decision-making skills, and understand how science and technology are used to change society.

Problems for students to work on can be multidisciplinary in nature. This learning is excellent for the underserved and the underrepresented population. These students can acquire scientific ways of thinking, talking, and writing through inquiry-oriented teaching. Journal writing can help students reflect on articles, videos, and information they have researched in several formats. A conceptual change occurs in the students. The scientific concepts and ways of thinking become part of the students' personal frameworks. Scientific knowledge is meaningful. Students become familiar with ways of describing, predicting, and concluding.

PROJECT 2061

Project 2061 is science for all Americans, not just the college-prep, high-scoring computer whiz kids. It reaches out to females, minorities, the disabled, and the average. Its goal is to have a scientifically literate population by the year 2061. The goals for the American Association for the Advancement of Science (AAAS) project are as follows:

- to become familiar with the natural world and recognize its diversity and unity
- to understand key concepts and principles in science
- to be aware of some of the important ways that science, math, and technology depend on one another
- to know that science, math, and technology are human enterprises and understand what that implies in regard to their strengths and limitations
- to develop the scientific way of thinking in students
- to use scientific knowledge and ways of thinking for individual and social purposes (Blosser 1990)

There are five criteria that assist faculty in assessing the curriculum to achieve the goal of scientific literacy. They include:

- utility—in terms of long-term employment and personal decision making
- social responsibility—the ability to make intelligent decisions on matters of a social and political nature that involve science and technology
- intrinsic value of knowledge—the understanding that information is critical and pervasive in our culture—an educated person needs to be information literate
- philosophical value—an aid to examine and investigate the larger questions of human meaning
- childhood enrichment—not only for later life but also to enrich the student's childhood (Blosser 1990)

Harty (1993) stated:

The most serious problems that face humanity today involve scientific problem-solving; acid rain, population growth, endangered species, resource depletion, drought and deforestation, contagious diseases, and addictions. Progress against these threats is handicapped without science and technology; yet the wisdom with which humans use that science and technology depends on the quality of their education. Without fostering the respect for nature and the interdependence of living things, human society endangers its own life-support systems.

Yager et al. (1995) described the failure of science education:

Studies of undergraduate physics and engineering majors revealed that most could only repeat the concepts and explanations advanced by scientists and perform only certain skills practiced in the laboratory. For 85–90% of the most capable students entering colleges as science and engineering majors, surprisingly little real learning occurred (if learning is defined as doing something with concepts and skills practiced in real-world situations). What is typically learned had little transfer to real world settings.

Real learning connotes use. Authentic learning comes from trial and error. Little, however, is known about how a learner moves from imitation to intrinsic ownership and from external modeling to internalization and competence (Reinsmith 1993).

Inquiry learning fosters interactive science learning through collaboration and communication about an event. The collecting, analyzing, and sharing of scientific data through extensive use of telecommunications are recommended. It is not enough to collect and analyze data; it is important to apply the knowledge to help solve problems. This is the essence of information literacy. Science should use hands-on laboratory investigations, sharing samples and data via telecommunications. A textbook can be too vague for understanding the underlying problems. Scientists use research through library media and electronic resources to fully understand a problem before developing a hypothesis for experimentation. The library media specialist can be invaluable to the science teacher in implementing the national science goals of the American Association for the Advancement of Science. The issues studied should be those that are problems in the real world. There should be diversity in the materials and the methods used.

Curriculum connections are encouraged among all disciplines, stimulating holistic thinking and reflecting on the ecology of living things. The library media specialist can be pivotal in fostering, developing, and initiating the curriculum connections. Rather than the linear thinking and tunnel vision represented by the traditional boundaries between subjects and perpetuated by textbook learning, this type of learning fosters creativity, investigation, and real-world involvement.

Weiss (1987) found that a sizable proportion of science teachers had not taken a course for college credit in their subject in the last ten years. In grades four to twelve, 90 percent of the students receive their knowledge from textbooks. Two publishers, Merrill and Holt, Rinehart and Winston, supply more than half of the textbooks. A sizable number of science teachers are using textbooks that are six years old. Many science educators have criticized textbooks for being too encyclopedic, perpetuating misconception, and not reflecting the latest pedagogy in how children learn.

Not having the most up-to-date information in a fast-changing dynamic area is a problem. Periodicals, online and CD-ROM databases, and Internet resources can provide the current thinking on various problems. Be sensitive to gender issues and incorporate hands-on science, research, and multimedia when explaining concepts.

TEACHING PROBLEM SOLVING

Problem solving assumes that students will become involved with the thinking operations of analysis, synthesis, and evaluation. These are higher-order thinking skills. Information-processing theory involves two processes that are inherently critical to the scientist and should be to the science student. The first is retrieval from memory of pertinent information. The second is the proper application of the information to the problem.

In genetics and biology, for example, reasoning can travel in two directions. One can reason and study a problem from the causes of the problem to the effects of the problem. In science one is also very much concerned with reasoning from the effects of the problem to find the cause of the problem. This intellectual activity is fundamental to AIDS research or in genetic engineering. Teachers, many times, are not trained in this type of thinking. Library media specialists are because of the nature of information literacy and their professional expertise.

Science teachers need to involve more proportional reasoning and logical deductive thinking in the problems they provide for their students. Lessons need to incorporate teaching and learning strategies to reduce students' math anxiety. Visual approaches for high-anxious students who are also deficient in proportional reasoning ability can be very successful (Gabel and Sherwood 1983).

MIDDLE SCHOOLS

The director of the United States Education Office of Educational Technology believes that middle schools are uniquely positioned for interdisciplinary instruction, hands-on activities, and team teaching. Schools hampered by an unclear vision find it difficult to develop a comprehensive technology plan and move ahead. Many middle schools cite funding, fear of new technology, and higher priorities as key reasons for not implementing more technology while still acknowledging its importance (Mancini 1995).

One example of an innovative science project that follows the guidelines of Project 2061 took place at Lake Gibson Middle School on Florida's west coast. There is a swamp behind the middle school, and students have taken soil samples and observed plant and animal life, including an occasional alligator. After heavy rains, the swamp land was in prime condition for research. Students took photographs of the area that they scanned into Hypercard to create presentations of specific environmental topics. They searched for environmental topics on the Internet. The library media specialist could work closely with the science teacher to ensure that students used all resources to discover information on their topics and the immediate environment that surrounded them. Tom Snyder's videodisk, the *Great Ocean Rescue*, was viewed to learn about marine life and ecology. Technology was a means within the curriculum to stimulate open-ended inquiry.

Dave Richard, the seventh-grade science teacher, stated, "We give students enough to understand a problem or question but never give them the answer." Grant money was raised by Dave to support projects like the swamp study and buy the computer equipment necessary to assist with the research. Technology followed the curriculum vision. Risk was necessary to step out and undertake something previously untried.

In Baltimore's Harbor District, students use an integrative approach to research science topics. A variety of interdisciplinary topics prepare them for technology in the working world. Most of the students are at risk and are from low-income homes where a computer is rare. Providing the technology at school and integrating it within a multidisciplinary approach has reduced suspensions from fifty to ten. The average attendance, according to Principal Craig Spellman, is up from 70 percent to 88 percent. Writing skills are among the best in the state, with an increase of twelve percentage points (Mancini 1995). Science CD-ROMs such as ADAM provide students with lifelike illustrations—for example, one of the circulation system—that a book cannot bring to life.

Ann Arbor High School worked closely with the University of Michigan to develop a program known as FOS (Foundations of Science Curriculum). It includes an interdisciplinary curriculum in biology, earth science, and chemistry. The program integrates these three sciences into a three-year, project-based program of study. The students discuss, evaluate, and write. Technology allows students to get answers for themselves rather than from teachers and provides the means for project-based science to be successful.

The purpose of the Water Contamination project is for the students to develop a genuine understanding of science and its relevance to their lives. They are being trained in the methodologies of the twenty-first–century work force. The project received a $1.5 million National Science Foundation grant. Teachers involved in the grant were given one hour of prep time each day to consult with each other while developing the class. The group believed that lecture/textbook-based science curriculum fails to encourage students to think for themselves. It does not foster the ability to communicate ideas through writing and speaking and has little relevance in the students' lives.

The FOS program used inquiry and experience to foster an environment where students could talk to each other, write, explore, evaluate, make decisions, and, in a phrase, "act like scientists." In the Water Contamination project small groups of students collected biological organism data from a stream. Chemical tests were conducted on the water samples. Physical assessments of soil, vegetation, and topology near the stream were made through the use of microcomputer-based laboratory probes and hand-held Newton computers.

Soloway (1996) described the importance of technology:

In our opinion, technology is the key to moving science teaching out of the 19th century—but not just because it's a late 20th-century invention. Technology allows students to seek out answers themselves instead of running to the teacher each time they don't understand something—or worse, passively sitting by as the teacher tells them everything they need to know. (Pryor and Soloway 1996).

Educational software tools were designed to support students in all aspects of the project planning, data gathering, analysis, visualizing, and modeling data sets. Creating multimedia presentations and publishing research on the World Wide Web was part of the project. ScienceWare is the name for the suite of scientific technological tools that were developed to enable the inquiry-based projects:

The ScienceWare suite currently includes: PlantOut, a collaborative project-planning and organizational tool; NIMBLE, a data collection tool that allows water-quality data to be collected directly from water to computer via Newtons and various probes; RiverBank, a database for water quality monitoring; VizIt, a data-visualization tool; the Classifier, a tool for building classification trees; Model-It, a tool for creating models and simulations of dynamic systems; RiverMUD, a virtual community centered on scientific modeling; Media Genie, a tool to assist in incorporating sound, pictures, movies, and hypertext links into a HyperCard stack; and Web-It, a tool that translates ClarisWorks documents directly into HTML for publication on the World Wide Web. (Pryor and Soloway 1996).

For more information on the project and the tools that were developed, electronic mail can be directed to AZP@umich.edu or soloway@umich.edu.

The Huron River Watershed Council, a part of the Michigan Department of Natural Resources, contacted students to test and assess the water quality of Traver Creek. In another community project, after assessing the quality of the drainage pond near the school, the students recommended planting a variety of plants that would relieve the area of its unpleasant odor.

Students standardized test scores rose—particulary in the essay portions, where they illustrated the deeper and more sophisticated knowledge gained in interpreting data and reaching conclusions. In these areas the students' knowledge was higher than students in biology classes.

MULTIMEDIA, INSTRUCTION, AND OUR EXPECTATIONS

Multimedia is a means to explain, visually depict, stimulate self-investigations, and create presentations of knowledge to share. It will pay for itself in more ways than just the financial one. It should be closely integrated into the curriculum and directly related to the goals and objectives of the curriculum. The second phase of a cognitive study of multimedia and its effects on sixth graders' learning relationship using text, animation, and captions indicated that there was greater recall, inference, and comprehension when the three forms of information were combined.

Personal exploration of the technology will assist students in becoming comfortable with the technology after training. After introducing the Internet, I often will have exercises that I think the students will find useful. After the students' first introduction, and hands-on experiences, I am amazed at how stimulated they are to explore the World Wide Web. Within a two-hour period, they will have tried the Universal Resource Locators with addresses I have provided or they will search for specific key words. Whether using various search engines, video- and audiotapes, chat groups, or electronic mail, or trying to find worldwide electronic mail addresses of friends or relatives, the students enjoy the freedom to navigate, think, and build bridges between the navigational interface, the content, and their mind.

This exploration allows the students to make the connections of how the Web works, how to access it from the training they have received, and how it can be useful and relevant to them. By stimulating their creative forces, they will develop a foundation of what the Web is and how it works. This experience was found to be very important to international students from Brazil and Japan. Both groups had distinctly different learning styles. They both shared the need for hands-on navigation and the time on task to explore for themselves, making connections and discovering relevance. For both groups an entire lecture on the Web would have been deadly.

There is a demand for multimedia, not only in the fine arts but also in the sciences. There are a large number of auditory and visual videodisks and CD-ROM products available. Multimedia products can help students practice decision-making skills in the health sciences. If instruction is too hazardous, difficult, or costly, simulation can provide experiences in such areas as chemistry.

Multimedia can assist in motivating students to learn more about a subject and see how the subject is related to other phenomena in the world.

CHEMISTRY SIMULATION

In chemistry, for example, if it is too hazardous or costly, or if the equipment is outdated to perform specific experiments, chemistry multimedia programs can assist. They allow students to collect and analyze data. If inadequate observations are made and consequently invalid conclusions are drawn, the program notifies the students. Students explore chemistry in different ways while learning the subject matter. In order to be effective the multimedia programs need to be thoughtfully and thoroughly integrated into the course content. The student can:

- learn about chemical reactions by applying the theoretical explanations
- control the experiment through the multimedia program by decision-making and problem-solving techniques practiced in the real world
- balance the equation
- view a simulation of the process at the molecular level
- test his/her understanding by responding to queries

Simulations are not a substitute for hands-on laboratory experiments. Many of the top research labs are concerned with the lack of real hands-on experimentation and analysis occurring in the public schools and four-year institutions.

In order for multimedia to work it must be an integral part of the course. Chromosome development is wonderfully illustrated on a video taken through a microscope on a biology laser disk. Tornadoes and their forces are better understood by viewing a video of the tornado through an earth science laser disk and seeing the destruction it can cause within a short time period. Visuals in science either at the library media center or in the classroom can open up portals in the mind for understanding previously difficult concepts. This is extremely important for at-risk student learning. There are wonderful resources for the study of science.

There is a positive quality learned. The student values the content learned because he or she is actively involved in processing the material. There is also efficiency of instruction. By seeing, hearing, and doing the senses assist in understanding and multiple intelligences are called into play.

MULTIMEDIA TOOLS

Multimedia Index

Multimedia tools come in a variety of forms. Multimedia tools for instruction include the multimedia index, hypertext, and simulations. The multimedia index provides a linear presentation of movies, film clips, and audio clips. One can type in the bar code or type the index number of the clip wanted into a remote control unit.

Hypermedia Programs

Hypermedia is utilized by videodisks, CD-ROMs, the Internet, and on-line networks to allow video images, photographs, audio, graphics, and text to be keyed to the appropriate text or to other images and used at the students' option. Simulated reality allows student observers to interact with a video sequence, or animation, conduct an experiment, initiate a decision tree or communicate within the simulation to effect or simply observe the course of events. A tutorial allows the student to be one-on-one with the instructor via the program. In order to move ahead one must exhibit learning.

Both hypertext and the index formats allow greater flexibility on the part of the user. Hypermedia stimulates a higher quality learning experience through relationships and connections. The logical order of the connections can be learned, but its flexibility and critical and creative potential lie in the students' ability to design and follow their own connections. Students can discover a set body of knowledge. However, if their content base is limited, they may need more structure. A teacher, student, or the library media specialist can develop a multimedia file that will automatically display and sequence the images, graphics, text, and videos.

Simulation imitates reality. The structure of the simulation can have a profound effect on student learning. Studies on teaching content and experiments found that in open-ended simulations students did not learn good approaches to conducting scientific experiments (Jones and Smith 1992). A good simulation will keep track of the lessons each student has completed. Learning is more efficient and more potent when it is guided by the instructor.

In order to understand the differences in the types of multimedia formats available, faculty need to be trained and have hands-on experiences to examine the multimedia materials against the framework of their curriculum. They also need to understand the logic, flexibility, and thought processes stimulated by the program. They need to analyze and evaluate them in the context of their curriculum. Then faculty can decide if they will make learning more efficient by developing a deeper understanding of the content.

A multimedia cart for classroom and library media presentations can include a microcomputer with the following:

- a minimum of 32 megabytes of RAM
- quick time
- video card and sound card or programs
- digital audio
- stereo sound
- CD-ROM

- videodisk player
- LCD Panel
- multimedia software

MATHEMATICS-SCIENCE PARTNERSHIP PROJECT

California State University at Bakersfield and Kern High School District in Bakersfield worked together to develop a partnership in mathematics and science entitled the Mathematics and Science Partnership Project (MSPP). Similar projects were conducted in New England using library media specialists as consultants. They received funding through the United States Department of Education and the IBM EduQuest Program. Thirteen high school teachers were involved with IBM state-of-the-art computer networks, hardware, and multimedia software. The teachers underwent intensive in-service for staff development to teach them how to use the technology in the classroom.

Linkway, which is the IBM version of Macintosh's Hypercard, was used as a multimodality software-authoring system to integrate graphics and text and to drive the interactive videodisk. The Personal Science Laboratory introduced highly accurate probes that measure temperature, movement, light intensity, sound, and pH. The Mathematics Exploration Toolkit was used in a variety of tasks that included simple computations as well as graphing complex calculus problems. Microsoft Works was used for its word-processing, database, and spreadsheet capabilities. Multimedia workstations included large color monitors, multimedia computers, and videodisk players.

The learning environment was expanded from the science textbook to include laboratory electronic probes, multimedia and computer applications programs, and library research. For example, one of the projects included the periodic table of elements. Chemistry classes studied the periodic table through group research and investigation. Chemistry students developed computer folders about each element. Groups of students working together had to research several elements. The students reviewed the information on an interactive laser disk and through the resources in all formats available in the library media center. They constructed Linkway folders on their computers. The folders included the written text from their research investigations linked to video, graphics, and video segments about their elements on the videodisks. They designed and constructed graphics that illustrated the various properties of their elements. Teachers who had been trained in the technology in their staff development classes linked all the folders together into one huge periodic table.

The students used the folders to prepare for exams. They exhibited creativity and individuality in their organization and representation of the elements. Students were involved. They worked on the projects before and after school. One student stated, "I enjoyed using technology in this class because it made the learning a little bit easier and a lot more fun. I enjoyed the freedom it granted me." Another student said, "I enjoyed using the technology in the lab because I had a better chance of collecting accurate data and . . . exposure to the technology is indispensable in today's workplace (PHYS-MA-TECH 1992).

Several of the observations and the outcomes of the projects indicated that

- technology changed teaching in the classroom
- extensive training was needed for teachers to be comfortable with integrating the technology into the classroom
- this type of learning improved student-teacher relationships

Very important outcomes of the project had not been predicted. These included the improved student-teacher relationships and the reduction in the amount of variance in student performance. Many times this type of learning is not provided to average and special needs students, as indicated in several studies. This environment fosters investigation and thinking, allowing students to perform at a much higher level. Students were heterogeneously grouped. Technology decreased the difference between the top and bottom groups. One teacher verified this conclusion: "The worst report from this year was better than the best reports from last year before we got into computers."

Students collected the data using the Personal Science Laboratory and received immediate feedback to assist in problem solving. Students examined their assumptions and developed alternative assessments. The benefits of this hands-on, inquiry-learning approach that integrated technology included less lecturing, more doing of science and math, improved feedback to students, more hypothesis generating, and more performance-based assessment as well as an increase in student motivation and teacher productivity.

Poor handwriting was overcome. Average and special needs students were able to turn in word-processed reports that were neat and organized with excellent spelling through the use of the spell checker. The online thesaurus also helped them to vary the words. The work of the below-average students significantly improved. The graphing capability of several of the programs also boosted the grades of the below-average student. The inquiry-based learning environment—fostering problem solving with technological tools, and using manipulative materials, the calculator, and the computer—greatly increased the achievement of the at-risk learner. One of the mathematics teachers stated, "Students who have good thinking abilities or other important academic abilities but who struggle with mathematical calculations caused by excess performance anxiety or faulty acquisition of appropriate heuristics are able to correctly solve complex problems by using the capabilities of computers and sophisticated calculators provided to the students" (PHYS-MA-TECH 1992).

IDEA

Another project was a component of the Iowa Distance Education Alliance (IDEA) and included science reform through distance education. The project promoted curriculum reform in five areas: science, math, foreign language, literacy, and vocational. The staff development and in-service training model is worthy of introduction. Studies (Mendrinos 1992a, 1994) conclude that if teachers are trained by the library media specialist or attend workshops that he or she developed, the faculty are more likely to develop classroom and curricular projects that use the technology and modes of thinking studied. This project includes an excellent model for teacher training. I would include the library media specialist in the staff training to promote joint curriculum development.

The model consists of:

- Two-week leadership conference for the most successful teachers from previous years who want to become part of the instructional team for future workshops.
- Three-week summer workshops at each new site for thirty teachers to develop new constructivist practices and strategies.
- Five-day science/technology/society content and curriculum development to take place in the classroom of all summer participants during September and early October.
- Three-day fall short course for thirty-fifty of the teachers including the thirty enrolled during the summer. This fosters the development of a month-long module in science/technology/society where constructivist practices are used along with an extensive assessment plan.
- Interim communication with central staff, lead teachers, and fellow participants. This occurs through a newsletter, special memoranda, monthly telephone contacts, and school/classroom visits.
- Three-day spring short course for the thirty to fifty teachers who participated in the fall. Focus is on the reports by the participants about their experiences with constructivist teaching and the results of the assessments (Yager, Dunkhase, Tillotson, and Glass 1995).

This model supports teacher learning in constructivist curriculum development, and provides teachers with assessment tools, feedback, and the means of sharing successful projects. It does not only occur once or twice during the year since there are mechanisms set up to keep it ongoing. The dual purposes consisted of increasing the participants' level of knowledge of current issues and reform in science education and the need to provide training.

Perrone (1994) in his synthesis of research on students' engagement and involvement concluded that it is not what is being taught but how it is being taught that is most crucial. He suggested these strategies for successful student involvement:

- Students should help define the content.
- Students should have time to wonder and to find a particular direction that interests them.
- Topics should foster a new way of seeing something common and/or investigate lingering questions.
- Teachers should encourage different forms of expression and respect student views.
- The best activities are those invented by teachers and their students.
- Students should create original and public products.
- Students should DO something.
- Students should sense that the results of their work are not predetermined or fully predictable.

Constructivist teaching encourages the use of alternative sources for information both from written materials and from the experts. The type of learning that is being recommended by Project 2061 involves the talents of library media specialists as partners with the science and multidisciplinary community. This change in thinking may account for the change in the survey data in 1996. In the 1992 survey only 53 percent of the library media specialists offered in-service workshops. All of the library media specialists in the 1996 survey offered in-service workshops.

In 1992 science teachers (17%) had the least exposure and participation in the in-service workshops and had the least understanding of CD-ROM technology. In the 1996 survey, science teachers (97%) were the largest group participating in in-service staff development workshops that incorporated educational technology into the curriculum. They were also the largest users of the videodisks and followed social studies teachers in the use of CD-ROM laser disks. Science teachers along with social studies teachers were the largest groups to work with the library media specialist to integrate educational technologies within the curriculum. As I was tabulating the surveys, even for this small sample, there appeared to be a remarkable change. The AAAS recommendations for Project 2061 strongly support inquiry-based learning, technology, and research that are complemented and enhanced by the skills of the library media specialist.

THE SCHOOL IS A ZOO

Twelve miles outside of Minneapolis is the School of Environmental Studies in Apple Valley, Minnesota (Smith 1996). The school is located on the grounds of the Minnesota Zoo. It is home to 400 eleventh- and twelfth-grade students. They are surrounded by 2,700 animal species, and 500 acres of wetlands. Technology is integrated into every area of the school—English, social studies, and the environmental sciences. The focus is to produce innovative student thinkers. One of the projects uses the wetlands as a real-world laboratory. Students are researching the wetlands in terms of the environment, economics, government law, its effects on endangered species, and its interrelationship with water agreements.

Students are involved in constructing knowledge. Brad Johnson, one of the teachers at the school stated, "We'll do a set of activities, typically outside the school, that mirror what people do in the real world. Then we'll do some background reading and little lights will go off. The kids, will say, I saw that. Now I understand." Students create multimedia presentations of their research and findings through computer presentation programs such as PowerPoint.

NASA

A chapter on integrating science in the curriculum would not be complete without referencing the fantastic work that NASA has done in sharing its research, providing lesson plans, videos, graphics, and images on the Internet and the World Wide Web, through CD-ROM laser disks, videos, videodisks, and print materials (see Figure 6.2).

There have been national concerns about the quality and effectiveness of science teaching and the need to restructure the U.S. science curricula. These efforts are focusing on the need to:

Figure 6.2
NASA Web Site Logo

- understand the earth
- infuse more content regarding the modern understanding of the earth into the K–12 science curricula
- develop an earth systems education framework
- develop earth systems education projects (Mayer 1996)

Several initiatives by NASA promote using technology to communicate and involve students in scientific inquiry learning. Students are voyagers on the NASA space shuttles that are studying space and the earth. They can view the images, videos, graphics, video segments, and the text of the investigations on the World Wide Web. They can also talk with real scientists who are on location investigating and exploring the earth and space.

NASA has developed the Information Infrastructure Technology and Applications Program (IITA). Its goals are to:

- develop affordable, innovative K–12 projects, technologies, and applications that can be widely disseminated to the educational community
- use NASA activities to inspire students to undertake high technology careers using the Internet
- integrate network and computer literacy into the teaching process
- develop Internet-based curriculum enhancement tied to NASA information of interest to teachers and students
- develop projects focused on early levels of education and underserved students (http://quest.arc.nasa.gov//nk12/index.html)

NASA/Ames in Moffett Field, California, has developed the Internet initiative to meet these goals. It has organized various interactive online projects that connect classrooms with ongoing science and engineering work. Students have access to the professionals who are doing real-time science work. They are provided with background information on their research. NASA experts are available online and also via electronic mail. Past projects involved going live on Antarctica as the NASA scientists investigated this icy continent and the ozone hole. Students were part of the Galileo spacecraft encounter with Jupiter. This previous year students participated in the project Live from the Stratosphere, which enabled students across America to take a virtual trip aboard NASA's Kuiper Airborne Observatory (see Figure 6.3).

Many of the NASA projects are integrated multimedia projects and are accompanied by live television PBS-supported programs. They also include print materials and hands-on online activities. Students can post messages and read their peer comments from around the world using the Internet. Internet World Wide Web sites for the project feature video, graphics, and images from the NASA mission.

Figure 6.3
Live from the Stratosphere

To stay informed of new projects send e-mail to: listmanager@quest.arc. nasa.gov. Leave the subject blank, and in the message body write: subscribe sharing-nasa first name last name.

NASA/Ames also offers videos on using the Internet in the classroom. These videos may be freely duplicated for education. They include:

- Global Quest: The Internet in the Classroom
- Connecting to the Future
- Global Quest II: Teaching with the Internet

Full information about these titles is available by sending e-mail to: video-info@quest.arc.nasa.gov.

The NASA Mission to Planet Earth Web site is remarkable. Located at http://www.hq.nasa.gov, it has extensive information on all topics of the earth investigations being undertaken by NASA scientists (see Figure 6.4).

Figure 6.4
Welcome to NASA's Mission to Planet Earth

Students can look at the images taken by radar from the satellites, or the teacher can use the images, videos, and graphics for classroom demonstrations and explanations of changes that are occurring. The information is up to date and is sometimes technical, but many of the discoveries from the ongoing explorations are not part of any textbook.

Is this information only for secondary school science classes? As a former elementary teacher who taught science, I would definitely use the resources in the K–12 classrooms. Of course, explanations can vary, but the images are priceless.

Asteroid and Comet Collisions with Earth is one of the projects investigated by Mission to Planet Earth scientists.

Kilometer-sized asteroids and comets cause global scale disasters when they hit Earth. Ames' researchers found that the Chixulub crater in the Yucatan Peninsula is the site of an impact 65 million years ago that killed the dinosaurs. Known as the K-T impact, it led to massive extinctions throughout the biosphere, while it paved the way for the ascent of mammals and the rise of humans. (Toon, Zahnle, and Morrison 1996)

Mission to Planet Earth has folders and posters on their scientific missions. These are available from NASA/Ames in Moffet Field, California. With the availability of remote sensing and image processing through the Mission to Planet Earth sites, a discussion and understanding of remote sensing and image processing becomes necessary.

NASA, which had previously concentrated on space exploration, began Mission to Planet Earth (see Figure 6.5). In the spring of 1994, a series of shuttle-based multiseasonal earth observation missions began. These missions are called the Space Radar Laboratory and use Shuttle Imaging Radar and the Mapping of Air Pollution from Space instruments. The purpose of the shuttle missions is to discover more about the processes at work in our planet. Supersites around the globe have been chosen for intense study by the Space Radar Laboratory. Topics for study include:

Figure 6.5
Mission to Planet Earth

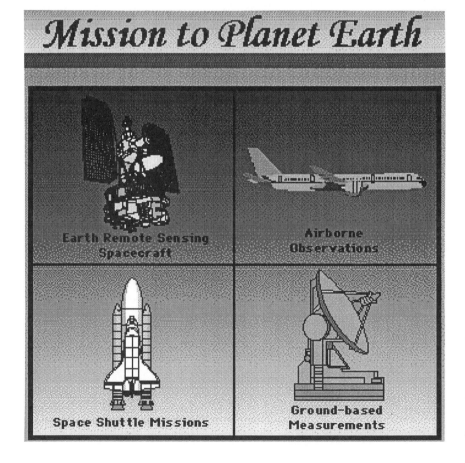

I. The state of the earth

- vegetation greenness
- topical wet/dry season (tropical forests)
- rain
- flooding
- snow
- soil moisture
- seasonal freeze and thaw
- burning
- dust storms
- ice edge
- volcanoes and earthquakes

II. Dynamic surface phenomena

- overview of ocean features and documentation
- ecology (including the rain forest and the Sahara)
- hydrology
- geology
- rain and clouds

TEACHER ENHANCEMENT WORKSHOPS

Teacher education workshops are being held at the University of Arizona's Image Processing Center (http://ipt.lpl.arizona.edu) and at Foothill College's Digital Mapping and Image Processing Center (http://earth.fhda.edu). Both World Wide Web sites include other resources on the Internet related to these technologies. Both centers are also developing curriculum materials on the Web and are using multimedia technologies to integrate these technologies in the curriculum.

Foothill College's Digital Mapping and Image Processing Center is part of the National Science Foundation's project on remote sensing, image processing, and Geographical Information Systems (see Figure 6.6). Foothill is one of twelve community colleges that are part of the grant. The project's goal is to develop an earth systems science curriculum using technologies that can be used at the community college level to educate and train students for higher education and careers using these technologies. Secondary school teachers may be able to adopt some curriculum activities for their classrooms. Enhanced faculty workshops are held to instruct teachers in these areas. Foothill College's Digital Mapping and Image Processing Center will provide the images for the curriculum and the image-processing workshops. The World Wide Web page at http://earth.fhda.edu will assist in disseminating information on the workshops and the project. It provides

Figure 6.6
CCITT Project

links to other sites using and exploring these technologies worldwide. An interactive bulletin board allows messages and responses to be posted and sent. A listserv has also been developed to further curriculum development among the nation's remote community colleges.

Secondary school science teachers and library media specialists can seek out the information on this Web page. Geographical Information Systems is represented and can be another very rich source of information.

The University of Arizona's Image Processing Center for Teaching Projects is utilizing images from NASA and Landsat to develop curriculum for K–12 science education.

Raphael and Greenberg (1995) explained how technologies can be used:

Scientists—or students—create images by scanning or photographing objects with a digital or video camera, a process that translates a picture into a matrix of dots, or digits. Virtually any set of measurements (light, temperature, x-rays and so on) can be compiled in a rectangular array of numbers and then displayed on a computer screen as a photographic quality image. With image processing scientists— or students—can edit, analyze, and enhance these digital images to gain more information from the data. The methods they can use can distinguish shades, colors, and relationships not visible to the human eye. For example, scientists use the technology to create digital images of the earth from interplanetary space probes; doctors, to manipulate images generated during CAT scans; and meteorologists, to create weather maps from satellite information.

Students are given images developed by the Image Processing for Teaching Project and can observe, enhance, and magnify them. The images are a series of mathematical numbers that the student can measure, graph, analyze data, and solve problems with. Image processing is an extremely useful tool for the at-risk student. It has helped many of them in understanding the relationships between math and science.

Gayle Wilson has the largest number of Chapter 1 students of any high school in Albuquerque, New Mexico. Two-thirds of the freshman in her math and computer classes do not graduate. Sixty percent read below grade level. Image processing is used to improve her students' skills in math, science, technology, and communication. Students work in pairs and use scanners, video cameras, the Internet, and digital still cameras along with the image-processing activities presented on the CD-ROM disk. The experience for these students has been very positive, changing attitudes and overcoming major hurdles in the process.

Real-world problems can be analyzed and understood through the application of remote sensing, image processing, and GIS. Lyme disease is one example:

Lyme disease is currently the most commonly reported vector borne disease in the United States. . . . In this study, remote sensing (RS) and geographic information system (GIS) technologies provided an efficient means to charactrerize and model the relationships between landscape elements that contribute to Lyme disease transmission risk in Westchester County, New York. . . . This finding suggests that a RS/GIS technique, which identifies the spatial distribution of these landscape patterns, can help generate predictions of Lyme disease risk within areas of the Northeast that are similar to Westchester County. (Dister 1996)

Lyme disease is of serious concern to all parents in the Northeast. It is a real-world problem that students are familiar with. By investigating Lyme disease through the Internet, imaging, GIS, electronic and print resources, the library media specialist and science teacher can simulate a scientific investigation.

Jeff Lockwood, a physics teacher at Sahuaro High School in Tucson, Arizona, uses image processing as part of the students' astronomy research. His students formulate hypotheses, organize and collect data, and write their results as well as an abstract. One of his students at risk of dropping out was turned on to learning.

Mike, a sophomore with what Lockwood called "an abysmal grade point average," including failure in college algebra, entered the astronomy research class a few years ago. Although Mike liked computers, he hadn't found a way to apply them to his academic work. In Lockwood's class, Mike did nearly 10 times the work required by each student, classifying 2,000 volcanic edifices on Venus. Last year, he and a student in Vancouver, Washington explored whether there are associations of small volcanic edifices with major geologic features on Venus. The two did all the work themselves, through e-mail, and presented their research at the conference in Houston. . . . Last year Mike entered the University of Arizona majoring in physics. (Raphael and Greenberg 1995)

The studies quoted in previous chapters indicated that most at-risk students do well on standardized tests. Mike was turned on to learning in an inquiry-based real-world environment. Lesson plans and units that integrate educational technology and information literacy within the curriculum take time to develop. However, the results are more than worth the effort!

Information on workshops for staff development training using image processing and lesson plans are available on the Image Processing for Teaching World Wide Web site (http://ipt.arizona.edu). Joe Freeman, a teacher from Field Elementary School in Mesa, Arizona, wrote that after a short two-day IPT workshop,

I was jazzed about implementing it in my computer lab curriculum. . . . One of my favorite units is Greek culture. The students are taught how archeologists use shards of pottery to gain insight into ancient civilization. The creative lesson called Piecing Together the Past has actually allowed students to manipulate shards on the computer screen to make their own pottery. The task seems simple at first until they realize they must draw on their prior knowledge of Greek culture and design to come up with the correct answers. (http://ipt.lpl.arizona.edu)

E-mail can be sent to Joe Freeman at JAFreeman@eworld.com.

AT-RISK STUDENTS AND SCIENCE

Students seeking the best employment opportunities will need a good grasp of science, math, and computer technology. At-risk students have problems to overcome that are reflected in cognitive differences. Many students experience family stress, which can include poverty, unemployment, and other problems that they engender. Cultural and racial bias may be the underlying reason they are encouraged to take less challenging and nonacademic courses of study. If they have a disability, the students may be "tracked" out of technical courses because of the misconception that they cannot function safely in the lab and could never work in science (Schwartz 1987).

Students who are at risk or average learners should be exposed to the same types of experiences that the above average and college track students have. Their programs should be high quality and long term. At-risk students need enrichment, hands-on experience, and need to be evaluated frequently with feedback. Their courses need a strong purpose, relevance, and direction and should be taught by competent teachers who enjoy working with this target population. Recontextualization is important to present scientific concepts in a problem-solving approach that is embedded in familiar contexts. Relating math and science learning to future careers and job opportunities will increase student attention, comprehension, and retention. An alternative learning environment such as the library media center can promote research, electronic telecommunication, using the Internet, or working on a field study. A different learning environment can be an important stress-reducing strategy. Cooperative social interaction on specifically designed problem-solving tasks is important for females and minorities.

To increase science achievement for this target population, science programs should feature smaller classes and working more closely with the teacher and the library media specialist on motivational, structured hands-on lab and research activities involving multimedia and computer technology. Students also need increased time on task. Small, mixed-ability cooperative groupings work well. Students can solve problems independently, and help each other develop inquiry and scientific literacy.

The Internet is a phenomenal research tool for science. Lesson plans, career information, medical textbooks with multimedia illustrations from major universities, and the latest scientific research from around the world are available and are a hint of the power of this network of networks. Faculty and students can harness the power of the Internet for their own learning.

Following are some of the exceptional multimedia science resources that are recommended by school library media specialists.

Videodisks

Tom Snyder
Great Ocean Rescue
Great Solar System Race

National Geographic
Human Body
The Cell
Restless Earth
Planetary Manager

Videodiscovery
Science Discovery: Science Sleuths
BioSci II
Physics at the Indy 500

Optical Data
Windows on Science: Life Science
Windows on Science: Physical Science

ABC Interactive
The Great Quake of '88

NASA
Space Shuttle Images

CD-ROM Laser Disks

A.D.A.M.® Essentials: "A.D.A.M. Essentials is an excellent reference and study tool for introductory human anatomy. The anatomical terminology and content within A.D.A.M. Essentials are tailored to advanced secondary school biology programs or introductory college-level courses. In addition to its approximate 100 layers of dissectible anatomical images and two views, A.D.A.M. Essentials contains 38 narrated animations for study of basic physiological concepts, and six challenging interactive puzzles" (http://www.adam.com).

NASA

SIR-C CD-ROMS are available from the EROS Data Center. You can also call, fax, or e-mail the EROS Data Center:

Phone: (605) 594–6116
Fax: (605) 594–6589
E-mail: edc@eos.nasa.gov

EDC DAAC User Services
EROS Data Center
Sioux Falls, SD 57198

SIRCED01—contains a pre-launch look at the SIR-C/X-SAR mission, the sites to be covered, and the science planned for the mission. SIRSED02—contains the Space Shuttle Endeavor Mission results in pictures and videos with lesson plans that utilize the mission results to teach students about our changing earth.

USGS Digital Maps on CD-ROM
Horizons Technology, Inc.
3990 Ruttin Road
San Diego, CA 92123

Internet Resources

ASK ERIC—Lesson plans, curriculum guides, ERIC Digests, and ERIC citations and abstracts
   http://ericir.syr.edu/ithome/askeric.html

Badger—San Francisco Geo-Data over the Internet
   http://www.svi.org/badger.html

CCITT NSF Grant in Image Processing, Remote Sensing, and GIS
   http://earth.fhda.edu

Discover Magazine—Editor's Web Tour
   http://www.dc.enews.com/magazines/discover/webtur.html

Discover Magazine—School Science Program
   http://www.enews.com/magazines/discover/page7.html

Education Sites—Internet museums, online libraries, major science "hot spots" and K–12 resources
   http://www.fn.net/education.html

Eisenhower National Clearinghouse (ENC)
   http://www.enc.org

ENC—outstanding worldwide science resources on the Internet
   http://carson.enc.org:80/ressci.htm

Explorer—Network database system for contributing, organizing, and delivering education resources (instructional software, lab activities, and lesson plans)
   http://unite2.tisl.ukans.edu/

Geodata Information Systems—A wealth of digital cartographic and environmental data
   http://cger.uiowa.edu/servers/servers_geodata.html

Image Processing for Teaching Center, University of Arizona
http://ipt.lpl.arizona.edu

Insanely Great Science Websites—Over 100 links to some of the most popular science websites
http://ww.eskimo.com/~billb/edu.html

Mathematics, Science, and Technology—University of Missouri—Columbia College of Education maintains this site. 100 links to major math, science, and technology resources
http://tiger.coe.missouri.edu.mathsci.html

NCGIA—National Center for Geographic Information and Analysis. "NCGIA is a research consortium funded by the National Science Foundation. Its primary mandate is to conduct basic research in geographic information analysis and its related technology."
http://bbq.ncgia.ucsb.edu:80
http://www.ncgia.ucsb.edu/education/

SciEd—Science and Mathematics Education Resources. Titles range from anthropology to earth science to pseudoscience. Science Reference Shelf included
http://www-hpcc.astro.washington.edu/scied/science.html

Science Learning Network—Funded by National Science Foundation and Unisys Corporation. Alliance of six science museums supporting teacher development in science pedagogy
http://www.omsi.edu/sln/sln.html

World Wide Virtual Library—www.w3.org. Thematic guide on the use of satellite remote sensing to study the human dimensions of global environmental change
http://www.ciesin.org/TG/RS/RS-home.html

U.S. Geologic Survey—Water resources, weather, digital maps
http://www.cr.usgs.gov

NASA

Goddard DAAC (Distributed Active Archive Centers): "The Goddard Distributed Active Archive Center (DAAC) provides data and related services for global change research and education. We are funded through NASA's Earth Observing System (EOS) as a source of information about the upper atmosphere, atmospheric dynamics, and the global biosphere. We aim to be a useful facility to help you study the natural and human processes that influence Earth's climate."
http://daac.gsfc.nasa.gov.

Langley DAAC
http://eosdis.larc.nasa.gov

Marshall DAAC
http://wwwdaac.msfc.nasa.gov

Earth Data and Imagery

- Mission to Planet Earth Home Page
  http://www.hq.nasa.gov/office/mtpe/
- AVHRR Land Pathfinder
  http://xtreme.gsfc.nasa.gov
- JPL TOPEX/POSEIDON Images
  http://podaacc-www.jpl.nasa.gov/topex
- AVISO TOPEX/Poseidon data
  http://192.134.216.41
- Oceans SST Pathfinder (NOAA/NASA)
  http://sst-www.jpl.nasa.gov
- NASA/JPL Imaging Radar Homepage
  http://southport.jpl.nasa.gov
- SIR-C/SsSAR images
  http://www.jpl.nasa.gov/mip/earth.html
- World Wide Web Library: Oceanography
  http://www.mth.uea.ac.uk/ocean/oceanography.html

Many times, average, special needs, and below-average students have exceptional music, artistic, and multimedia abilities. With the use of a computer, software, electronic research tools, and the Internet, their hands-on discovery, exploration, and research presentations may meet or exceed our expectations.

The following case study incorporates the tremendous potential of the Internet in an inquiry-based, real-world learning experience for at-risk students. Andrew Ross taught in the Teach for America program (1–800–TFA–1230) and is also involved with the Libraries for the Future progam. Located in the projects of Washington, D.C., the name of the school has been changed but the case study is true. It has integrity and exudes a powerful commitment toward the education of all students.

Andrew Ross, Assistant Professor
Department of Biology
Prince George's Community College
(202) 265–8180
e-mail: tyger@erols.com

TECHNOLOGY FOR AT-RISK YOUTH

Demographics

Weston Junior High Alternative School is a seventh through ninth grade middle-level public school that serves an extremely unique population. Students are 100 percent African American and 95+ percent of the student body live in public housing in the surrounding southeast corridor of Washington, D.C., in the Anacostia neighborhood. Over 70 percent of the students at Weston are enrolled in the alternative program, which serves students who are in school as a condition of probation, drug rehabilitation programs, or teenage-parenting programs.

The school is extremely underresourced. The library is minuscule and had no computer until late 1993. Indeed, the school possessed very little in the way of technology; administrators and school system officials refused to provide expensive equipment to the school, based on its location at the locus of most of the city's serious criminal activity. Students who attend Weston are, for the same reasons, very unskilled in computer use. Most have never used a computer for anything other than a video game.

Because of poor administration at the school, the school had been unable to obtain many of the government funds for which it was eligible. Tallies of the student body and their financial information were done haphazardly and with little care. Most students who attend Weston have had precious little previous success in education; many have been completely alienated from academics and therefore arrive prepared for failure. It is precisely this attitude that creates a self-fulfilling prophecy for so many of these children.

Obtaining Technology

In order to implement any program that utilizes computer technology, I first had to obtain computers for the school. I began in the fall of 1993, soliciting donations of old computer systems on the Internet. I acquired a Macintosh SE system, an Apple Image Writer, and a Macintosh Plus system for my classroom within weeks of posting a message to various technology-related news groups. It was with this very outdated equipment that I began to work.

Later in the year, when students had become familiar with the technology and had begun to create some amazing products, I took my students' work and approached the school system for more funding. Eventually, I applied for and obtained funding through the Gifted and Talented Programs Division for four up-to-date Macintosh systems, an Internet connection, a 14.4 baud modem, a color scanner, and two color printers. Additionally, another grant from an outside source provided my classroom with another excellent Macintosh system, another printer, and another modem.

Once the new computers arrived, students in my classes decided that the best use of the original two computers and the printer would be in the library. With that, we donated the systems to the library, and several students from each class acted as on-site experts to help the librarians use the systems.

Academic Projects

The program that I began at the school involved a project-based curriculum for two of my classes. Students were split into mixed-ability-level cooperative groups of four people and worked throughout the semester on a project on a subject that they found fascinating. Students worked during the class periods on the computers, doing searches of the Internet through search engines, obtaining text and picture information through the World Wide Web and Gopher. During the classes, I moved from group to group, assisting students and guiding them so that they could put together a cohesive product from the massive amount of information that they were all able to obtain. Many students found experts such as scientists, doctors, lawyers, and professors with whom they began e-mail correspondence. This virtual mentoring excited both the experts and my students.

The program also had an after-school component that involved other teachers and the library media specialist at the school. Every group had an advisor/teacher/library media specialist who would be available at least once every week to counsel students on their progress, help with research and information location, and provide feedback on the projects. In this way, I created an environment wherein I was not the sole guide. Students were able to obtain advice from several teachers and the library media specialist on-site, as well as from their e-mail mentors.

At the conclusion of every semester, students put together a finished product. Projects ranged in scope from research papers and posters, to poetry (workshops with writers from the University of Miami), African dance (with guidance from an anthropologist in Ghana), a rap project (with input given by the staff of *Vibe* magazine), and a short play on AIDS (advised by a local teen AIDS organization and by Horizons Youth Group in Chicago). In essence, the projects that the students completed at the end of the semester reflected collaboration with people from hundreds of miles away, and this broadened perspective created a much richer result. I should point out that in most cases, the virtual mentors played a role that was limited to reading what students had written or created and giving criticism and advice. Today, with CU-SEE-ME and other videoconferencing software, the opportunity exists for visual and aural cross-talk between mentor and student.

The students presented their projects one afternoon to the entire student body of the school and invited parents to come to the school in the afternoon to share their successes. In addition, I worked with the local public library so that after the semester ended, the students' projects went on display in the library for several months. This display allowed members of the community to see what students had achieved, and it gave the library an opportunity to showcase how members of the local community had made the most of electronic media and moved into the information age.

Students appreciated the opportunity to educate the members of the community about the Internet as well as the individual topics that their projects covered. It is through exactly this sort of integration of school, community, and global infrastructure that students were able to empower themselves and begin to view their roles in society as something other than predetermined. For the first time in many students' lives, they had made a real, positive impact on their world, one which resonated hundreds of miles away.

Sara A. Murray, Media Specialist
Brown Barge Middle School
151 East Fairfield Drive
Pensacola, FL 32503
(904) 444–2700

DESCRIPTION

Electronic Learning magazine described Brown Barge Middle School (BBMS) as "a typical '50's elementary school set in an unprepossessing environment—a low-slung red-brick building with four wings, encircled by a cyclone fence, perched on the edge of interstate I-110" (Siegel 1994). Definitely not state of the art, at least from the outside!

People frequently ask us about our name—Brown Barge was named for two prominent Pensacola African American female educators of the 1950s. After being closed for a number of years, it was reopened in 1987 as the first middle-grade magnet school in Escambia County, a district of approximately 43,000 students with twelve middle schools, six high schools, and sixty elementary schools. Since we are a magnet program, our racial makeup reflects that of the county—slightly more than one-third of our students are from minority backgrounds.

Our faculty applied to work in this new program knowing that the curriculum would not continue the "status quo," and two years later, largely through the example of a visionary principal, Camille C. Barr, the faculty had become convinced that restructuring to a totally integrative curriculum would be our mission. (More about that in a moment.) Wrestling with the many issues required to develop this new curriculum is a story for another time! Having implemented our vision, we have been operating under this model for the last four years.

Brown Barge Middle School's Model:
Characteristics of a Changing Curriculum

TOTALLY INTEGRATED CURRICULUM
which is

RESOURCE-BASED
in which
TEXTBOOKS ARE RESOURCES
and where
TECHNOLOGY IS A TOOL—
a means, not an end
SUPPORTED BY SCHOOL-BASED MANAGEMENT
BY AN EMPOWERED FACULTY
implementing
THEMATIC INSTRUCTION through STREAMS
which are
LEARNER-CENTERED
because topics are derived from
SURVEYS OF STUDENTS, PARENTS, AND FACULTY.

Teachers use
RESTRUCTURED TEACHING METHODS—
Stream-flexible scheduling, teaching teams, & cross-grade level
instruction, integrating technology &
ALTERNATIVE INSTRUCTION & EVALUATION METHODS:
Co-operative, active, authentic, hands-on learning using portfolio
assessment with teachers as facilitators.

I think it is critical that educators and people interested in education have this background information because this changing paradigm profoundly affects the role of the media specialist and the media center's resources.

TECHNOLOGY

Technology is an important tool in supporting Brown Barge's integrative curriculum. We have a local area thin-wire Ethernet network and two Digital Alpha AXP-150 servers (15Gb of memory each) running Windows NT networking software. Two IBM file servers are also on the network, and they serve a variety of programs that are accessible from any IBM classroom on the network. One is a CD-ROM server that makes available networked CD-ROMs such as SIRS, *World Book*'s Information Finder, and *Grolier*'s Electronic Encyclopedia. Our electronic catalog, Alexandria, is also available via the network. The second server is the WICAT Integrated Learning Program. Every student takes a CAT test and works on curriculum that they may have trouble in.

There are also three main MAC servers. One is a CD-ROM server that every student has access to through the network. Titles include SIRS, SIRS Researcher, *Grolier*'s, and SIRS Discoverer. Josten's Integrated Learning

Series is the second file server. Josten is similar to WICAT and provides assistance with a variety of subjects. The third file server houses Edunetics (ILS). It contains a variety of science software.

Upon enrolling at BBMS, each student is issued a VAX account number, and those accounts are where most student and faculty work is kept. We have approximately 530 middle schoolers (6–8 grade), and we have approximately 250 Macintosh computers of varying models and 200 IBMs. (See the schematic of our network.)

In each wing of the school there is a Macintosh computer lab consisting of twenty to twenty-nine computers. There are also two IBM labs with twenty-six computers in each. The IBMs have the Columbus Series with Illustrated Manuscript, a multimedia program that allows you to research everything from Hamlet to the authors of today. It also includes a social studies program with multimedia presentations from the period of the cavemen to the information age.

With this amount of hardware, it would be impossible not to have someone on site to maintain it and equally impossible for that person to be the media specialist. Fred Pippen, our technology coordinator, keeps this now-aging network running. Although we work very closely together, we do very different things.

Every classroom at Brown Barge has an MMP—a multimedia platform. Designed by the faculty, an MMP houses a Samsung 29-inch TV, a Magnavox VCR, a Pioneer laser disk player, a Umax scanner, and a Macintosh IIci with CD peripheral. The Apple IICI includes a video capture card, video display card, and audio card for multimedia presentations. This is where students work to assemble their multimedia presentations. Our library management program, Alexandria for the Macintosh, makes it possible for any student or teacher to access the media center's electronic card catalog from any room in the school—no more middle schoolers dawdling down the hallways to "see if a book is in"! Included is a partial list of other networked and "stand-alone" software available to students and faculty.

CURRICULUM

In order to understand how students and faculty use this technology, one must first have some understanding of how Brown Barge's curriculum operates. The first thing Mrs. Barr gave each of us when we joined the faculty was a copy of Dr. James Beane's slim book, *The Middle School Curriculum: From Rhetoric to Reality*. Combining Beane's ideas of using surveys to identify themes of significance to middle schoolers with the faculty's conviction of the importance of teaching higher-level thinking skills, we began developing our concept of an integrative curriculum. In retrospect we realize that this curriculum has been on an evolving continuum that began with a traditional curriculum, evolved to an interdisciplinary one, then to a multidisciplinary one, next to transdisciplinary one, and finally an integrative curriculum. We have been teaching in this new paradigm for four years.

Using the result of the surveys of students, parents, and faculty suggested by Beane, we developed themes based on the interests and concerns the three groups expressed. The themes are called Streams. I have included a list of this year's Streams to give an idea of their variety. Students sign up at the end of each year for their three preferences for the coming year. Technology is, again, an invaluable tool at this time—monitoring what Streams students have already had, and, equally important, ensuring that each child has a balance among the language arts/social studies and math/science Streams.

After the Streams to be taught for a new year are determined, the Stream teams begin planning, both formally in scheduled meetings and informally with me and other faculty not necessarily on their current Streams. Much of the discussion centers on resources to support Stream simulations, and the culmination of the activities that have gone on in the Streams. Technology tools are important resources here—look again at the sources that can be accessed from the network or through "stand-alone" items that Streams have checked out from the media center to use in their respective Stream wings.

ELECTRONIC RESOURCES

The following computer-networked titles can be accessed in every classroom in the school:

Alexandria electronic card catalog
World Book's New Illustrated Information Finder
Grolier's Electronic Encyclopedia
Social Issues Resources Series (SIRS)

Other resources available, but not on the network include:

Mammals: A Multimedia Encyclopedia
CIA World Factbook
Guinness Disk of Records
Small Blue Planet: The Real Picture Atlas
Time Almanac
Columbus
The Presidents

Laserdisk titles that are available include:

GTV: Geographic Perspectives in American History
ABC News Interactive: Martin Luther King, Jr.
The Great Solar System Rescue
The Physics of Flight: Videodiscovery
Musee d'Orsay
American Art from the National Gallery
The Visual Almanac: An Interactive Multimedia Kit (Voyager)
Our Biosphere: The Earth in Our Hands (Smithsonian)

ROLE OF THE LIBRARY MEDIA SPECIALIST

In thinking about my responsibilities as media specialist in a restructured, integrative curriculum over the past four years, I realized they could all be grouped under one of the three headings Information Power suggests: information specialist, instructional consultant, and teacher. To personally put this theory into practice—to practice the reality, not just the rhetoric—I decided that after three years of developing integrative curriculum, it was time for me to teach it.

Several things made my going into the classroom possible—a supportive principal, a tolerant faculty, and another teacher who is also a media specialist but chooses to be a classroom teacher. The feedback from the team I worked with was that, over and over, they saw me experiencing the same issues they had gone through two years earlier when we first implemented a totally integrated curriculum. As well as being an invaluable learning experience for me, my classroom teaching was very interesting to all of us, demonstrating that learning to teach in this environment is clearly a developmental process.

After having had a trimester's experience in the Global Awareness Stream in 1995, we decided that the following year I would teach an afternoon activity class, "Introduction to the Internet" in the same Stream. This course would be a trial run for Brown Barge, and several things were immediately necessary: (1) an Internet connection, (2) an Acceptable Use Policy (AUP), and (3) a curriculum.

Through the generous help of Dr. Alberta Canas of the University of West Florida's (UWF) Human and Machine Cognition Institute, we were able to secure an Internet connection. When Dr. Canas had offered UWF's first "virtual" class on the Internet, I was one of the 150 students who registered. After Mr. Pippen and I described the class we wanted to offer to our students, Dr. Canas supplied the connections we requested. We began with only four, thinking that students could work together in groups of six or seven, but we quickly realized that four were not enough. Dr. Canas eventually allowed us to use eight lines, which worked very well for our purposes. If districts do not have Internet connections yet and there is a college or university nearby, media specialists might try the route we followed.

The next issue was to formulate an Acceptable Use Policy for Brown Barge. Even though our district did not yet have Internet access, the school board has drafted a policy "for the assessing of Internet resources in District schools." Two key requirements were that "the principal of each school will be responsible for developing an Internet access policy prior to the District implementation of this service at that school" and that "this policy is to be developed in concert with the School Advisory Council." At my request, a team of teachers was assembled to develop the guidelines and then present them to our School Advisory Council. It took about two months for the draft to be reviewed and revised by the various groups, but we finally have our own AUP.

Two extremely useful resources are available from the Internet for media specialists and others who are in the process of formulating their own AUPs. A free electronic magazine that focuses on the impact of new technology on education and teaching, called *From Now On: The Educational Technology Journal*, is available on the World Wide Web at <http://www.pacificrim.net/-mekenzie/>. A second excellent source is from *Classroom Connect*, a monthly publication one subscribes to that helps educators integrate the Internet and its resources into the K–12 curriculum. On your World Wide Web browser, it is available at ftp://ftp classroom.net/wentworth/Classroom-Connect/aup=faq.txt.

To integrate my lessons into the flow of the Global Awareness Stream, I attended all the team's planning sessions and participated in some of their simulations if time permitted. The promise for this Stream reads: "Understanding today's world and its cultures requires a global perspective which looks at 1) common issues shared by all nations, 2) analyzes the history and background of these issues, and 3) develops ways of dealing with them using technology as an increasingly useful tool in information-sharing, research, and development."

One of the three simulations students carry out is the creation of a travel diary. The assignment given to students follows this case study. (See Global Awareness Stream, Simulation 2: Travel Diary.) To give students some ideas about locating information for their countries, I discovered an excellent hands-on lesson that the staff at Zenger Media (a division of the Social Studies School Service) developed. Since we did not have time to carry out all four tasks, I modified Task #1, see "Trip to Vietnam," to our purposes. After students completed this activity, they were to use this model as a template to locate information on their respective countries. The students were excited about both actually being on the Internet and locating information in this new format! Rick Allen's narrative is an example of how one student described his experiences.

THE FUTURE

One of Brown Barge's unique attributes is that our faculty has been simultaneously creating a totally integrated curriculum while incorporating a huge infusion of technology. We have several continuing challenges ahead of us. One is to plan, budget for, and continuously upgrade existing older hardware to be able to use increasingly sophisticated software. A second is to maintain the model being pioneered in this intensive curriculum. A third is to keep integrating developing technology tools into our continuously developing curriculum. We strive to meet the challenge of education for the future.

Brown Barge Middle School has been the recipient of many awards and honors. Several include: ESE/FEFP Pilot School, 1995–96; William Alexander Award for Outstanding Middle Schools, 1994; and Red Carpet School Award, 1993.

GLOBAL AWARENESS STREAM—SIMULATION 2: TRAVEL DIARY

Name:

Date:

TOR:

You are an American tourist traveling in your assigned country for a minimum of ten days. You may be any age you choose and you may be traveling or visiting your country for any reason, such as business, touring, exchange student, visiting a friend or relative, and so forth. Create a travel diary that describes what you see and experience in your country and expresses your reactions and feelings.

Your travel diary must include five dated entries. You have been researching and studying many areas of your country's culture, geography, and economy in your classes as preparation for this simulation. As you prepare your entries, you need to include the following topics and you may use this as a checklist:

- Geography
- Time change
- Famous landmarks and tourist attractions
- Holidays/Festivals/Celebrations
- Shopping and using currency
- Clothing or traditional costumes
- Eating
- Transportation
- Religion

- Games/Sports/Recreation
- Words or phrases
- Other items of your choosing, that is, music, current issues (optional)

In addition to your five entries, your travel diary must also include these items:

- A map of your country on which you have drawn your itinerary
- A packing list (consider your country's climate, weather, and the time of year)
- A snapshot/picture (copied from a book) for each entry

You will be evaluated on the following criteria:

- Written communication (content and creative writing)
- Research (factual information you have learned in your classes as a result of your work with computer resources and books)
- Conscientiousness (your best effort to complete this project as described, to have a diary that is neat and well done, and to turn it in on time)
- All entries and items are to be mounted on card stock, which will be provided for you.

This project is due Wednesday, April 3. Please turn it in to your delegation's ambassador.

Bon Voyage!

TRIP TO VIETNAM

Name:

TOR:

Date:

TOI: Mrs. Murray, Mrs. Towns

Imagine that you have the opportunity to travel to Vietnam and you spend ten days there exploring whatever features of the country you wish. In this series of activities, your group will visit different sites on the Internet and World Wide Web to try to find basic facts about Vietnam that travelers should know. Although this exercise is specific to Vietnam, the tasks outlined can be applied to the study of any country, so this model could be used to develop activities for any of the countries being studied in the global awareness classes.

As you move through the exercise, you will be asked to do a number of different things, including downloading text and graphics, finding specific locations on the Web, and answering questions about the geography and culture of Vietnam. At certain points you will be asked to save information that you have downloaded in a folder on the desktop; at other times you will simply write answers in the spaces provided here.

Let us get started !

Task #1

(Note: the following information is found under the Social Studies School Service site located at http://www.socialstudies.com. Select online resources and then Vietnam.)

Select the online resources link under bookmarks, then select Vietnam. Scroll down to the "Cycle Through Vietnam" feature (it is the eighth one) on the Social Studies School Service site. Begin reading the contents of this virtual field trip, and answer the questions as you go.

1. Who is describing his experiences on this trip for us?
2. How many miles would the bike ride cover?
3. From what major city did it begin and what city was the final destination?
4. Were there many signs or evidence that a devastating war had taken place?
5. What things made cycling tough?
6. Who arranged this trip? Why?

To save time, when your group reaches the vertical picture of the Vietnamese people on page 2, scroll to the bottom of the page and click on page 3 to continue researching.

7. What makes biking in Hanoi a challenge?
8. Who was "Uncle Ho?"
9. What was unusual about the old university in Hanoi?
10. Would you like to be a puppet master in a water puppet show? Why or why not?
11. What was the general response of the Vietnamese people to this trip?
12. Describe some of the landmarks/sights in northern Vietnam that particularly struck Jay as being unique to this country.

RICK ALLEN'S NARRATIVE

During the Global Awareness Stream, I took a class on the Internet. I learned what is available to me on the Internet for the classes. I found that the Internet has many fun and educational activities to offer. Since the Internet is so addictive, I am always around a computer. Therefore, I have gotten much more familiar with them. During the week of classes I learned more about computers and what they can provide.

The Internet has everything from an encyclopedia to your mail address. I received information on the African sleeping sickness in the encyclopedia. It is a disease I had to research. The pictures were helpful because I could see the picture that the text was trying to describe.

After experiencing the Internet, I was able to type about twenty words a minute, instead of only twelve. I was making progress every day. Now, I am more familiar with the computer. I am able to look up programs and documents faster and easier.

At school our computers are logged onto Netscape. When I was on the Internet at school, I had two addresses to look up for the teacher to find information on the Republican party. First, I went on to CNN's home page. There were articles on world conflict. Then I went into the *New York Times'* home page. I was in the sports section, but Mrs. Murray told me to go into the local section. It was about the primary, and it gave me information on the Republican party.

Through all of the classes, I have learned that the Internet is a very good learning tool. When you are online you can look up different home pages or talk to people in Chicago. The Internet has helped me accomplish my goal to be able to type faster. There are literally millions of addresses so it never gets boring and there are new ones being added every hour. The Internet is a great advance in our technology. I would recommend the Internet to anyone who asked.

Mary Ellen Scribner
Westwood High School
Round Rock Independent School District
12400 Mellow Meadow Drive
Austin, TX 78750–1824
(512) 464–4033
Fax (512) 464–4020

Westwood High School opened in 1981 as the second high school in the Round Rock Independent School District (ISD), a community located on the north edge of Austin, the state capital. Today Westwood is one of three high schools, six middle schools, and twenty-one elementary schools serving the district's approximately 25,000 students. Such rapid growth has required that much of the district's capital outlay go to the construction of new buildings and that personnel costs consume most of the other available monies. Thus, less than adequate funding has been available for the planning, implementation, and utilization of technology.

Westwood is located in a middle-class suburban area and serves 1,900 students in grades nine through twelve. The racial/ethnic composition of the student body is 85 percent white (not Hispanic), 7 percent Hispanic, 3 percent African American, 5 percent Asian or Pacific islander, and less than 1 percent Native American. Many parents of Westwood students are employed by high tech firms or institutions of higher education located in the area and have very high expectations of the schools that their children attend. This year efforts to meet these expectations led to Westwood being named a Blue Ribbon School by the U.S. Department of Education and being named one of the top 155 public high schools in the United States and one of sixty-three cited for overall excellence by *Redbook*'s fifth annual America's Best Schools project. These efforts have relied on making the best use of available technology resources as well as finding different ways to acquire new or additional technology.

The library media center (LMC) acquired its first computers in 1983, two Apple IIe's! One of the computers was placed in the LMC workroom and was used primarily by the staff to print bibliographies, overdue notices, catalog cards, and so forth. The other computer was made available in the LMC for faculty and student use, mostly for word processing. Eventually, a few software programs were acquired that students could use to review or sharpen their foreign language skills, create puzzles, and so forth.

In 1984 we acquired a stand-alone CD-ROM station to run the SIRS (Social Issues Resources Series), which was a favorite library resource but which had overwhelmed us in paper format. Partial funding for each of these acquisitions was provided by Austin Community College, which used our LMC on a limited basis for some instructional support.

After much research and lobbying by the director of District Media Services and the library media specialists, Round Rock ISD administrators agreed in 1988 to fund automated circulation for the high school libraries. Follett Software Company's Circulation Plus was selected as the system to be used. At Westwood a plan was developed to accomplish this during the summer vacation so that no service time would be lost through either closing the library for a period of time or doing the work "on the fly," which we thought would slow service and which would probably result in an inferior database as well. The two library media specialists, assisted by two students hired on an hourly basis, worked through the summer to bar code and enter each book and piece of audiovisual software into the database. A 3-M Tattle Tape security system was installed at the same time, and members of the National Honor Society inserted the security strips in the books as a service project.

In early 1993 I served on the Library Technology Task Force, which prepared a report entitled "Accessing the Past, Present, and Future: Technology in the Round Rock ISD Library Media Centers." This report focused on the school library media program's attempt to meet specific objectives adapted from the American Association of School Libraries, *Information Power: National Guidelines for School Library Media Programs* (American Association of School Libraries 1988):

to provide intellectual access to information through systematic learning activities at all grade levels and in all curriculum areas

to provide physical access to information through (a) a carefully selected and systematically organized collection of diverse learning resources; (b) access to information and materials outside the library media center and school building; and (c) instruction in the operating of equipment necessary to use the information in any format.

to provide learning experiences that encourage users to become discriminating consumers and skilled creators of information

to provide leadership, instruction, and consulting assistance in the use of instructional and information technology and the use of sound instructional design principles

to provide resources and activities that contribute to lifelong learning while accommodating a wide range of differences in teaching and learning styles and in instructional methods and interests

to provide a facility that functions as the information center of the campus

to provide resources and learning activities that represent a diversity of experiences, opinions, social and cultural perspectives, supporting the concept that intellectual freedom and access to information are prerequisite to effective and responsible citizenship in a democracy

Technology needs were identified in the areas of automation, resource sharing, telecommunications, and information processing. Concerning library automation, the task force wrote:

As numerous educational paradigms shift or are reshaped, an imperative for automating the school library media center emerges from the realization that these libraries are rapidly being changed from storehouses of knowledge into centers for managing communications and information for the students and the staff. In order for students and staff to effectively access and process the information needed to interact responsibly with each other and society, local area information networks utilizing electronic access to library records and CD-ROM technology are essential.

The district administration and board of education adopted a plan to automate the library media centers from the high schools down over a period of five years.

At Westwood we sought additional monies from campus funds and, once again, from Austin Community College. As we had done when circulation was automated, we also looked for ways to make the available funding go further. We chose to do as much of the retrospective cataloging as we could possibly do ourselves and used the money allocated for that purpose to purchase an additional CD-ROM tower. We now have a network of twelve IBM student stations, three printers, and the circulation desk computer. In addition to the online catalog, the following databases are available on the library network: *World Book*'s Information Finder; UMI Resource One; SIRS Renaissance; Monarch Notes; Time Almanac; College Bluebook; Energy; Granger's Guide to Poetry; and CD Newsbank. The old NewsBank hardware is being retired, and the former SIRS stand-alone station is used to access single-user programs: The Presidents; Mammals; Picture Atlas of the World; American Journey 1945–1986; Statistical Abstract of the United States; Endangered and Threatened Species; and History of the World.

A task force composed of the director of District Media Services and four library media specialists (of which I am one) has just completed a grant application for $170,000 of funds designated by the Seventy-fourth Texas Legislature for Projects for Educational Technology. The receipt of these funds would allow the implementation of a plan that focuses on achieving three major objectives during the period of the grant:

- providing twenty-four–hour remote access to electronic library resources for high school students and staff
- providing access to traditional and electronic library resources for unserved high school students and staff on remote campuses during the regular school day
- providing a mechanism for the location and sharing of both traditional and electronic resources housed in the high school libraries among all district campuses

Grant funding would provide for the purchase and the installation of communication servers, software, telecommunication lines, and facsimile machines. Students and staff would be able to remotely connect to the three high school libraries' local area networks on which reside online catalogs of the libraries' resources and an array of CD-ROM databases. Laptop computers equipped with modems, communications software, and word-processing software would be made available for check out at the three high school libraries to allow students and staff who do not have access to computers at home to participate. Facsimile machines would allow for physical document delivery to remote campuses as well as to the middle and elementary schools within each high school's area.

During the 1992–1993 school year I became frustrated by unsuccessful efforts to get adequate word-processing capability for students and staff in the LMC. I was also concerned that a Macintosh writing lab located in the English Department was not being effectively used or adequately supervised. I proposed to the new campus principal that she relocate the Macintosh lab to the accounting classroom, which was separated from the

LMC by only a locked door and put it under the supervision of the LMC staff. Within two weeks, another classroom had been found for accounting, the door had been unlocked, and the Macintosh computers had been relocated to the newly vacated accounting classroom. And we were interviewing for a technology center coordinator because the principal very wisely realized that the LMC staff could not do it all by themselves! The writing lab quickly became a multipurpose technology center; the door between the LMC and the technology center is seldom closed as students and staff go back and forth between the two very complementary facilities accessing, synthesizing, and processing information.

Goals and guiding principles for the library media center itself have evolved over the years just as the whole Library Media Program has evolved from a collection of mostly print materials, a few filmstrips, and 16mm films circulated by the Regional Service Center to an online catalog of 22,000 volumes, networked CD-ROM databases, computer programs, laser disks, and videocassettes. Presently, the goals of the Westwood High School LMC state that students will:

- develop the habits of lifelong reading and lifelong learning
- demonstrate their ability to locate, identify, and select resources using a variety of media
- demonstrate their ability to apply reference and research skills in retrieving ideas and information from a variety of resources, including electronic databases and other emerging information technologies
- demonstrate their ability to use higher-order thinking to evaluate, organize, analyze, and synthesize information and ideas for both problem solving and decision making
- recognize that the school library media center is an integral part of a global information network

Just as site-based decision making has given the entire faculty and staff a voice in over-all campus management, full participation of the senior library media specialist in the staff leadership team has provided the vehicle for cross-curricular and collaborative planning and practice. *The Big Six Guide to Information Problem-Solving* developed by Michael B. Eisenberg and Robert Berkowitz is the model for much of this collaborative effort. Both library media specialists and several lead teachers have received extensive staff development in the Big Six model, which is outlined as follows:

1. Task Definition:
   - Define the problem
   - Identify the information needed

2. Information Seeking Strategies:
   - Brainstorm all possible sources
   - Select the best sources
3. Location and Access:
   - Locate sources (intellectually/physically)
   - Find information within sources
4. Use of Information:
   - Engage (e.g., read, hear, view)
   - Extract relevant information
5. Synthesis:
   - Organize information from multiple sources
   - Present the result
6. Evaluation:
   - Judge the result (effectiveness)
   - Judge the process (efficiency)

The Big Six model is most effective when lesson plans for LMC visits are the result of joint planning by the teacher and the library media specialist. With this in mind, the two library media specialists have assigned themselves responsibilities for consulting with classroom teachers along departmental lines, based on their interests and areas of expertise. One works with the English Department, and the other works with the Science and Math Departments. Both, however, work with the Social Studies Department due to its heavy and varied use of the LMC. This collaborative approach has been especially important in meeting the new challenge of creating learning opportunities and project assignments that make valid use of the CD-ROM databases and reasonable use of the printer without arbitrarily limiting what or how much a student can print.

To further update our LMC programs to reflect the steadily increasing available technology, we are presently developing a sequential set of benchmarks. A library media specialist from each of the other two high schools worked with me to propose the following eleventh and twelfth grade benchmarks:

The library should play a key role in developing student information literacy and should help students make the transition from high school to college or the workplace by making sure students have a thorough knowledge of how to access and retrieve information from network or online sources.

By grades eleven and twelve students should have developed basic information skills of access, selection, evaluation, application, and synthesis. In the final two years of high school, students should develop competency in the independent use of materials:

Students will be able to access network or online databases independently, using on-screen instructions.

Students will become highly competent in Boolean searching strategies.

Students will be able to determine whether or not materials are appropriate for their use based on the assignment parameters and available information, not limiting materials to those physically available in the library.

Students will be knowledgeable in the use of interactive technologies, access to the Internet, and distance learning.

Students will be knowledgeable about systems of information classification and subject headings. College-bound students, in particular, should become aware of Library of Congress classification.

The Texas Education Network, or TENET as it is known by Texas educators, was authorized through the leadership of the Seventy-first Texas Legislature and developed by the collaborative efforts of the Department of Information Resources, the Texas Education Agency, and the University of Texas. TENET fosters innovation and educational excellence across the state through a transparent communications infrastructure that enables educators to move information across the barriers of time and space. For the unbelievably low cost $5.00 per year, every educator in the state can have this access. In Round Rock ISD, a Train-the-Trainer program has been developed that provides training through staff development to enable one person on each campus to be regularly updated and trained to teach others on the home campus. I am the trainer for the Westwood High School faculty and have succeeded in getting about 75 percent of our staff on TENET. I have created handouts for two staff development workshops, which I periodically present to faculty and staff: "Managing Your Tenet E-Mail" and "Accessing the Tenet World Wide Web Server Using Lynx." I am also one of twenty-five Round Rock ISD educators piloting SLIP accounts for TENET with the expectation that all TENET accounts will be upgraded to SLIP accounts within a year's time.

In the LMC we use TENET to assist teachers in a number of ways. For example, the Texas Education Agency has just released TEKS (Texas Essential Knowledge and Skills) in all content areas, and we either provided instructions and assistance for downloading or actually downloaded these files for each department. We were able to do this first in the draft stage and then the final versions. Each library media specialist monitors several listservs for the benefit of the entire staff. As Westwood has completed the application process and been accepted into the International Baccalaureate program, I have been able to get questions answered and collect information, ideas, and suggestions from the IBM listserv. These printouts are collected in a notebook that is kept in the library for teachers to review.

Access to the Internet is presently available on only two "communication stations" in the LMC, which limits student access to advanced students or special projects. We are presently working on two proposals to extend Internet access to all students on a more equitable basis. Developing an Acceptable Use Policy that is acceptable and applicable districtwide has become a major stumbling block, but we are working that out even as we seek funding to transform our communication stations into a communications lab. A pilot "senior thesis" class this year has used the LMC Internet access extensively to obtain primary source material from around the world. The teacher and I have guided these seniors onto the Internet to search out information or to search the University of Texas catalog, and we have also served as the conduit for international e-mail. On numerous occasions I have been startled to find in my e-mailbox messages in Spanish from the rebels hiding in the jungles of Chiapas! If our current proposals are funded, we will have a lab of ten to fifteen access stations next year and will be utilizing the Internet in more and more areas of the curriculum. Collaboration and communication with our feeder schools have been enhanced by the use of TENET; for example, high school science classes have answered questions posed by elementary students at our feeder schools via TENET. This year the student members of Amnesty International for which I serve as faculty advisor has received its biweekly Urgent Action Network alerts via e-mail.

The main challenges to developing an outstanding technology program are, of course, funding, and finding the time to focus on technology along with the myriad of other responsibilities that seem to be constantly added to the library media specialist job description. Getting a strong infrastructure and a viable training program established are the keys to any future successful implementation and utilization of technology.

Lynn McCree
Martin Junior High School
1601 Haskell
Austin, TX 78702–5412
(512) 476–5436
Fax (512) 320–0125
e-mail: lmcc@tenet.edu

A CD-ROMANCE

"Martin Junior High School has an advanced computer technology lab program with an Apple Macintosh Writing Lab available to all students, a Macintosh Mathematics lab, eight Macintosh computers and six LCD units for instructional use in the classroom, as well as IBM computer and software for our . . . English yearbook layout.

The Scholastic Process Writer, used in our Writing Lab, is a collection of tools and activities that assists students with the writing process. This program helps students discover and organize what they have to say about a topic as well as facilitates effective and creative self-expression.

MacSile is a collaborative learning environment which encourages the development of independent and cooperative learning skills for students at all grade levels and across all subject areas. The Martin Junior High School mathematics students are using this environment to develop and share strategies for solving complex problems.

Daedalus is an integrated writing environment. It divides writing into three distinct phases: invention and pre-writing, composition, and revision. This system is being used by students to compare ideas and write story problems.

Through Daedalus, MacSile, and TENET, Martin Junior High School students are able to communicate, elaborate, and enhance their learning with students from other middle schools in the Austin area and the University of Texas.

The Martin library is one of the most progressive in Austin I.S.D. Our library CD-ROM Network System provides students and teachers access to the most current research information available for instruction and investigation" (Welcome to Martin Junior High School 1996).

It was during the summer of 1992 that I first realized what a boon the CD-ROM is for students who are book phobic. Martin was the host for middle school summer school that year, so students from all over the district who had failed descended on the library to do research.

I had one encyclopedia CD-ROM, and the lines began to form. The word quickly spread that all one had to do was find a subject, print it out, and highlight the interesting sections. All the bibliographic information was printed out with the information. The students and I were elated with this machine that would print out good-looking information on our subjects. Getting a source of information was so easy that the students kept right at it and finished their papers for the first time in their lives.

For most of these students, research in the past had consisted of one discouraging step after another: trying to find the right volume of the encyclopedia, trying to take notes, trying to get the paper organized. Now in one step, they were halfway there. Naturally, we had to explain to a few that they were not all the way there—that there is a difference between a printout and a student's report! Actually, although plagiarism is discussed often on the Net, we have not been troubled greatly.

After the students had their printouts, I passed out markers for them to highlight important and interesting information. Since they had such neat notes, complete with the source listed, they began to realize they could do research. Having made such a good beginning, they rapidly found two more sources and wrote their first research papers.

I have heard tales of students printing out reams of unwanted paper, turning in information as reports, and so forth. This has not happened thus far at Martin. My library aides and I suggest to the user what a reasonable amount of printing would be and show them how to limit it. I have also found that every student in school can use the CD-ROM effectively: gifted and talented, honors, special education—every student. One of my best student aides was from special education.

We were all proud, and I quickly realized that I needed to make CD-ROMs accessible to everyone. I needed a CD-ROM network where students could use a CD-ROM simultaneously—if a class was studying poetry they all needed poetry. From the time of the first tentative planning (since this was cutting edge in 1992), we realized the need for CD-ROM networking. That fall we installed a CD-ROM server that now has seven CD-ROM drives. They are connected to six workstations located in the library and in the social studies classes. Research at Martin is easy and fun.

CD-ROMs are so easy to use that no teacher in-service is needed. They fit in with all the other reference sources easily. Some of our CD-ROM titles include *World Book*'s Information Finder, Encarta, Magazine Index (Information Access), Discovering Authors by Gale Research, Granger's Poetry, SIRS (which is used in science and for social issues), Microsoft Bookshelf, and Musical Instruments. I have never felt that books and electronic sources of information were mutually exclusive. Both are used as needed.

The CD-ROM network area has been a source of pride for our school. We purchased it with money from the PTA, the Governor's Performance Award, and district money that was given to us after an instructional audit revealed that our small population (550 seventh through ninth graders) prevented us from buying some of the technology other schools had. We use the network every period for every research project. We have even used it as a recruiting tool, which is the project I am going to describe. Although some may find doing research a strange activity to use for recruitment, it fits in with our belief that learning is so much fun that it may become a lifelong activity.

"The sixth-grade teachers in our feeder schools were invited to bring their classes to Martin to do research using the Marshall Cavendish Cultures of the World series and the Microsoft CD-ROM Musical Instruments. While some of the students were working on mouse practice in the MAC writing lab across the hall, others were using the books and the CD-ROM in the library. The Martin visitors were assigned a seventh-grade buddy to help them to feel more at home. Together the teams work on a short data retrieval project that involves using the computer and other library resources" (Mgebroff 1995).

The subject matter was chosen because the sixth graders study world history throughout the year. It also emphasizes one of our main goals: "to produce citizens who accept the diversity of today's world and who willingly develop positive attitudes toward different cultural, racial, ethnic, religious and gender groups." A copy of the activity follows.

Austin is completing a fiber optic system. When we become connected, we will have direct access to the Internet. At that time I expect students to use it regularly for research. The eighth-grade English classes study the Holocaust, and we did journey to Jerusalem One to gather information. We hope to be able to interview survivors on the Internet. I use it daily to brainstorm with other people in my field on several listservs and I forward interesting-sounding projects to the appropriate teachers. Our teachers are being trained, for the most part, by the Educational Service Center. I simply help them get started on a one-to-one basis.

In addition to the Internet, we hope to expand the multimedia reports done by students. In our writing lab we use a scanner, and we plan to add HyperStudio. In our media-journalism class we plan to produce a multimedia Martin news show. We are in the process of becoming a multi-intelligence academy, so we are excited about making alternative ways of communicating available to students.

I have been a librarian for twenty-five years, and I think these are exciting and interesting times that we live in. The technology has been a real asset to the library and the students!

LESSON PLAN: CULTURES OF THE WORLD

Martin Jr. High

Country:

Student:

Teacher:

Using Cultures of the World or the Infopedia, describe in your own words two interesting things you learn about:

CULTURES OF THE WORLD

Arts

    1.

    2.

Leisure

    1.

    2.

Festivals

    1.

    2.

Food

    1.

    2.

Music: find the musical instruments mentioned in the book. Using the CD-ROM Musical Instruments, listen to them and print a picture of your favorite instrument from that country.

Dr. Ron C. Rescigno, Superintendent
Hueneme School District
205 North Ventura Road
Port Hueneme, CA 93041
(805) 488-3588
Fax (805) 986-8755

Dr. Rescigno testified before the Subcommittee on Telecommunications and Finance:

The Hueneme School District is a community of racial, language and economic diversity characteristic of Southern California. Using interactive network technology we changed the basic culture of several of our public schools by focusing on (1) the organization and management of public school education; (2) curriculum; and (3) student achievement. The District evolved through various stages of information transformation starting with the development of Smart Classrooms, i.e., computer managed multi-media classroom environments. We graduated from local area networks to wide area networks and ultimately to worldwide networks. Students are achieving far beyond their peers in similar communities in California at levels that foreshadow success in the highly competitive information age.

Twelve years ago, students in the Hueneme School District scored right in the middle in such subjects as math, reading science, and history compared to similar schools and districts in the state of California. Today, average student test scores in this K–8 district near Santa Barbara have risen to above the eightieth percentile. Perhaps even more impressive, though, academic researchers using the Cornell Critical Thinking Test have found that average student critical-thinking abilities have risen from the fortieth percentile to the eightieth percentile when measured against their peers.

As with most social change, pinpointing the source of these dramatic improvements is a difficult thing to do. But the teachers and parents in the Hueneme District attribute the difference at least in part to the fact that the last twelve years have been marked by a substantial investment in educational technology, including computers, networking, and teacher training. Today, the Hueneme School District has one of the most innovative technology infrastructures in the nation, as well as a carefully crafted program for integrating technology into curricula as varied as science and history.

With nearly one computer per student distributed across classrooms and libraries, and TV monitors and video equipment in every room, Hueneme schools are well equipped on the technology front. But the teachers and the administrators have gone another important step forward by literally redesigning the physical layout of their classrooms to make optimum use of the technology and maximize teacher-student interactions. In Hueneme's "smart classrooms" students no longer sit in rows behind desks and listen passively to lectures. Instead, computers and video monitors have been integrated into "learning pods" in which students work together, facing each other.

This dynamic learning is made possible by a number of networks that link schools in the district to each other and to the Internet and other national networks. All eleven schools, the district office, and maintenance facilities have local area networks that are linked to the Hueneme Wide Area Network (HWAN), which, in turn, is linked to the Internet. Cable linkages, provided by the local cable company, Jones Intercable, Inc., connect all district classrooms, enabling videoconferencing lessons across the district. And one school, Blackstock Junior High School—a state of California Model Technology school site—also has an advanced fiber optic local area school network, which will be replicated in other district schools within the next twelve months. This junior high is also connected to a national, wide area network that includes several schools from other states and the MCI laboratory in Richardson, Texas.

For Hueneme students, technology and connectivity provide an exciting learning environment in which they can master educational basics while learning skills that prepare them for the future. At Blackstock Junior High, for example, each day begins with a live schoolwide video broadcast of the day's events that is scripted, produced, recorded, and transmitted over the internal video network by the students. With the touch of a button, students in a social studies class bring geography to life with digitized terrain maps, recordings of national anthems, and video clips of life and culture in other nations. Science students can watch and tinker with computerized physics experiments—for example, simulated stress testing of student-designed surfaces—that would be otherwise virtually impossible to carry out. A direct connection to the Lawrence Livermore Laboratory Cray computers allows students to review alternative strategies for solving complex math and science projects.

The dramatically changed learning environments in Hueneme did not appear overnight. Rather, they are the product of years of experimentation and trial. The district started out twelve years ago with one computer lab in a single school. Classroom use of computers began after one teacher agreed to spend a semester designing a science classroom with individual computer stations set up to teach different science concepts—the smart classroom was born. Since then, teachers have designed rooms for other subjects, ranging from math to English to social studies, and have utilized "time away from instruction" to design new curricula that take advantage of the new learning environments.

"We gave six teachers a full year off from classroom teaching to think through the technology and connectivity they wanted, the physical layout of the classrooms, and the ways in which they could integrate technology into their courses," explained Dr. Ron Rescigno, district superintendent. "They were encouraged to attend conferences and to network with other teachers and professionals associated with technology. Obviously, we still provide real-time support to our teachers and special technology courses on an ongoing basis, but the ability of these six teachers to completely focus on creating their own technology environments has made a huge difference. Talk to any one of those teachers or their students—they are delighted." In 1995, the twelfth-generation smart classroom design of learning pods and videoconferencing capability was unveiled for student use.

None of the benefits engendered by technology and connectivity in the Hueneme District would have been possible without the combined support of the district administration, school board, parents, and community leaders. Rescigno has provided vision, leadership, and moral support to the critical agents of change, the teachers. "We have a clear focus on technology," he said. "The key is to keep experimenting—pushing the envelope—and then integrate what you learn into the next deployment of technology. Teachers here know they are taking risks when they use educational technology, but they know they have the support of the district. I don't think we are anywhere near to having perfected classroom use of technology. I do not know if we will ever perfect it. There will always be new developments to consider."

THE ELEVENTH-GENERATION SMART CLASSROOM

At Hueneme, the stimulus is toward learning networks, unlike traditional schools. This learning system is supported by funding from grants, the private sector, and with work with the university. The learning network is flexible and dynamic. This superintendent understands the power of technology, the role of the teachers, and the need for curriculum development, teacher training, and classroom design. In regards to the students, especially the high-risk population that predominates throughout the district, technology has moved from computer-assisted instruction to integrative learning in the twelve years of access.

Emphasis is on student interaction and written communication. Operating under the premise that students will use computers to analyze data rather than perform drills of basic facts, critical-thinking skills have improved and achievement has increased. Students use software to manipulate text, graphics, and video images in ways that promote exploration and discovery.

The eleventh-generation smart classroom resembles the computer design of the Levy Library at the University of Southern California. At the Levy Library a similar hexagonal cluster is designed with panels on either side of the student's computer area to provide privacy. The round conference table can accommodate collaborative learning with two or three students at each computer station because the desk surface is large enough. At the Levy Library all the stations are networked to the Internet and provide access to CD-ROMs and software.

At Hueneme the structure is maximized for collaborative learning. There are no panels to separate the students. The computers are also networked to software, CD-ROMs, and the Internet. A description follows from the brochure entitled "Prototype 11th Generation Smart Classroom—Math":

The Smart Classroom infrastructure provides the capacity and the connectivity for all data, voice and video applications to be delivered to the learner in a seamless and interlocking fashion. . . . The functional guidelines for the "Math Smart Classroom" are generated to mask the physical contact between each individual, groups of students and the teacher. The design emphasizes the importance of human dynamics by creating a five-workstation cluster design (i.e., turtles) with each work station resembling a conference table for six students. One of the major learning of this turtle environment is to have six students working in a collaborative mode as they interact with one another and through computer simulated activities. Each turtle has one chair that is designated as the "captain chair" and provides the human and the technology leadership for problem solving. The computers are suppressed and located within the desks. They do not take away from classroom discussions or intrude on other classroom activities when the students are not using them.

The teacher workstation sits on a platform and includes a monitor, CPU, a color printer, and a color scanner beneath the desktop. The teacher workstation is designed to give the teacher eye contact with all students and provides for a spectrum of devices and tools. The teacher workstation will control an overhead projection system mounted into the ceiling with a motorized screen to be used for large groups and direct instructional strategies as well as a large series 80 35 inch ProScan television. All analog multi-media equipment will be housed in the teacher station, as well as the student-teacher instructional feedback network.

The Smart Classroom has two video cameras with connectors to the Jones INET system (interactive distance learning). One camera and lens is dedicated to each turtle and works off of the five remote microphones located at each turtle. A second camera and lens is dedicated to the teacher and is controlled from a portable wireless mike attached to the teacher. A 7 bay CD-ROM tower is also connected to the classroom.

JONES INTERCABLE, INC.

The partnership with Jones Intercable, Inc., has provided the system with point-to-point and point-to-multipoint transmission connecting schools and classrooms. Real-time video, audio, and data are delivered to students and teachers. This interactive multiple-direction system is being used to create the "virtual" classroom. This includes live interaction with computer simulations between and among remote classroom sites; live class debates between and among students from different school locations; teacher staff development with scholar experts; student articulation between schools; online transmission of top news stories of the week; and live information on national and international weather.

SCHOOLS—CONNECTED

The latest venture includes a partnership between MCI and Pyramid Technologies, working to create a new concept of education delivery and services: Hueneme, Berryessa, in San Jose, California, and the Savannah-Chatham County schools in Georgia are involved in a demonstration project to study and implement distance learning utilizing the following components:

- distance instruction/teleconferencing
- video on demand
- interactive multimedia classes

Student achievement was evaluated by the University of Southern California and results showed a strong positive improvement from 1984 levels and levels in comparable California districts. The United States Department of Education recognized the district as a National A+ District for Breaking the Mold.

STANFORD'S MEYER LIBRARY—THE FLEXIBLE CLASSROOM

One of the most flexible designs for a classroom/library computer lab is located at Meyer Library at Stanford University. I am including this in the book because it can easily be replicated as a state-of-the-art library classroom at any level. Meyer Library is the media and technology center. There is a traditional teaching computer lab where the desks are in rows with computers on the desktops. Students peer from behind the computers to the large projection screen at the front of the classroom. Teachers and librarians had designed the room but were frustrated by the lack of flexibility and creativity in the teaching situation. Students can easily lose interest in the lecture or presentation and begin exploring with the computers before them.

The staff of the Stanford University Libraries/Academic Information Resources Group raised the following concerns in 1994:

Such a facility encourages illustrated lectures and individual work with the computers, and discourages other forms of teaching that occur quite frequently in most colleges and universities, such as discussions, class projects, and work in small groups. Could a computer teaching facility be designed to support a wider range of teaching styles, especially these more dynamic and social ones?

This structured, rigid computer design did not lend itself to using multimedia in a collaborative learning situation. The library's technology specialists formed a committee composed of teachers, librarians, and students to research, design, test, and then implement the best design for an instructional technology classroom. A prototype lab operated in Sweet Hall during the 1994–1995 academic year. Charles Kerns from the library and the Curriculum Development Lab and Dr. Decker Walker, a professor in the School of Education with graduate education students, conducted a study and wrote a report that outlined the physical and technical specifications for the new lab. The report included the affect that the flexible teaching lab would have on different teaching styles. Kerns stated: "We designed a room for innovative teaching and learning in which computers play an important role. We did not design a room full of computers in which, by the way, you can teach."

Flexible Class Lab

The room is designed to be portable and flexible and to accommodate varying pedagogical styles. The use and configuration of the room is set up to support the instructional and learning needs of the teacher and the students. How is this possible? Network and electrical connections are located on the floor, which is comfortably carpeted. As many as six stations can be accommodated in the area of one outlet. Rainbow-colored bean bag chairs can be arranged in any formation. Triangular tables can be combined in circles, hexagons, and in a variety of other shapes to encourage group thinking and collaboration.

The large closet within the room stores the file servers and portable computers, which can be wheeled out on a cart. The students can use the Macintosh 540 laptop computers and connect them to the wired network through the floor connections arranged in abundance throughout the room. The modular tables and chairs can be configured in any number of ways or not used. A teaching station is also portable and on a cart. It consists of digital video recording and playback with a connection to the file servers and SUNet, a digital scanner and a printer. The back-lit projection system allows the blinds to be opened when students are viewing the projection screen. This allows the sunshine and the beauty of the outdoors to come in and does not create the dark atmosphere that most projection screens require for proper viewing. The projection system can switch from a video system to a computer system in milliseconds. Noise has been eliminated and lighting zones help control the atmosphere needed for creative classroom thought.

Figure 7.1
The Flexible Classroom, Meyer Library

Instruction

The modular, comfortable room does not make one feel as if he or she is in a sterile, technical environment. One of the teachers, Marjorie Ford, a lecturer in Writing and Critical Thinking, uses the room because it encourages communication, ad hoc collaboration, and openness in an informal atmosphere. Electronic mail is facilitated through the networks and provides for more accessibility with her students. Her freshman course, Writing for Change, stimulates a community of writers with audience and society as the central issues. The students are easily engaged in writing in this environment.

Professor John Barson of the French Department also prefers this environment. His students are engaged in project-oriented, student-driven methods, and the flexible classroom serves them well. It fosters multimedia project development, incorporating images, text, and voice-overs and using the software program he designed called Stay Tooned. The classroom fosters spontaneity.

Interestingly, faculty have to write a proposal to be scheduled to use the flexible lab. The learning has to incorporate creativity, innovation, and multimedia in order to be acceptable for use. The Curriculum Development Lab staff will assist the faculty in developing curriculum proposals utilizing the multimedia technologies to promote and increase student thinking and learning ("Flexible class-lab" 1996).

It is an interesting concept and one that might work very well for all groups of students, including those with special needs and average abilities. However, the groups should not be too large. There is an intimacy, comfort, collaborative environment that could be lost in chaos if the group is too large and unfocused. The report, provided at http://www-leland. stanford.edu/group/CDL/report.html, discusses the importance of technical support, preplanning, and teacher training. If this concept can work for you in your situation or has strong potential, I strongly recommend reading the report and reflecting on the substance, comparing it with your needs, financial resources, and library/class/flexible scheduling.

Epilogue

Reflect on the research presented, the changing landscape in educational opportunity, information resources, and the twenty-first–century workplace. I hope that the need to develop an active-learning and critical-thinking environment will manifest itself in your library media center. In partnerships with your faculty through the use of educational technology in the curriculum, create a stimulating environment for the at-risk learner, encouraging him or her to succeed and surpass your expectations. I have observed students who were considered average, special needs, or below average, soar.

I believe it is our responsibility and our legacy to increase the literacy levels of all students in a dynamic, active hands-on environment. The research indicates educational technology, inquiry learning, and information literacy integrated within the curriculum increase student achievement. Reach out and contact the successful library media specialists and schools for more information. Contact NASA for involvement in their ongoing educational opportunities.

I leave with a quote from Lynn McCree, "I have been a librarian for twenty-five years, and I think these are exciting and interesting times that we live in. The technology has been a real asset to the library and the students!"

Appendix A:
Computer Skills for Information Problem Solving: Learning and Teaching Technology in Context

Michael B. Eisenberg and Doug Johnson

This curriculum guide is an excerpt from "Computer Skills for Information Problem Solving: Learning and Teaching Technology in Context," *ERIC Digest* (March 1996), prepared by Michael B. Eisenberg and Doug Johnson for the ERIC Clearinghouse on Information & Technology, Syracuse, N.Y. (ED number pending, IR 055 809). All intext citations for Appendix A can be found in the References and Suggested Reading section at the end of Appendix A. Asterisked (*) items are specific to Internet use.

There seems to be clear and widespread agreement among the public and educators that students need to be proficient computer users—students need to be "computer literate." However, while districts are spending a great deal of money on technology, there seems to be only a vague notion of what computer literacy really means.

* Can the student who operates a computer well enough to play Doom be considered computer literate?
* Will a student who has used computers in school only for running tutorials or an integrated learning system have the skills necessary to survive in our society?
* Will the ability to do basic word processing be sufficient for students entering the workplace or post-secondary education?

Clearly not. In too many schools, most teachers and students still use computers only as the equivalent of expensive flash cards or electronic worksheets. The productivity side of computer use in the general content area curriculum is neglected or grossly underdeveloped (Moursund, 1995).

There are, however, some encouraging signs concerning computers and technology in education. For example, it is becoming increasingly popular for educational technologists to advocate integrating computers into the content areas. Teachers and administrators are recognizing that computer skills should not be taught in isolation, and that separate "computer classes" do not really help students learn to apply computer skills in meaningful ways. This is an important shift in approach and emphasis. And it's a shift with which library media specialists have a great deal of familiarity.

Library media specialists know that moving from isolated skills instruction to an integrated approach is an important step that takes a great deal of planning and effort. Over the past 20 years, library media professionals have worked hard to move from teaching isolated "library skills" to teaching integrated information skills. Effective integration of information skills has two requirements:

1. the skills must directly relate to the content area curriculum and to classroom assignments, and
2. the skills themselves need to be tied together in a logical and systematic information process model.

Schools seeking to move from isolated computer skills instruction will also need to focus on both of these requirements. Successful integrated information skills programs are designed around collaborative projects jointly planned and taught by teachers and library media professionals. Computer skills instruction can follow the same approach. Library media specialists, computer teachers, and classroom teachers need to work together to develop units and lessons that will include . . . computer skills, general information skills, and content-area curriculum outcomes.

A meaningful, unified computer literacy curriculum must be more than "laundry lists" of isolated skills, such as:

* knowing the parts of the computer
* writing drafts and final products with a word processor
* searching for information using a CD-ROM database

While these specific skills are certainly important for students to learn, the "laundry list" approach does not provide an adequate model for students to transfer and apply skills from situation to situation. These curricula address the "how" of computer use, but rarely the "when" or "why." Students may learn isolated skills and tools, but they will still lack an understanding of how those various skills fit together to solve problems and complete tasks. Students need to be able to use computers flexibly, creatively and purposefully. All learners should be able to recognize what they need to accomplish, determine whether a computer will help them to do so, and then be able to use the computer as part of the process of accomplishing their task. Individual computer skills take on a new meaning when they are integrated within this type of information problem-solving process, and students develop true "computer literacy" because they have genuinely applied various computer skills as part of the learning process.

The curriculum outlined below, "Computer Skills for Information Problem-Solving," demonstrates how computer literacy skills can fit within an information literacy skills context (American Association of School Librarians 1995). The baseline information literacy context is the Big Six Skills process (see . . . Eisenberg and Berkowitz cites). The various computer skills are adapted from curricula developed by the state of Minnesota (Minnesota Department of Education 1989) and the Mankato Area Public Schools (Mankato Schools Information Literacy Curriculum Guideline). These basic computer skills are those which all students might reasonably be expected to authentically demonstrate before graduation. Since Internet-related skills are increasingly important for information problem-solving, they are included in this curriculum, and are noted by an asterisk.

Some computer literacy "skills" competencies which do not seem to fit into this information processing model, and which may or may not be important to have stated include:

* knowing the basic operation, terminology, and maintenance of equipment
* knowing how to use computer-assisted instructional programs
* having knowledge of the impact of technology on careers, society, and culture
* computer programming
* specialized computer applications like music composition software, computer assisted drawing and drafting programs, mathematics modeling software, etc.

Listing computer skills is only a first step in assuring all our children become proficient information and technology users. A teacher supported scope and sequence of skills, well designed projects, and effective assessments are also critical. Many library media specialists will need to hone their own technology skills in order to remain effective information skills teachers. But such a curriculum holds tremendous opportunities for library media specialists to become vital, indispensable staff members, and for all children to master the skills they will need to thrive in an information rich future.

Computer Skills for Information Problem-Solving: A Curriculum Based on the Big Six Skills Approach (copyright 1996 Michael B. Eisenberg, Doug Johnson, and Robert E. Berkowitz)

1. TASK DEFINITION

The first step in the information problem-solving process is to recognize that an information need exists, to define the problem, and to identify the types and amount of information needed. In terms of technology, students will be able to:

A. Use e-mail, and online discussion groups (e.g., listservs, newsgroups) on the Internet to communicate with teachers regarding assignments, tasks, and information-problems.*

B. Use e-mail, and online discussion groups (e.g., listservs, newsgroups) on the Internet to generate topics and problems and to facilitate cooperative activities among groups of students locally and globally.*

C. Use desktop conferencing, e-mail, and groupware software on local area networks to communicate with teachers regarding assignments, tasks, and information problems.

D. Use desktop conferencing, e-mail, and groupware software on local area networks to generate topics and problems and to facilitate cooperative activities among groups of students locally.

E. Use computer brainstorming or idea generating software to define or refine the information problem. This includes developing a research question or perspective on a topic.

2. INFORMATION SEEKING STRATEGIES

Once the information problem has been formulated, the student must consider all possible information sources and develop a plan for searching. Students will be able to:

A. Assess the value of various types of electronic resources for data gathering, including databases, CD-ROM resources, commercial and Internet online resources, electronic reference works, community and government information electronic resources.*

B. Identify and apply specific criteria for evaluating computerized electronic resources.

C. Assess the value of e-mail, and online discussion groups (e.g., listservs, newsgroups) on the Internet as part of a search of the current literature or in relation to the information task.

D. Use a computer to generate modifiable flow charts, Gantt charts, time lines, organizational charts, project plans, and calendars which will help the student plan and organize complex or group information problem-solving tasks.

3. LOCATION AND ACCESS

After students determine their priorities for information seeking, they must locate information from a variety of resources and access specific information found within individual resources. Students will be able to:

A. Locate and use appropriate computer resources and technologies available within the school library media center, including those on the library media center's local area network (e.g., online catalogs, periodical indexes, full-text sources, multimedia computer stations, CD-ROM stations, online terminals, scanners, digital cameras).

B. Locate and use appropriate computer resources and technologies available throughout the school including those available through local area networks (e.g., full-text resources, CD-ROMs, productivity software, scanners, digital cameras).

C. Locate and use appropriate computer resources and technologies available beyond the school through the Internet (e.g., newsgroups, listservs, WWW sites via Netscape, Lynx or another browser, gopher, ftp sites, online public access library catalogs, commercial databases and online services, other community, academic, and government resources).*

D. Know the roles and computer expertise of the people working in the school library media center and elsewhere who might provide information or assistance.

E. Use electronic reference materials (e.g., electronic encyclopedias, dictionaries, biographical reference sources, atlases, geographic databanks, thesauri, almanacs, fact books) available through local area networks, stand-alone workstations, commercial online vendors, or the Internet.

F. Use the Internet or commercial computer networks to contact experts and help and referral services.*

G. Conduct self-initiated electronic surveys conducted through e-mail, listservs, or newsgroups.*

H. Use organizational systems and tools specific to electronic information sources that assist in finding specific and general information (e.g., indexes, tables of contents, user's instructions and manuals, legends, boldface and italics, graphic clues and icons, cross-references, Boolean logic strategies, time lines, hypertext links, knowledge trees, URLs etc.) including the use of:
    1. search tools and commands for stand-alone, CD-ROM, and online databases and services (e.g., DIALOG commands, America Online, UMI, Mead);

2. search tools and commands for searching the Internet (e.g., Yahoo, Lycos, WebCrawler, Veronica, Archie).*

4. USE OF INFORMATION

After finding potentially useful resources, students must engage (read, view, listen) the information to determine its relevance and then extract the relevant information. Students will be able to:

A. Connect and operate the computer technology needed to access information, and read the guides and manuals associated with such tasks.
B. View, download, decompress and open documents and programs from Internet sites and archives.*
C. Cut and paste information from an electronic source into a personal document complete with proper citation.
D. Take notes and outline with a word processor or similar productivity program.
E. Record electronic sources of information and locations of those sources to properly cite and credit in footnotes, endnotes, and bibliographies.
F. Use electronic spreadsheets, databases, and statistical software to process and analyze statistical data.
G. Analyze and filter electronic information in relation to the task, rejecting non-relevant information.

5. SYNTHESIS

Students must organize and communicate the results of the information problem-solving effort. Students will be able to:

A. Classify and group information using a word processor, database or spreadsheet.
B. Use word processing and desktop publishing software to create printed documents, applying keyboard skills equivalent to at least twice the rate of handwriting speed.
C. Create and use computer-generated graphics and art in various print and electronic presentations.
D. Use electronic spreadsheet software to create original spreadsheets.
E. Generate charts, tables and graphs using electronic spreadsheets and other graphing programs.
F. Use database/file management software to create original databases.
G. Use presentation software (e.g., PowerPoint, HyperStudio, Aldus Persuasion) to create electronic slide shows and to generate overheads and slides.
H. Create hypermedia and multimedia productions with digital video and audio.

I. Create World Wide Web pages and sites using hypertext markup language (HTML).*

J. Use e-mail, ftp, and other telecommunications capabilities to share information, products, and files.*

K. Use specialized computer applications as appropriate for specific tasks, e.g., music composition software, computer assisted drawing and drafting programs, mathematics modeling software.

L. Properly cite and credit electronic sources of information in footnotes, endnotes, and bibliographies.

6. EVALUATION

Evaluation focuses on how well the final product meets the original task (effectiveness) and the process of how well students carried out the information problem-solving process (efficiency). Students may evaluate their own work and process or be evaluated by others (i.e., classmates, teachers, library media staff, parents). Students will be able to:

A. Evaluate electronic presentations in terms of both the content and format.

B. Use spell and grammar checking capabilities of word processing and other software to edit and revise their work.

C. Apply legal principles and ethical conduct related to information technology related to copyright and plagiarism.

D. Understand and abide by telecomputing etiquette when using e-mail, newsgroups, listservs and other Internet functions.*

E. Understand and abide by acceptable use policies in relation to use of the Internet and other electronic technologies.*

F. Use e-mail, and online discussion groups (e.g., listservs, newsgroups) on local area networks and the Internet to communicate with teachers and others regarding their performance on assignments, tasks, and information-problems.*

G. Use desktop conferencing, e-mail, and groupware software on local area networks to communicate with teachers and others regarding student performance on assignments, tasks, and information problems.

H. Thoughtfully reflect on the use of electronic resources and tools throughout the process.

ADDENDUM

Included here are skills and knowledge related to technology that are not part of the computer and information technology curriculum. These items should be learned in context, i.e., as students are working through various assignments and information problems using technology. Students will be able to:

A. Know and use basic computer terminology.

B. Operate various pieces of hardware and software—particularly operating systems—and be able to handle basic maintenance.

C. Understand the basics of computer programming. Specific courses in computer programming should be part of the school's curricular offerings.

D. Understand and articulate the relationship and impact of information technology on careers, society, culture, and their own lives.

Note: Permission is granted for educational use or reprint of all or parts of this curriculum as long as the authors are properly and prominently credited.

The Big Six Skills Approach
to Information Problem Solving
(copyright Eisenberg and Berkowitz, 1988)

The Big Six is an information literacy curriculum, an information problem-solving process, and a set of skills which provide a strategy for effectively and efficiently meeting information needs. The Big Six Skills approach can be used whenever students are in a situation, academic or personal, which requires information to solve a problem, make a decision or complete a task. This model is transferable to school, personal, and work applications, as well as all content areas and the full range of grade levels. When taught collaboratively with content area teachers in concert with content-area objectives, it serves to ensure that students are information literate.

THE BIG SIX

1. Task Definition
    1.1 Define the task (the information problem)
    1.2 Identify information needed in order to complete the task (to solve the information problem)

2. Information Seeking Strategies
    2.1 Brainstorm all possible sources
    2.2 Select the best sources

3. Location and Access
    3.1 Locate sources
    3.2 Find information within the source

4. Use of Information
    4.1 Engage in the source (read, hear, view, touch)

4.2 Extract relevant information

5. Synthesis

    5.1 Organize information from multiple sources

    5.2 Present the information

6. Evaluation

    6.1 Judge the process (efficiency)

    6.2 Judge the product (effectiveness)

REFERENCES AND SUGGESTED READING

American Association of School Librarians. (1995, November). Information literacy: A position paper on information problem solving. *Emergency Librarian, 23*(2), 20–23. (EJ number pending, IR 531 873). Also available from the American Association of School Librarians.

California Media and Library Educators Association Staff. (1993). *From library skills to information literacy: A handbook for the 21st century.* Englewood, Colo.: Libraries Unlimited, Inc. (ISBN: 0–931510–49–X)

Coulehan, J. L. (1995). Using electronic mail for a small-group curriculum in ethical and social issues. *Academic Medicine, 70*(2), 158–163. (EJ 499 651)

Doyle, C. S. (1994). *Information literacy in an information society: A concept for the information age.* Syracuse, N.Y.: ERIC Clearinghouse on Information & Technology. (ED 372 763)

Eisenberg, M. B., and Berkowitz, R. (1988). Curriculum initiative: An agenda and strategy for library media programs. Norwood, N.J.: Ablex.

———. (1992). Information problem solving: The big six skills approach. *School Library Media Activities Monthly, 8*(5), 27–29, 37, 42. (EJ 438 023)

Eisenberg, M. B., and Ely, D. P. (1993). Plugging into the "Net." *Emergency Librarian, 21*(2), 8–16. (EJ 471 260)

Eisenberg, M. B., and Small, R. V. (1993). Information-based education: An investigation of the nature and role of information attributes in education. *Information Processing and Management, 29*(2), 263–275. (EJ 462 841)

Eisenberg, M. B., and Spitzer, K. L. (1991). Information technology and services in schools. In M. E. Williams (Ed.), *Annual Review of Information Science and Technology: Vol. 26* (pp. 243–285). Medford, N.J.: Learned Information, Inc. (EJ 441 688)

Garland, K. (1995). The information search process: A study of elements associated with meaningful research tasks. *School Libraries Worldwide, 1*(1), 41–53. (EJ 503 407)

Johnson, D. (1995a). Captured by the web: K–12 schools and the world-wide web. *MultiMedia Schools, 2*(2), 24–30. (EJ 499 841)

———. (1995b). The new and improved school library: How one district planned for the future. *School Library Journal, 41*(6), 36–39. (EJ 505 448)

———. (1995c). Student access to the Internet: Librarians and teachers working together to teach higher level survival skills. *Emergency Librarian, 22*(3), 8–12. (EJ 497 895)

Kuhlthau, C. C. (1993). Implementing a process approach to information skills: A study identifying indicators of success in library media programs. *School Library Media Quarterly, 22*(1), 11–18. (EJ 473 063)

———. (1995). The process of learning from information. *School Libraries Worldwide, 1*(1), 1–12. (EJ 503 404)

Mankato Schools Information Literacy Curriculum Guideline. Internet WWW page, at URL: (version current at 11 March 1996).

McNally, M. J., and Kulhthau, C. C. (1994). Information search process in science education. *Reference Librarian, 44*, 53–60. (EJ 488 273)

Minnesota Department of Education. (1989). *Model learner outcomes for educational media and technology*. St. Paul, Minn.: Author. (ED 336 070)

Moursund, D. (1995, December). Effective practices (part 2): Productivity tools. *Learning and Leading with Technology, 23*(4), 5–6.

Pappas, M. L. (1993, September). A vision of school library media centers in an electronic information age. *School Library Media Activities Monthly, 10*(1), 32–34, 38. (EJ 469 122)

———. (1995). Information skills for electronic resources. *School Library Media Activities Monthly, 11*(8), 39–40. (EJ 499 875)

Todd, R. J. (1995a). Information literacy: Philosophy, principles, and practice. *School Libraries Worldwide, 1*(1), 54–68. (EJ 503 408)

———. (1995b). Integrated information skills instruction: Does it make a difference? *School Library Media Quarterly, 23*(2), 133–138. (EJ 497 921)

Wisconsin Educational Media Association. (1993). *Information literacy: A position paper on information problem-solving*. Madison, Wis.: WEMA Publications. (ED 376 817). (Portions adapted from Michigan State Board of Education's Position Paper on Information Processing Skills, 1992).

This ERIC Digest was prepared by Michael B. Eisenberg, director of the ERIC Clearinghouse on Information & Technology and professor of Information Studies, Syracuse University, Syracuse, N.Y., and Doug Johnson, district media supervisor for Mankato Public Schools, Mankato, Minn.

ERIC Digests are in the public domain and may be freely reproduced and disseminated.

ERIC Clearinghouse on Information & Technology, Syracuse University, 4–194 Center for Science & Technology, Syracuse, NY 13244–4100; (315) 443–3640; (800) 464–9107; Fax (315) 443–5448; Internet: eric@ericir.syr.edu

This publication was prepared with funding from the Office of Educational Research and Improvement, U.S. Department of Education, under contract no. RR93002009. The opinions expressed in this report do not necessarily reflect the positions of OERI or ED.

Appendix B: Citing Information Resources on the Internet

The following are World Wide Web sites that present a style sheet for citing information resources on the Internet:

Citation Guides for Electronic Documents. <http://www.nlc-bnc.ca/ifla/I/training/ citation/citing.htm> (August 12, 1996)

Harnack, Andrew, and Gene Kleppinger. *Beyond the MLA Handbook: Documenting Electronic Sources on the Internet.* <: http://falcon.eku.edu/honors/beyond-mla> (August 12, 1996)

Bibliography

AIM LAB. (1996, August 12). Urbana-Champaign: University of Illinois, College of Agriculture, Consumer and Environmental Sciences. <http://w3.ag.uiuc. edu/AIM/>

Ahlgren, Andrew. (1993, February). Creating benchmarks for science education. *Educational Leadership.*

Ambruster, Bonnie B. et al. (1983). *The role of metacognition in reading to learn: A developmental perspective.* (Reading Education Report No. 40.) Urbana, IL: Center for the Study of Reading. (ED 228618).

American Association for the Advancement of Science. (1989). *Science for all Americans.* Washington, DC: AAAS. (ED 309059).

American Association for the Advancement of Science. (1992a). *Project 2061.* Washington, DC: AAAS.

American Association for the Advancement of Science. (1992b). *Update: Project 2061.* Washington, DC: AAAS.

American Association of School Libraries. (1988). *Information power: National guidelines for school library media programs.* Chicago: AASL.

American Library Association. (1996). *Equity on the information superhighway: Problems and possibilities.* Chicago: ALA.

Ammon, Paul, & Ammon, Mary Sue. (1990). *Using student writing to assess and promote understanding in science.* (Occasional Paper No. 16.) Berkeley, CA: Center for the Study of Writing. (ED 316864).

Applebee, Arthur N. et al. (1986). *The writing report card: Writing achievement in American schools.* Princeton, NJ: Educational Testing Service; Washington, DC: Office of Educational Research and Improvement. (ED 273994).

Arritt, Susan. (1993). The living earth book of deserts. Pleasantville, NY: The Reader's Digest Association, Inc.

Asher, Carol. (1982). Microcomputers: Equity and quality in education for urban disadvantaged students. *ERIC/CUE Digest, 19.*

Association for Advancement of Computing in Education. (1993). *Technology and teacher evaluation annual 1993.* Charlottesville, VA: AACE. (ED 355937).

Ausubel, D. (1978). *Educational psychology A cognitive view* (2nd ed.). New York: Holt, Rinehart and Winston.

Balajthy, Ernest. (1987). What does research on computer-based instruction have to say to the reading teacher? *Reading Research and Instruction, 27*(1), 54–65.

Bard, Nancy. (1993, Winter). Networking CD-ROM's: A case study. *Journal of Youth Services in Libraries.*

Barr, Hugh. (1994, July/August). Social studies by electronic mail. *The Social Studies,* 170–73.

Barr, Mary A., & Healy, Mary K. (1988, Winter). School and university articulation: Different contexts for writing across the curriculum. *New Directions for Teaching and Learning, 36,* 43–53. (EJ 382431).

Barron, Linda et al. (1989, December). Enhancing learning in at-risk students: Applications of video technology. *ERIC Digest.* Syracuse, NY: ERIC Clearinghouse on Information Resources. (ED 318464).

Beck, I. L. (1989). Reading and reasoning. *Reading Teacher, 42*(9), 876–82. (EJ 388672).

Behrmann, Michael M. (1995, January). *Assistive technology for students with mild disabilities.* Council for Exceptional Children, Reston, VA: ERIC Clearinghouse on Disabilities and Gifted Education, Reston, VA. (ED 378755).

Bell, Sharon McCoy. (1995, September). Rules to train by (training teachers to use technology). *Electronic Learning, 15*(1), 16.

Benedicks, William, Jr., & Felton, Randall G. (1994, July/August). An interactive multimedia review. *The Social Studies, 85*(4), 185–86.

Beuter, John H. (1995, January/February). A different spin. (Environmental protection in Oregon). *American Forests, 101*(1–2), 14(2).

Bevilacqua, Ann. (1989, August). *Hypertext: Behind the hype.* Syracuse, NY: ERIC Clearinghouse on Information Resources.

Blosser, Patricia. (1989). *Teaching problem solving—secondary school science.* Columbus, OH: ERIC Clearinghouse on Science, Math and Environmental Education. (ED 309049).

Blosser, Patricia et al. (1989). *Selected procedures for improving the science curriculum.* (Science Education Digest No. 2.) Columbus, OH: ERIC Clearinghouse for Science, Math and Environmental Education. (ED 325303).

Blosser, Patricia. (1990). Current projects and activities in K–12 science education curriculum development. Columbus, OH: ERIC Clearinghouse on Science, Math and Environmental Education.

Booker, Ellis. (1995, February 27). Time to unweave the Web, explore the site. *Computerworld 29*(9), 65.

Boone, William J. et al. (1995). Teachers' attitudes towards distance learning technology in a Science/Society Global Issues Course. *Journal of Computers in Mathematics and Science Teaching, 14*(3), 305–23.

Bos, Candice S. (1982). Getting past decoding: Assisted and repeated readings as remedial methods for learning disabled students. *Topics in Learning and Learning Disabilities, 1,* 51–57.

Bower, G. H., & Hilgard, E. R. (1981). *Theories of learning.* Englewood Cliffs, NJ: Prentice Hall.

Brady, H. Robert. (1994). An overview of computer integration into social studies instruction. *Social Education, 58*(5), 312–14.

Brandt, R. (1993). On teaching for understanding: A conversation with Howard Gardner. *Educational Leadership, 50*(7), 4–7.

Bransford, J. D., Sherwood, R. D., Hasselberg, T. S., Kinzer, C. K., & Williams, S. M. (In press). Anchored instruction: Why we need it and how technology can help. In D. Nix, & R. Spiro (Eds.), *Advances in computers and instruction.* Hillsdale, NJ: Lawrence Erlbaum Associates.

Brass, James. (1996). *Fire control and fire impact: The Yellowstone experience.* Moffett Field, CA: NASA Ames Research Center, Earth Sciences Division.

Bright, Twyla L. (1991). *Integrating computers into the language arts curriculum.* Paper presented at the Indiana Fall Language Arts Conference. (ED 326884).

Brockman, F. (1993). Personal correspondence. (F. Brockman is program director of the Rudolph Awards for Scientific Excellence URASEe, Rudolph Research, Flanders, NJ) ·

Burnett, G. (1994, February). Technology as a tool for urban classrooms. *ERIC Digest, 95.* New York: ERIC Clearinghouse on Urban Education. (ED 368809).

Calkins, Lucy. (1986). *The art of teaching writing.* Portsmouth, NH: Heinemann. (ED 263613).

Carnine, Douglas, & Kinder, Diane. (1985). Teaching low performing students to apply generative and schema strategies to narrative and expository materials. *Remedial and Special Education, 6*(1), 20–30. (EJ 316930).

Carr, K. S. (1988). How can we teach critical thinking? *Childhood Education, 65*(2), 69–73. (EJ 382605).

Carroll, Nicole. (1996, June). Many school computers are outdated. *USA Today.*

Connecting schools and employers. (1995, May/June). *Change,* 39.

Citroen. (1988). Class of 2000: The good news and the bad news. *The Futurist, 22,* 9–15.

Clark, C. R. (1992). Cognitive science: The scientific basis of emerging information technologies. *Australian Psychologist, 27*(1), 17–21.

Coats, Kaye et al. (1990). Ideas from teachers. *Writing notebook: Creative word processing in the classroom, 7*(4), 40–41. (EJ 408372).

Cochran-Smith Marilyn. (1991). Word processing and writing in elementary classrooms: A critical review of related literature. *Review of Educational Research, 6*(1), 107–55. (EJ 425124).

Cohen, Inez, & Elmer, Jan. (1995). *Basic library and information competencies: A unified state-wide approach.* Sacramento: Chancellor's Office of California Community Colleges.

Cohen, Kathleen. (1993, Winter). Can multimedia help social studies teachers? Or are videodiscs worth the expense? *Social Studies Review, 32*(2), 35–43.

Collins, A. (1990). Cognitive apprenticeship and instructional technology. In L. Idol & B. F. Jones (Eds.), *Educational values and cognitive instruction: Implications for reform.* Hillsdale, NJ: Lawrence Erlbaum Associates.

Collins, Norma Decker. (1993). *Teaching critical reading through literature.* Bloomington, IN: ERIC Clearinghouse on Reading, English and Communication. (ED 363869).

Collins, Norma Decker. (1994). *Metacognition and reading to learn.* Bloomington, IN: ERIC Clearinghouse on Reading, English and Communication Skills. (ED 376427).

Coombs, Norman. (1992, March/April). Teaching in the Information Age. *EDUCOM Review, 27*(2).

Congressional Office of Technology Assessment. (1995, April). *Teachers and technology: Making the connection.* Washington, DC: Office of Technology Assessment.

Couch, Kenneth. (1994, May). The German apprenticeship experience: A comparison of school-to-work models. *Current.*

Courtois, Martin P. et al. (1995, November/December). Cool tools for searching the web. *ONLINE, 19*(6), 15.

Crane, Beverly. (1993, Winter). Information technology: Stepping stone to the future. *Social Studies Review, 32*(2), 44–49.

CSU Council of Library Directors. (1994). *Transforming CSU libraries for the 21st century.* San Jose: California State University.

Daiute, Collette. (1985). Using microcomputers in elementary language arts instruction. *ERIC Digest.* (ED 264575).

Daugherty, M., & Wicklein, R. (1993, Spring). Mathematics, science, and technology teachers' perceptions of technology education. *Journal of Technology Education, 4*(2), 30–45.

Daulton, D. (1996). Personal correspondence from the Library Media Specialist listserv LM_NET.

De Mey, M. (1992). *The cognitive paradigm.* Chicago: The University of Chicago Press.

DiGisi, Lori Lyman, & Yore, Larry D. (1992). Reading comprehension and metacognition in science: Status, potential and future direction. Paper presented at the Annual Meeting of the National Association for Research in Science Teaching, Boston. (ED 356132).

Dister, Sheri. (1996). *The center for health applications of aerospace related technologies: Predicting Lyme disease in Westchester County, New York.* Moffett Field, CA: NASA Ames Research Center, Earth Sciences Division.

Dossey, J. D., Mullis, I. V., Lindquist, M. M., & Chambers, D. L. (1988). *The mathematics report card: Are we measuring up?* Princeton, NJ: Educational Testing Service. (ED 300206).

Eastern Oregon State College. (1995, September). Handout on distance learning. Presented at the Internet Conference, Sheraton Gateway, Chicago, IL.

Ediger, Marlow. (1991). *Interest, social studies, and the emerging adolescent.* Position paper. (ED 365601).

Eisenberg, Michael, & Johnson, Doug. (1996). *Computer skills for information problem solving: Learning and teaching technology in context.* Syracuse, NY: ERIC Clearinghouse on Information Science. (EDO–IR–96–04).

Elmer-Dewitt, P. (1991, May 20). The revolution that fizzled. *Time, 137,* 48–49.

Estrin, Herman. (1993). *Teaching minority students to write effectively.* Bloomington, IN: ERIC Clearinghouse on Reading, English and Communication Skills. (ED 358487).

Everhart, Barbara Link. (1991). *Parent involvement with at-risk students: A case study (at risk students, CAI, THC Program).* Ann Arbor, MI: Dissertation Abstracts International. (AAD92–04435).

Farr, Roger. (1991). *Portfolios: Assessment in language arts.* Bloomington, IN: ERIC Clearinghouse on Reading, English and Communication Skills. (ED 334603).

Farr, Roger, & Tone, Bruce. (1994a). *Portfolio and performance assessment: Helping students evaluate their progress as readers and writers.* Orlando, FL: Harcourt Brace and Co.

Farr, Roger, & Tone, Bruce. (1994b). *Theory meets practice in a language arts assessment*. Bloomington, IN: ERIC Clearinghouse on Reading, English and Communication Skills. (ED 369075).

Fear-Fenn, M., & Kapostasy, K. K. (1992). Math + science + technology = vocational preparation for girls. Columbus: Center for Sex Equity, The Ohio State University. (ED 341863).

Feuerstein, R., Rand, Y., Hoffman, M. B., & Miller, Y. (1980). *Instrumental enrichment*. Baltimore, MD: University Park Press.

Finn, Chester E. (1995, May 29). Will they ever learn? *National Review, 47*(10), 26.

Finneran, Kevin. (1995, Winter). School daze (reforming the science education system). *Issues in Science and Technology, 12*(2), 94.

Fisher, K. (1990). Semantic networking: The new kid on the block. *Journal of Research in Science Teaching, 27*(10), 1001–1018.

Fisher, K. M., & Lipson, J. I. (1985). Information processing interpretation of errors in college science learning. *Instructional Science, 14*, 49–79.

Flexible class-lab opens in Meyer. (1996, January 22). *Speaking of Computers: A newsletter for the Stanford academic community*. Stanford, CA: Stanford University.

Flinn, Jane Zeni. (1986). *The role of instruction in revising with computers: Forming a construct for "Good Writing."* St. Louis: University of Missouri. (ED 274963).

Flynn, L. L. (1989). Developing critical reading skills through comparative problem solving. *Reading Teacher, 42*(9), 664–68. (EJ 388670).

Franklin, Sharon (Ed.). (1988). *Making the literature, writing, word processing connection: The best of the writing notebook* (2nd Ed.). Eugene, OR: Creative Word Processing. (ED 312644).

Freire, P. (1985). *The politics of education*. New York: Bergin & Garvey.

Frisk, Philip. (1989). *Black English and the Henry Higgins Project. Avoiding disempowering interventions into Black English*. Paper presented at the conference on College Composition and Communication, Seattle, Washington. (ED 348673).

Fulton, K. (1993, March). Teaching matters: The role of technology in education. In D. Carey, R. Carey, D. A. Willis, & J. Willis (Eds.), *Technology and teacher education annual 1993* (1–6). Charlottesville, VA: Association for Advancement of Computing in Education. (ED 355937).

Gabel, Dorothy, & Sherwood, Robert. (1983). Facilitating problem solving in high school chemistry. *Journal of Research in Science Teaching 20*(2): 163–77.

Galst, Liz. (1996, July). Ogletree warns agains race, class divisions in cyberspace. *American Library Association Annual Meeting Cognotes, 5*, Wrapup, 1.

Gastright, Joseph F. (1989, April). Don't base your drop-out program on somebody else's problem. *Bulletin, 8* (Phi Delta Kappa Center on Evaluation, Development and Research).

Gehl, John. (1995, January/February). Info Vertigo. *Educom Review*.

Gere, Anne Ruggles (Ed.). (1985). *Roots in the sawdust: Writing to learn across the discipline*. Urbana, IL: National Council of Teachers of English. (ED 262419).

Gerstner, Louis. (1995, August 22). *USA Today*, editorial.

Gertz, Ellen A. (1994). *Enhancing Motivation and Reading Achievement: Intervention Strategies for the Underachieving Middle School Student*. (Ed.D. Practicum, Nova Southeastern University.) (CS 011760).

Getting to know desktop GIS. (1995). Redlands, CA: Environmental Systems Research Institute, Inc.

Gluck, G. H. (1993, May 2). Florio, pupils sample magic of math and science. *Sunday Star Ledger*, 55.

Gorman, Eric. (1994, September 15). History comes alive on the little screen. *NEA Today*, 13(2).

Greenan, J. P., & Tucker, P. (1990, Fall). Integrating science knowledge and skills in vocational education programs. *Journal for Vocational Special Needs Education*, 13(1), 19–22.

Halasz, F. G. (1988). Reflections on notecards: Seven issues for the next generation of hypermedia systems. *Communications of the ACM*, 31(7), 836–52.

Hamilton-Wieler, Sharon. (1988). Writing as a thought process: Site of a struggle. *Journal of Teaching Writing*, 7(2). (EJ 391833).

Hamilton-Wieler, Sharon. (1989, October). Awkward compromises and eloquent achievements. *English Education*, 21(3), 152–69. (EJ 397676).

Hansen, J. (1987). *When writers read*. Portsmouth, NH: Heinemann. (ED 282226).

Hanson, R., & Siegel, D. F. (1988). The effects on high school seniors of learning to read in kindergarten. *Technical Report No. 1*. Garden Grove, CA: Hanson Research Associates. (ED 341967).

Hanson, R., & Siegel, D. F. (1991). The long-term effects on high school seniors of learning to read in kindergarten: A twelve-year follow-up study. (ED 323494).

Hardie, Crista. (1996, May 6). Motorola readies ADSL video IC for '97 entry. *Electronic News*, 42(2115), 52.

Harris, Jane. (1990). *Text annotation and underlining as metacognitive strategies to improve comprehension and retention of expository text*. Paper presented at the Annual Meeting of the National Reading Conference, Miami. (ED 335669).

Harste, J. et al. (1988). *Creating classrooms for authors*. Portsmouth, NH: Heinemann. (ED 320168).

Harty, Sheila. (1993). Project 2061: Systemic reform of K–12 education for science literacy. *Journal of Science Education and Technology*, 2(3).

Haury, David. (1993, March). *Teaching science through inquiry*. Columbus, OH: ERIC Clearinghouse for Science, Math and Environmental Education.

Heath, Philip. (1988, September). Science/technology/society in the social studies. *ERIC Digest*. Bloomington, IN: ERIC Clearinghouse for Social Studies/Social Science Education.

Henry, Tamara. (1995, September 20). A call for high-tech classrooms. *USA Today*, D1.

Herman, Joan et al. (1992). *A Practical Guide to Alternative Assessment*. Alexandria, VA: ASCD. (ED 352389).

Heterick, Robert C., Jr., & Gehl, John. (1995, January/February). Information technology and year 2020. *Educom Review*, 30(1), 22–25.

Hillocks, George, Jr. (1982). The interaction of instruction, teacher comment, and revision in teaching the composing process. *Research in the Teaching of English*, 16. (EJ 268134).

Horn, R. E. (1989). *Mapping hypertext: The analysis, orgranization, and display of knowledge for the next generation of on-line text and graphics*. Lexington, MA: The Lexington Institute.

Hull, D. M. (1990, Summer). Interdisciplinary relationships in technical education: The CORD Perspective. *Journal of Studies in Technical Careers*, 12(3), 253–67. (EJ 434009).

Information Society 2000: A Danish strategy for the information society. (1996, January 9). Available at http://www.fsk.dk/fsk/pub/info2000-uk/.

Investor's Business Daily. (1995, March 10), A15.

Irving, Larry, & Breeden, Laura. (1995, March/April). Universal access: Should we get in line? *Educom Review.*

Jenkinson, Edward. (1992). *A professor responds by computer to the writing of elementary students.* Bloomington, IN: ERIC Clearinghouse on Reading and Communication Skills. (ED 341061).

Johnson, Doug et al. (1995). *Suggested professional staff technology competencies.* Mankato, MN: Mankato Public Schools.

Jonassen, D. H. (1988). Designing structured hypertext and structuring access to hypertext. *Educational Technology*, 13–16.

Jones, Beverly. (1991, Spring). Cognitive sciences: Implications for art education. *Visual Arts Research, 17* (University of Illinois Press).

Jones, Loretta, & Smith, Stanley G. (1992, January/February). Can multimedia meet our expectations? *Educom Review, 27*(1).

Jordan, W. R., & Follman, J. M. (Eds.). (1993). Using technology to improve teaching and learning. *Hot topics: Usable research.* Victoria, BC, Canada: British Columbia Ministry of Attorney-General; Greensboro, NC: Southeastern Regional Vision for Education. (ED 355930).

Keogh, B. K., & Hall, R. J. (1983). Cognitive training with learning disabled students. In A. Meyers & W. Craighead (Eds.), *Cognitive behavior modification.* New York: Plenum.

Key internet demographics & future prospects. (1997, January 27). Available at http://www.netbiz-marketing.com.

Kinnaman, Daniel E. (1993, September). Technology and situated cognition. *Technology and learning, 14*(1), 86.

Kinzer, C. K., & Risko, V. J. (1988). *Macrocontexts to facilitate learning.* Paper presented at the 33rd Annual Conference of the International Reading Association, Toronto, Ontario.

Kumar, David D., Helgeson, Stanley L., & White, Arthur L. (1994). Computer technology-cognitive psychology interface and science performance assessment. *ETR&D, 42*(4).

Kumar, David D., Helgeson, Stanley L., & White, Arthur L. (1995). A study of the effect of Hypercard and traditional pen-paper performance assessment methods on expert-novice chemistry problem solving. *Journal of Science Education and Technology.*

Kumar, David D., & Helgeson, Stanley L. (1995). Trends in computer applications in science assessment. *Journal of Science Education and Technology, 4*(1), 29–36.

Kurfiss, Joanne. (1985, December). Do students really learn from writing? *Writing Across the Curriculum, 3*(1), 3–4. (ED 293123).

Kurth, Ruth J. (1986). *Using word processing to enhance revision strategies during student composing.* Paper presented at the Annual Meeting of the American Educational Research Association, San Francisco. (ED 277049).

Langer, Margaret Anne, & Neal, Judith Chibante. (1987). Strategies for learning: An adjunct study skills model. *Journal of Reading, 31*(2), 134–39. (EJ 359218).

Lankard, Bettina. (1993). *Integrating science and math in vocational education.* Columbus, OH: ERIC Clearinghouse on Adult, Career, and Vocational Education. (ED 355456).

Large, Andrew. (1995, June). Multimedia and comprehension and the relationship among text, animations and captions. *Journal of the American Society for Information Science, 46*(5), 340–47.

Lee, Yvonne. (1996, July 1). Vendors team up to build ADSL networks; trials planned across the country. (Asymmetric Digital Subscriber Loop). *InfoWorld, 18*(27), 10.

Lehr, Fran. (1995). *Revision in the writing process.* Bloomington, IN: ERIC Clearinghouse on Reading, English and Communication Skills.

Levin, J. A. (1989). Observations on electronic networks. *The Computing Teacher, 17*(6), 30–35.

Levinson, Eliot. (1994, March). When a program "fails," how a mid-course correction can overhaul a floundering technology program. *Electronic Learning, 13*(6), 18.

Lindsay, P. H., & Norman, D. (1977). *Human information processing* (2nd ed.). New York: Academic Press.

Lisowski, Marilyn. (1985). Science-technology-society in the science curriculum. (Special Digest No. 2.) Columbus, OH: ERIC Clearinghouse for Science, Math and Environmental Education. (ED 274513).

Lulla, K. (1993). Personal correspondence.

McCormick, Patricia. (1995, April). What children really learn on computers. *Parents Magazine, 70*(4), 109.

McKenzie, Jamieson. (1993). *Administrator's at risk: Tools and technologies for securing your future.* Bloomington, IN: National Education Service.

Maddaus, George. (1994, Spring). Symposium: Equity and educational assessment. *Harvard Educational Review, 64*(1).

Mageau, Therese. (1995, September). Has technology made the curriculum obsolete? *Electronic Learning, 13*(1), 16.

Mancini, Gail H. (1995, November/December). Charting the course? (Middle schools combine technology and curriculum). *Electronic Learning,* 22.

Mann, D. (1986). Can we help dropouts? *Teacher's College Report,* 87.

Mann, Dale. (1989, September). Effective schools as a dropout prevention strategy. *NASSP Bulletin, 73*(518), 77–83. (EJ 396507).

Materials technology: The common core skills that are shaping the future. (1990). Richland, WA: Battelle Pacific Northwest Laboratories and Richland School District 400; Ellensburg, WA: Central Washington University; Portland, OR: Northwest Regional Educational Laboratory. (ED 327735).

Mayer, Victor. (1993). Earth systems education. *ERIC Digests.* (ED 359049).

Meichanbaum, Donald. (1981). *Teaching thinking: A cognitive-behavioral approach* (127–41). Paper presented at the Society for Learning Disabilities and Remedial Education, New York.

Mendrinos, Roxanne. (1992a). Applications of CD-ROM technology for reference purposes: A survey of secondary school library media specialists in Maine and Pennsylvania. *Dissertation Abstracts.* (University Microfilms No. 9217458).

Mendrinos, Roxanne. (1992b, February). CD-ROM and the at-risk student. *School Library Journal.*

Mendrinos, Roxanne. (1994). *Building information literacy: A guide to schools and libraries.* Englewood, CO: Libraries Unlimited.

Menn, Don. (1993a, October). Holier than educational multimedia. *PC World.*

Menn, Don. (1993b, October). Multimedia in education: Arming our kids for the future. *PC World,* 52.

Menn, Don. (1993c, October). Teacher in a box: The debate over multimedia learning. *PC World,* 62.

Mgebroff, J. W. (1995, December 21). Martin Jr. High program demystifies secondary school campus. *West Austin News,* 1.

Miller, John W. (Ed.). (1993, March). *Students at risk: Pitfalls and promising plans.* Papers from the Annual Conference on Students at Risk, Savannah, Georgia. (ED 362593).

Montague, Marjorie. (1990). Computers and writing process instruction. *Computers in the Schools, 7*(3), 5–20. (EJ 420378).

Muth, K. Denise. (1987). Structure strategies for comprehending expository text. *Reading Research and Instruction, 27*(1), 66–72.

National Assessment of Educational Progress. (1992). *The 1990 science report card: NAEP assessment of fourth, eighth, and twelfth graders.*

National Commission on Excellence in Education. (1983). *Nation at risk: The imperative for educational reform.* Washington DC: U.S. Government Printing Office. (ED 226006).

National Council for the Social Studies. (1993). *Curriculum standards for the Social Studies, Draft 2.* Washington, DC: NCSS.

National Council for the Teachers of Mathematics. Commission on Standards for School Mathematics. (1989). *Curriculum and evaluation standards for school mathematics.* Reston, VA: NCTM. (ED 304336).

National Research Council. (1993). National science education standards: An enhanced sampler. (A working paper of the National Council on Science Education Standards and Assessment.) Washington, DC: NRC. (ED 360175).

National Science Teacher's Association. (1990–1991). Science/technology/society: A new effort for providing appropriate science for all (position statement). In *NSTA Handbook* (47–48). Washington DC: NSTA.

Nebraska Department of Education. (1993). *A Strategic Plan for Social Studies in Nebraska.*

Nellis, M. Duane. (1994, January/February). Technology in geographic education: Reflections and future directions. *Journal of Geography, 93*(1), 36–39.

The new literacy: Beyond the three Rs. (1992, September). *Electronic Learning, 12*(1), 28.

Newman, J. (1984). Language learning and computers. *Language Arts,* 61. (EJ 425124).

Nikiforuk, Andrew, & Howes, Deborah. (1995, September). Why schools can't teach. *Saturday Night,* 22.

Norman, Carolyn F. (1996, March). *Information competency in the California community colleges: A status report.* Chancellor's Office staff report to the Educational Policy Committee of the Board of Governors.

Northup, T., Barth, J., & Kranze, H. (1991). Technology standards for social studies: A proposal. *Social Education, 55,* 218–20.

Novak, J. D. (1977). *A theory of education.* Ithaca, NY: Cornell University Press.

Novak, J. D., & Gowin, D. B. (1984). *Learning how to learn.* New York: Cambridge University Press.

Novelli, Joan. (1990, September). Fast new ways to break the September ice. *Instructor*, 91.

O'Connor, James, & Brie, Raymond. (1994). Mathematics and science partnerships: Products, people, performance and multimedia. *Computing Teacher, 22*(1).

Office of Technology and Assessment. (1993). *Adult literacy and new technologies: Tools for a lifetime.* Washington, DC: OTA.

Office of Technology Assessment. (1995). *Teachers and technology: Making the connection.* Washington, DC: OTA.

Ognes, Eva, & Koker, M. (1995, July/August). Teaching for understanding: An issue-oriented approach. *Clearing House, 68*(6), 343.

Olson, Mary W. (1991). Portfolios: Education tools. *Reading Psychology, 12*(1), 73–80.

O'Rourke, Ann, & Philips, David. (1989). *Responding effectively to pupils' writing.* (Writing Research Report No. 2.) Wellington, New Zealand: New Zealand Council for Educational Research. (CS 213090).

Osborne, M., & Freyberg, P. (1985). *Learning in science: Implications of children's knowledge.* Auckland, New Zealand: Heinemann.

Owston, Ronald D. et al. (1991). The effects of word processing on student writing in a high computer access environment. *Technical Report*, 91–93. York, Ontario: York University Centre for the Study of Computers in Education. (ED 341365).

Palumbo, David, & Bermudez, Andrea. (1994). Using hypermedia to assist language minority learners in achieving success. *Computers in the Schools, 10*(1/2), 171–88.

Pea, R. (1989, January). *Distributed intelligence, new media, and the processes of education.* Lecture delivered at the Cognition and Educational Symposium, University of Oregon, Eugene, Oregon.

Perelman, L. (1990, December 10). A new learning enterprise: The technology revolution comes to education. *Business Week, 3191*, 12ED–20ED.

Perrone, V. (1994). How to engage students in learning. *Educational Leadership, 51*(5), 11–13.

Phillips, Theodore Hart. (1992). Impact of a computer based process writing curriculum upon the written language and self-esteem of residentially placed at-risk students. *Dissertation Abstracts International, 53*, 06–A. (AAD92–28369).

PHYS-MA-TECH: An integrated partnership. (1992). DeKalb: Northern Illinois University.

Potter, Christopher, & Klooster, Steven. (1996). *Using satellite imagery to understand the global exchange of greenhouse gases between the terrestrial biosphere and the atmosphere.* Moffett Field, CA: NASA Ames Research Center, Earth Sciences Division.

Pritz, S. G. (1989). *The role of vocational education in developing students' academic skills.* (Information Series No. 340.) Columbus, OH: ERIC Clearinghouse on Adult, Career, and Vocational Education. (ED 326692).

Pryor, Amanda, & Soloway, Elliot. (1996, March/April). Practicing authentic science. *Electronic Learning, 15*(5), 34.

Puccio, P. M. (1993). *The computer-networked writing lab: One instructor's view.* Bloomington, IN: ERIC Clearinghouse on Reading, English and Communication Skills.

Raphael, Jacqueline, & Greenberg, Richard. (1995, October). Image processing: A state-of-the-art way to learn science. *Educational Leadership, 53*(2), 34–37.

Reinsmith, W. A. (1993). Ten fundamental truths about learning. *The National Teaching and Learning Forum, 2*(4), 7–8.

Riecken, T. J., & Miller, M. R. (1990). Introduce children to problem solving and decision making by using children's literature. *Social Studies, 81*(2), 59–64. (EJ 413991).

Riley, Richard W. (1995, Winter). Connecting classrooms, computers and communities. *Issues in Science and Technology, 12*(2), 49.

"Riskline." (1993, March 17). *USA Today*, p. 5D.

Robinson, Ann. (1985). *The effects of teacher probes on children's written revisions*. Macomb, IL: Western Illinois University. (ED 276053).

Ruiz, Nadine T. (1991, May). *Effective instruction for language minority children with mild disabilities*. Council for Exceptional Children, Reston, VA: ERIC Clearinghouse on Handicapped and Gifted Children. (ED 333621).

Satellite Imagery FAQ (1997, March 11). <http://www.geog.nott.ac.uk/remote/faq=1.html>.

Scaife, M. (1989). Education, information technology and cognitive science. *Journal of Computer Assisted Learning, 5*, 66–71.

Schon, Donald. (1983). *The Reflective Practitioner*. New York: Basic Books, Inc.

Shroeder, Eileen E. (1991, November). *Interactive multimedia computer systems*. Syracuse, NY: ERIC Clearinghouse on Information Resources. (ED 340388).

Schwartz, Wendy. (1987). *Teaching science and math to at risk students*. New York: ERIC Clearinghouse on Urban Information.

Self, Judy (Ed.). (1989). *Plain talk about learning and writing across the curriculum*. Richmond: Virginia Department of Education.

Senge, Peter N. (1994). *The fifth discipline: The art and practice of the learning organization*. New York: Doubleday.

Sensenbaugh, Roger. (1993). *Writing across the curriculum: Toward the year 2000*. Bloomington, IN: ERIC Clearinghouse on Reading, English and Communication Skills. (ED 354549).

Shavelson, R. J., Lang, H., & Lewin, B. (1993). *Indirect approaches to knowledge representation of high school science: On concept maps as potential authentic assessments in science*. A project report of the National Center for Research on Evaluation, Standards and Student Testing, Los Angeles, California.

Shelley, Gary, Cashman, Thomas, & Jordan, Kurt. (1996). *Netscape Navigator: An introduction*. Danvers, MA: Boyd & Fraser Publishing Company.

Sherwood, R. D., Kinzer, C. K., Bransford, J. D., & Franks, J. J. (1987). Some benefits of creating macrocontexts for science instruction. Initial findings. *Journal of Research in Science Teaching, 24*, 417–35.

Siegel, Donna, & Hanson, Ralph. (1992). *Prescription for literary: Providing educational experiences*. Bloomington, IN: ERIC Clearinghouse on Reading, English and Communication Skills.

Siegel, Jessica. (1994, September). Walking a new walk: Technology use at Brown Barge Middle School, Pensacola, Florida. *Electronic Learning, 14*(1).

Simic, Marjorie. (1993a). *Guidelines for computer-assisted reading instruction*. Bloomington, IN: ERIC Clearinghouse on Reading, English and Communication Skills. (ED 352630).

Simic, Marjorie. (1993b). Publishing children's writing. *ERIC/REC Digest*. (ED 363884).

Simic, Marjorie. (1994). *Computer-assisted writing instruction*. Bloomington, IN: ERIC Clearinghouse on Reading, English and Communication Skills.

Sizer, T. (1992). *Horace's school*. Boston: Houghton Mifflin Co.

Smith, Carl B. (1994). *Helping children understand literary genres*. Bloomington, IN: ERIC Clearinghouse on Reading, English and Communication Skills. (ED 366985).

Smith, Carl B., & Sensenbaugh, Roger. (1992). *Helping children overcome reading difficulties*. Bloomington, IN: ERIC Clearinghouse on Reading, English and Communication Skills. (ED 344190).

Smith, Hedrick. (1995, August 27). Future jobs less college-oriented. *San Jose Mercury News*, 11A.

Smith, Maureen M. (1996, March/April). This school is a zoo. *Electronic Learning*, 15(5), 26.

Snyder, Bill. (1995, May 29). Stay in school. *PC Week, 12*(21), A1.

Snyder, Ilana. (1993, Spring). Writing with the word processor: A research overview. *Educational Research*, 49–67.

Sommers, Nancy. (1982). *Revision strategies of student writers and experienced adult writers*. Washington, DC: National Institute of Education. (ED 220839).

Sorenson, Sharon. (1991). Encouraging writing achievement: Writing across the curriculum. Bloomington, IN: ERIC Clearinghouse on Reading, English and Communication Skills. (ED 327879).

Sowa, J. F. (1984). *Conceptual structures: Information processing in mind and machines*. Reading, MA: Addison-Wesley Publishing Co.

Steffens, Henry. (1988). *The value and difficulties of teaching the history of science and technology in secondary schools* (p. 17). Paper presented at the Annual Meeting of the American Historical Association, Cincinnati, Ohio. (ED 306182).

Stoddard, A., & Bosnick, J. (1993). Technology, thinking and teamwork. In *Students at risk: Pitfalls and promising plans*. Papers from the Annual Conference on Students at Risk, Savannah, Georgia. (ED 362593).

Strickland et al. (1987). *Using computers in the teaching of reading*. New York: Teacher's College Press.

Tei, Ebo, & Stewart, Oran. (1985). Effective studying from text. *Forum for Reading*, 16(2), 46–55. (ED 262378).

Tharp, Mike. (1996, May 13). Woodmen, spare that tree: In Oregon, environmental activists battle the U.S. Forest Service. *U.S. News & World Report, 120*(19), 36.

Toffler, Alvin. (1990). *Powershift: Knowledge, wealth, and violence at the edge of the 21st century*. New York: Bantam Books.

Tone, Bruce, & Winchester, Dorothy. (1988). Computer-Assisted Writing. *ERIC/REC Digest*. (ED 293130).

Toon, Owen, Zahnle, Kevin, & Morrison, David. (1996). *Asteroid and comet collisions with Earth*. Moffett Field, CA: NASA Ames Research Center, Earth Sciences Division.

Tsikalas, Kallen. (1995, April). Internet-based learning: Mostly students use the Net to socialize. *Electronic Learning*, 14(7), 14.

Tucker, Marc. (1987). Information technology and the schools: A personal perspective. In *Technology and students at risk of school failure*. Proceedings of the Conference. Bloomington, IN: Agency for Instructional Technology. (ED 295590).

Tucker, Robert. (1995, November/December). Distance learning programs: Models and alternatives. *Syllabus, 9*(3), 42–46.

Turned on to reading & writing. (1992, May/June). *Electronic Learning, 11*(8), 12.

Update on: Word processing, multimedia and literacy. (1993, November/December). *Electronic Learning, 13*(3), 10.

U.S. Department of Labor. (1991). What work requires of schools. A SCANS Report for America 2000: Executive Summary.

Using fairy tales for critical reading. Bonus Activity Book. (1991). *Learning, 19*(8), 23–42. (EJ 427873).

Valencia, Sheila (1990). A portfolio approach to classroom assessment: The whys, whats, and hows. *The Reading Teacher, 43*(4), 338–40. (EJ 403672).

Virginia Department of Education. (1993, January 20). *Survey results: School divisions identify and serve at-risk students.* Presentation to the Elementary and Secondary Education Subcommittee of the House Appropriations Committee.

Von Glasersfeld, E. (1992). Questions and answers about constructivism. In M. K. Pearsall (Ed.), *Scope, sequence and coordination of secondary school science: Vol. 2: Relevant research* (p. 169). Washington, DC: National Science Teachers Association.

Walker, Anne. (1988). Writing-across-the-curriculum: The second decade. *English Quarterly, 21*(2), 93–103. (EJ 378669).

Wandersee, J. H. (1990). Concept mapping and the cartography of cognition. *Journal of Research in Science Teaching, 27*(10), 923–26.

Washington State Library/Media Directors' Council. (1994). *Information competency: An initiative for integrated learning.* (Position statement).

Watt, D. (1982). Education for citizenship in a computer-based society. In Robert J. Seidel (Eds.), *Computer Literacy.* New York: Academic Press.

Webster, Kathleen, & Paul, Kathryn. (1996, January). Beyond surfing: Tools and techniques for searching the Web. *Information Technology.*

Weiss, Iris R. (1987). *Report of the 1985–86 National Survey of Science and Mathematics Education.* Durham, NC: Research Triangle Institute. (ED 292620).

Weiss, Iris. (1988, April). Indicators of science and mathematics education: Providing tools for state policymakers. Paper commissioned by Science/Mathematics Indicators Project, Council of Chief State School Officers, Washington, DC. (ED 295844).

Weller, K. (1993). *Effects of four instructional methods for teaching the geography of Kansas water resources.* Unpublished doctoral dissertation, Kansas State University, Manhattan.

Whitehead, A. N. (1929). *The aims of education.* New York: Macmillan.

Wiggins, Grant. (1993). Assessment: Authenticity, context, and validity. *Phi Delta Kappan,* p. 75. (EJ 472587).

Wilson, M. (1988). Critical thinking: Repackaging or revolution? *Language Arts, 65*(6), 543–51. (EJ 376160).

Winograd, Ken. (1991). *Writing, solving and sharing original math story problems: Case studies of fifth grade children's cognitive behavior.* Paper presented at the Annual Meeting of the American Educational Research Association, Chicago, Illinois. (ED 345936).

Wittrock, M. (1988). *The Future of Educational Psychology*. Unpublished manuscript.

Wolcott, Linda. (1994, Spring). Understanding how teachers plan. *School Library Media Quarterly*.

Womble, Gail G. (1984). Process and processor: Is there room for a machine in the English Classroom? *English Journal, 73*(1), 34–37. (EJ 291267).

Wong, Bernice Y. L., & Wilson, Megan. (1984). Investigating awareness of a teaching passage organization in learning disabled children. *Journal of Learning Disabilities, 17*(8), 77–82. (EJ 308339).

Woods, David D. (1986). Cognitive technologies: The design of joint human-machine cognitive systems. *The AI Magazine*.

Woods, David D. (1988). Cognitive engineering: Human problem solving with tools. *Human Factors, 30*(4), 415–30.

Word processing, multimedia and literacy. (1993, December). *Electronic Learning*, 10.

Worsley, Dale, & Mayer, Bernadette. (1989). *The art of science writing*. New York: Teachers and Writers Collaborative. (ED 304702).

Yager, Robert, Dunkhase, John, Tillotson, John, & Glass, Lynn. (1995, October). Science-technology reform via distance education terminology. *Tech Trends*, 19.

Yager, R., McLure, J. & Weld, J. (1993). Applying science across the curriculum. *Educational Leadership 50*(8): 79–80.

Yates, G.C.R., & Chandler, M. (1991). The cognitive psychology of knowledge. Basic research findings and educational implications. *Australian Journal of Education, 35*(2), 131–53.

Yoder, Sue Logsdon. (1993). Teaching, writing, revision: Attitudes and copy changes. *Journalism Educator*, 47.

Young-Hawkins, La Verne. (1993, December 3). *Technology education teacher preparation for students at risk*. Paper presented at the Annual Conference of the American Vocational Association, Nashville, Tennessee, October 3–7, 1993.

Ziegler, Bart. (1995, April). Stop the Presses. *Wall Street Journal*, 1.

Zoni, Stephen. (1992, August). *Improving process writing skills of 7th grade at-risk students by increasing interest through the use of networks, word processing software and telecommunications technology*. Education specialist practicum, Nova University. (ED 350624).

Index

ABOUT THE AUTHOR

ROXANNE BAXTER MENDRINOS holds a Ph.D. in Curriculum, Instruction and Administration and is Library Systems Administrator at Foothill College in Los Altos, California. Her book *Building Information Literacy Using High Technology: A Guide for Schools & Libraries* (1994) was nominated for the 1996 American Library Association Literature Award. She is the recipient of the League of Innovation Innovator of the Year Award, the NISOD Excellence in Teaching Award, and the Massachusetts Special Pathfinder Award for Extraordinary Leadership in Educational Technology. She is the author of numerous papers on educational technology and the library media program.